Managing Your Money Online For Dummies®

D1128303

Managing Your Money Online: The Short Course

This Cheat Sheet and the Internet can help you make the most of your long-term finances by reorganizing what you have today. Try each step in the following table and record your results in the form on the flipside of the cheat sheet.

Five Easy Online Steps to Improving Your Finances

Action	How You Accomplish It Online
1. Refinancing your mortgage	If interest rates have fallen by ½ to ¾ of a point since you took out your mortgage, check online mortgage lenders and brokers to see whether refinancing your mortgage can result in a lower monthly payment (see mortgage-x.com/general/average_rates.asp).
2. Lowering your credit card rates	Check your credit rating at www.myfico.com and correct any problems. If your credit score is 720 or better you need to get the best rates. Collect all your cards and determine the annual percentage (interest) rates (APRs). Use the credit card issuer's toll free number and ask for a reduced credit card rate. For a telephone script, see www.bankrate.com/brm/news/cc/20020415a.asp.
3. Refinancing or shortening car loan	When you purchase a car, you usually get a car loan for 5 years. Consider getting a car loan for 3 years and pocketing the difference in interest. Or if you already owe $7,500 or more on your car loan (and your car is worth that amount or more) use the Internet to check out refinancing (www.eloan.com).
4. Lowering insurance rates	Concentrate on the 5 essential types of insurance policies (medical, disability, life, property, and auto). If you haven't reviewed your policies in the last year, do so now. See whether you can lower the premiums and consider consolidating your policies with 1 or 2 providers. You may be able to save 5% to 10% of the premium. See InsWeb (www.insweb.com) for more information.
5. No PMI insurance	Mortgage insurance (called private mortgage insurance — PMI) is required if your down payment was 20% or less. If your home has appreciated, you may own more than 20%. If so, you shouldn't have to pay $16 to $50 per month in mortgage insurance. Find an online appraisal at www.electronicappraiser.com.

For Dummies: Bestselling Book Series for Beginners

Managing Your Money Online For Dummies®

Cheat Sheet

Your Monthly Results

Enter the amounts you've saved from the Five Easy Online Steps to Improving Your Finances from the opposite page on the lines provided below. Use the total amount of extra money to reduce bills or maximize your 401(k), IRA, or savings accounts. You can automatically transfer your extra savings by using online banking.

1. **Refinancing your mortgage** $_____
2. **Lowering credit card interest rates** $_____
3. **Refinancing or shortening car loan** $_____
4. **Lowering insurance rates** $_____
5. **No PMI insurance** $_____
   Total amount of extra money $_____

Online Financial Terms Worth Knowing

✔ **Account aggregation:** A service that enables you to view your online financial accounts from one page rather than having to log onto different Web sites to see each of your individual accounts. Only one password is required, and you can view all your accounts (such as credit card, mortgage, broker, and so on) from one place regardless of where they originate. Basically, account aggregation works like an online personal finance organizer. Egg Money at www.egg.com is an example of a free account aggregator.

✔ **Click-and-brick banks:** Banks with traditional branch offices and online banking services with browser-based Internet technology. An example of a click-and-brick bank is Bank of America (www.bankofamerica.com).

✔ **Credit score:** A single number, based on an individual's credit history, that measures that individual's credit worthiness. Credit scores are derived by using algorithms. The most widely used credit score is called FICO, for Fair Issac Co., which developed it. Try the free FICO score simulator at www.myfico.com.

✔ **E-bills:** Billing statements delivered to customers electronically over the Internet or other online network. For an example of how e-bills can help you get control of your bill paying, take the free demo at CheckFree (www.checkfree.com).

✔ **Phishing scams:** One of the latest online scams. Internet scammers cast about and go "phishing" for your financial information. Phishing uses spam or pop-up messages to deceive you into disclosing your credit card numbers, bank account information, Social Security number, passwords, or other sensitive information. Don't be a victim. Check out the Identity Theft Prevention and Survival Web site at www.identitytheft.org.

For Dummies: Bestselling Book Series for Beginners

Managing Your Money Online

FOR DUMMIES®

Managing Your Money Online

FOR

DUMMIES®

by Kathleen Sindell, PhD

WILEY

Wiley Publishing, Inc.

Managing Your Money Online For Dummies®
Published by
Wiley Publishing, Inc.
111 River St.
Hoboken, NJ 07030-5774
www.wiley.com

For general information on our other products and services, please contact our Customer Care Department within the U.S. at 800-762-2974, outside the U.S. at 317-572-3993, or fax 317-572-4002.

For technical support, please visit www.wiley.com/techsupport.

Wiley also publishes its books in a variety of electronic formats. Some content that appears in print may not be available in electronic books.

Library of Congress Control Number: 2004115153

ISBN: 0-7645-7210-5

Manufactured in the United States of America

10 9 8 7 6 5 4 3 2 1

1O/RW/RS/QU/IN

WILEY

About the Author

Kathleen Sindell is the author of *Investing Online for Dummies* (Wiley, 2005, 2002, 2000, 1999, 1998), *Safety Net: Protecting Your Business on the Internet* (Wiley, 2002), *Loyalty Marketing for the Internet Age* (Dearborn, 2000), *The Unofficial Guide to Buying a Home Online* (Hungry Minds, 2000). Dr. Sindell is contributing author to the *Encyclopedia of Computer Science* (Groves Dictionaries Inc., 2000) and online investing columnist for *Investor Direct* magazine (1999). She is the author of *A Hands-On Guide to Mortgage Banking Internet Sites*, a separate directory published by *Mortgage Banking Magazine* (2000, 1999, 1998, 1997) and *The Handbook of Real Estate Lending* (McGraw-Hill Professional Publishing, 1996). Dr. Sindell is an expert on electronic commerce and is an adjunct faculty member at the Johns Hopkins University MBA program. She is the former Associate Director of the Financial Management and Commercial Real Estate Programs for the University of Maryland, University College Graduate School of Management & Technology.

Dr. Sindell provides consulting and publications about management, security, finance, and real estate in the e-commerce environment. Her goal is to improve the quality of life and economic well-being of people and business organizations by providing information that they might not otherwise have or understand.

She received her B.A. in Business from Antioch University, an M.B.A. in Finance from the California State University at San Jose, and a Ph.D. in Administration and Management from Walden University, Institute for Advanced Studies.

Dedication

To my husband, Ivan Sindell, whose unwavering support helped make this book a reality.

Author's Acknowledgments

Managing Your Money Online For Dummies shows how you can use the Internet to maximize your personal wealth and represents my desire to help people take control of their finances by accessing quality online information. My thanks to Kathleen Cox, acquisitions editor, for her guidance. My thanks to Tim Gallan for being a terrific development editor and Neil Johnson for being an astute copy editor. My deepest appreciation to Wendy Taylor and Gerald Sindell of Thought Leaders Intl (www.thoughtleadersintl.com) for their representation of me for this project. Many thanks to Dan Chesler for his thorough technical review and all the people who work behind the scenes at Wiley Publishing, Inc.

I deeply appreciate my editorial assistant, Reuven Goren, who proofread the manuscript before it was submitted to the publisher.

My gratitude and a very special thank you to my brother-in-law, Gerald Sindell, for his profound counsel on everything relating to the business of publishing.

Publisher's Acknowledgments

We're proud of this book; please send us your comments through our Dummies online registration form located at www.dummies.com/register/.

Some of the people who helped bring this book to market include the following:

Acquisitions, Editorial, and Media Development

Senior Project Editor: Tim Gallan

Acquisitions Editor: Kathy Cox

Copy Editor: E. Neil Johnson

Technical Editor: Daniel L. Chesler, CMT, CTA (dan@charttricks.com)

Editorial Manager: Christine Meloy Beck

Editorial Assistants: Courtney Allen, Melissa S. Bennett, Nadine Bell

Cover Photo: © Royalty-Free/CORBIS

Cartoons: Rich Tennant, www.the5thwave.com

Composition

Project Coordinator: Nancee Reeves

Layout and Graphics: Andrea Dahl, Lauren Goddard, Denny Hager, Joyce Haughey, Stephanie D. Jumper, Barry Offringa, Heather Ryan

Proofreaders: Leeann Harney, Carl Pierce, Dwight Ramsey, Charles Spencer TECHBOOKS Production Services

Indexer: TECHBOOKS Production Services

Publishing and Editorial for Consumer Dummies

    Diane Graves Steele, Vice President and Publisher, Consumer Dummies

    Joyce Pepple, Acquisitions Director, Consumer Dummies

    Kristin A. Cocks, Product Development Director, Consumer Dummies

    Michael Spring, Vice President and Publisher, Travel

    Brice Gosnell, Associate Publisher, Travel

    Kelly Regan, Editorial Director, Travel

Publishing for Technology Dummies

    Andy Cummings, Vice President and Publisher, Dummies Technology/General User

Composition Services

    Gerry Fahey, Vice President of Production Services

    Debbie Stailey, Director of Composition Services

Contents at a Glance

Table of Contents

Introduction

● ●

*W*elcome to *Managing Your Money Online For Dummies* and the exciting world of online financial management. Regardless of whether you're experienced at planning your finances or are new to the Internet, this book guides you to Web-based resources that help you make better, more informed financial decisions than ever before. The Net offers an astounding amount of financial information, and *Managing Your Money Online For Dummies* provides clear instructions and ample illustration so you don't get lost in cyberspace.

About This Book

More and more Americans are turning to the Internet to find answers to their personal finance questions. *Managing Your Money Online For Dummies* shows you how to use the Internet to get more from what you already have and how to reach your personal financial goals without penny-pinching or giving up luxuries.

Everyone needs to make financial choices from "How much should I save?" to "How should I invest my retirement funds?" Knowing where to get up-to-the-minute information and being able to use it are necessary for anyone who wants to get a grip on his or her financial future.

More than ever before, individuals need to possess the tools and resources required to make informed decisions about their financial prospects. People who don't make financial plans using resources on the Internet may miss out on opportunities that their more enlightened neighbors can use to their advantage. The January 2003 results of a Pew Internet & American Life survey indicate that during the last two years, the Internet has played a crucial but important role in the decision-making of between 8 million and 14 million Americans for everything from purchasing of cars and making major financial decisions to getting more education and finding new places to live.

Current online financial planners already know that the Internet can be a robust, powerful, and profitable resource. However, the Internet is vast, ever-changing, and filled with surprises. *Managing Your Money Online For Dummies* provides ample, timely information about using the appropriate Internet resources to solve major personal financial management issues.

Managing Your Money Online For Dummies shows you how the Web can help you take control of your finances by pointing you to the best Web sites and providing easy step-by-step instructions for improved decision-making.

Foolish Assumptions

In writing this book, I assume you want to join the increasing ranks of middle-class millionaires by using online financial planning tools and resources. Middle-class millionaires didn't inherit their wealth or have access to surefire get-rich-quick formulas. These individuals became rich incrementally by developing plans and sticking to their strategies. I assume that you want to accumulate wealth by

- ✔ Using the Internet to take control of your personal finances, control spending, and whittle away debt.

- ✔ Getting more from what you already have and building personal wealth without penny-pinching or giving up luxuries.

- ✔ Protecting your assets by using the Internet to streamline your personal financial management, beef up savings, and plan for retirement.

If you're new to the Internet, I recommend getting a copy of *The Internet For Dummies,* Ninth Edition by John R. Levine, Carol Bardoudi, and Margaret Levine Young (Wiley). This book is great for anyone who needs help getting started with the Internet. *The Internet For Dummies* can help you hook up with local Internet providers, surf the Net, download free software, and join mailing lists or user groups.

If you're new to managing your personal finances online, check out Chapter 16. You want to be careful about what you download; it may be more than shareware. Find out how to select the right antivirus software, use firewalls, fight spam, and protect your online privacy. Chapter 17 offers warnings about online frauds, schemes, and deceptions.

Conventions Used in This Book

Although unfortunate, you're going to run into plenty of jargon from the world of money management, and the Internet for that matter, so when I define important terms that you need to remember, I highlight them in *italics*.

Occasionally I may wander a little off topic to discuss something technical or just something of interest. When that happens, you'll see what I'm talking about in a sidebar, which is book talk for special text that's set off in a box with a gray background. Check them out for the insight they add, but feel free to skip the ones that may not interest you.

When this book was printed, some Web addresses may have needed to break across two lines of text. If that happened, rest assured that we haven't put in any extra characters (such as hyphens) to indicate the break. So, when using one of these Web addresses, just type exactly what you see in this book, pretending that the line break doesn't exist.

How This Book Is Organized

Financial management is a broad topic. Don't feel bad if you have to use the table of contents and the index quite a bit. In fact, *For Dummies* readers are always encouraged to look through the table of contents and index for the topics that interest them the most. The chapters in this book stand on their own, so you don't have to read Chapter 11 to understand Chapter 12. Jump around and read the topics you want to know more about. *Managing Your Money Online For Dummies* is divided into six parts:

Part 1: Moving Your Money into Cyberspace

This part of the book explains how online management of your personal finances can save you time and money. You also gain an understanding of how handling your personal finances online enables you to get your ducks in a row before you have nothing left to lose, and you uncover where you're going money-wise with online tools and resources that can assist you in your financial planning. In addition, you discover how you can improve your credit rating and avoid late payments by using the Internet to pay your monthly credit-card and other bills.

Part 11: Saving Time and Money Online

In this section of *Managing Your Money Online For Dummies,* you grasp how using the Internet can shorten the time it takes to set up a budget. You find out how online banking is quickly becoming one of the most popular activities on the Web and how balancing your checkbook has never been easier. This section of the book also covers how you can easily purchase savings bonds and open high-yielding deposit accounts online. You get a handle on how you can use fee or free bill-paying services through the Internet and click-and-mortar banks. Just imagine, no more running to the post office or frantically looking for stamps!

Part III: Investing and Planning for the Future

Geared for individuals of all ages who are concerned with investing in their future and planning for an easy life after retirement, this part of *Managing Your Money Online For Dummies* shows you how to use the Internet to discover what type of investor you are and how you can maximize your personal wealth. You find out how to take advantage of Internet information about financial resources and maximize your savings to pay for your student's college education. You discover how to use online tools and sources to tell when it's near quitting time, how much you need, and how long your money needs to last during your retirement. Additionally, this part of *Managing Your Money Online For Dummies* helps you use the Internet to make it easy on yourself and your loved ones to settle your estate.

Part IV: Purchasing Online

Statistics show that each year millions of people investigate large purchases on the Internet. This section of *Managing Your Money Online For Dummies* shows you how to cut your time online and save money on big-ticket items. You find out how the Internet often is the easiest way to view homes and apply for a mortgage, and you discover how you can customize and purchase a new car online. Not in the market for a new car? Join thousands of other Internet users, and find out how you can purchase a used car online.

Part V: Protecting Your Money Online

See how you can make certain that a virus infection isn't fatal. Discover how to manage cookies and fight spam. You'll observe how Web-based and traditional scam artists both want the same thing — the money in your pocket. This section of *Managing Your Money Online For Dummies* also covers how to protect your family's financial health by using Web-based insurance calculators to determine how much insurance you need. You discover how to compare quotes online and search online for the best brokers, agents, or insurance companies.

Part VI: The Part of Tens

The Part of Tens provides new information in a condensed form about the top issues of online personal finance. See how you don't have to live from paycheck to paycheck. Discover how you can start small and then build on your use of the Internet to accurately and easily take control of your finances.

Next, visit ten handpicked Web sites and follow the easy self-help directions to discover whether you're swimming in debt. Find out how you can tell the difference between a real life preserver and a fraud.

Icons Used in This Book

For Dummies books use little pictures, called icons, to flag tidbits of important text. Here's what the icons mean:

Time is money. When you see these shortcuts or timesavers, read the information and think about how you can spend less time wrangling with your finances.

This icon is a type of sticky note. It points out the bottom line revealed to you here. You can easily go back and reread the important part of a chapter.

This heads-up warning helps you avoid mistakes and prevents you from getting trapped in an online scam or fraud.

You'll see this icon when I discuss nerdy technical information. You don't need to read it if you don't want to.

Where to Go from Here

You can start with Chapter 1 and read the whole book, or you can skip around and brush up on the topics that interest you at the moment. If you're new to the idea of managing money on the Internet, start with Part I. If you already have some of your dough in cyberspace, check out all the other cool stuff you can do in the rest of the book.

Feedback, Please

I'm always interested in your comments, suggestions, or questions. I'd love to hear from you. Please feel free to contact me in care of Wiley Publishing at 10475 Crosspoint Blvd., Indianapolis, IN 46256. Better yet, visit my Web site at www.kathleensindell.com or send me an e-mail message at ksindell@ kathleensindell.com.

Part I
Moving Your Money into Cyberspace

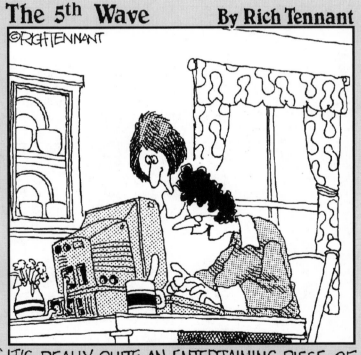

The 5th Wave   By Rich Tennant

"IT'S REALLY QUITE AN ENTERTAINING PIECE OF SOFTWARE. THERE'S ROLLER COASTER ACTION, SUSPENSE AND DRAMA, WHERE SKILL AND STRATEGY ARE MATCHED AGAINST WINNING AND LOSING. AND I THOUGHT MANAGING OUR BUDGET WOULD BE DULL."

In this part . . .

In this part of the book, I explain how online personal financial management can save you time and money. You soon find out how using the Internet to get your financial ducks in a row helps you achieve your financial goals.

Chapter 1

Managing Bucks with Clicks

In This Chapter

▶ Discovering your money personality through an online quiz

▶ Learning whether you're managing your dollars well

▶ Discovering how the Internet can help you build wealth

▶ Giving yourself an online financial makeover

A re you interested in accumulating wealth? Although the answer to this question may seem obvious, different people have different definitions of wealth. For some people, being wealthy means having a Cadillac with a chauffeur (remember *Driving Miss Daisy?),* but for other wealth seekers, being wealthy is taking world cruises or retiring comfortably in Florida.

Today, thousands of middle-class millionaires reside in America. These folks didn't inherit millions, they didn't become millionaires overnight, and they didn't hit the lottery. These wise individuals became rich incrementally, by simply facing their financial issues one at a time and using effective strategies to take control of their personal finances. At the end of the day, *wealth* is defined as building enough net worth to comfortably achieve your goals.

Using the Internet for Faster, Better Ways to Keep More Money

The Internet is ideal for everyone who wants to maximize personal wealth by making each and every dollar count. This book shows you how to get more from what you already have and how to reach your personal financial goals without penny-pinching or giving up luxuries.

There's no secret to becoming wealthy; all it takes is planning and discipline. Every day people find out that risky schemes, insider information, or even access to a closely held secret can't make them wealthy. The key to building wealth is organizing and maximizing your assets.

Wealth is created when your *inflows* (the amount of cash you receive) is greater than your *outflows* (the amount of cash you spend) over time. The greater your net worth, the wealthier you are. As you invest your excess cash in savings, securities, real estate, and related investments, your net worth grows.

When you spend every dime that you make, regardless of how much you make, you can never be wealthy. In other words, you need to save and invest, which means developing a plan to do so and sticking to it. At the end of the road, you'll find financial independence. So set a start date and get going. This book can help you every step of the way.

"What's Your Money Personality?" is a ten-question quiz that you can take at iVillage (www.ivillage.com). From your responses, you can discover whether you're a financial maven or a money novice. At the home page, click on "Money" and then click on "Quizzes" in the left margin.

Where Are You Now? An Online Mirror

When the stock market is improving, you may think it's time to start opening your brokerage statements. You may even be ready to sort out some of your other financial issues. Regardless of the reason, the present is a good time, if not the best, for taking control of your finances, getting back on track, and starting to accumulate wealth. Your first step is to start moving your financial information online so you can get and keep a bird's-eye view on what you need to focus on when getting your financial ducks in a row. For example, ask yourself these questions:

✔ Do I need to put a little life into my retirement savings? Check out Chapter 10 to discover how the Internet can help you determine how much you need to save for your retirement years.

✔ Should I pay off some debt? Thumb through Chapter 3 for online calculators that show the true cost of credit cards. You also can get online help with your decision-making.

✔ Should I increase or add insurance policies to protect my family? You can get online quotes for the insurance you need by using the information found in Chapter 18.

✔ How can I protect my nest egg? Go to Chapter 8 for help in selecting the online broker who's just right for you.

Don't try to tackle everything at once. Break your task into smaller achievable parts. Start with what's keeping you up at night, and then use the online strategies detailed in this book to organize your finances and maximize your net worth.

Giving Yourself an Online Financial Makeover

The Internet can help you set your financial goals. Establishing your financial objectives is a great way to plan for the future. By planning what you want to accomplish, you have a better chance of achieving your goals because you have the money to finance those objectives. Long-term goals, for example, can include owning a home, buying a car, saving money for your children's educations, and so on. Short-term goals cover the things you want to do today, next week, or within the next couple of months.

A personal financial plan can help you accumulate wealth and create a clear financial path for you and your family. Keep in mind that your financial plan needs to be flexible so you can accommodate life's little changes. Moreover, your personal financial plan needs to be

- ✔ **Realistic:** Make sure your goals are achievable.
- ✔ **Appropriate:** Make sure your goals are consistent with your personal lifestyle.
- ✔ **Time-specific:** Establishing milestones and deadlines along the way helps you reach your long-term goals.

Don't forget to include your personal values and to use your financial plan as a standard upon which you can base your decisions.

After you create a budget and a financial plan, you have a better idea of how much money you need to reach your financial goals. Table 1-1 shows you an online financial makeover that's designed to assist you in locating extra money for your short-term or long-term financial goals. What you'll soon discover is that by using online resources and looking at your entire personal financial picture you can make the most of your long-term finances by reorganizing the money you have today.

Table 1-1	The Online Financial Makeover
Categories	**Financial Makeover Questions and Online Resources**
Getting started	Are your savings and investments performing as well as they should? For the latest information about savings and investment returns, see Imoney.com (www.imoney.com) CBSMarketWatch (www.cbs.marketwatch.com) QuantumOnline.com (www.quantum-online.com)
Getting a handle on borrowing	Are you paying just the minimum monthly payment on your debts? Myfico.com (www.myfico.com) Creditinfocenter.com (www.creditinfocenter.com)
Taking advantage of lower interest rates	Can you negotiate a lower interest rate? You can often get your credit-card interest rate lowered with just one phone call. Bankrate (www.bankrate.com) Fiscal Agents (www.fiscalagents.com/learning cenre/credittips.shtml)
Determining your financial health	Do you know where you're spending your money? iVillage Cash Flow Calculator (www.ivillage.com/money/tools)
Managing your money	Are you tracking income and expenses by banking and paying bills online? MsMoney.com (www.msmoney.com) Checkfree (www.checkfree.com)
Protecting your assets	Are you prepared for an emergency? SmartPros (finance.pro2net.com/x32994.xml)
Protecting your future	Do you have enough insurance? InsWeb (www.insweb.com) Insure.com (www.insure.com) AccuQuote.com (www.accuquote.com)
Planning ahead	Can you afford the college of your child's choice? American College of Trust and Estate Counsel (www.actec.org)
Planning for retirement	Do you know how much to expect in Social Security benefits? Social Security Administration (www.ssa.gov)
Rebuilding your nest egg	Do you know how much you'll need to live on when you retire? T. Rowe Price Retirement Calculator (www.troweprice.com)
Investing in your future	Does your employer match your contribution to your retirement fund? How do you plan to invest the money? Kathleen Sindell's Online Investment Program (www.kathleen sindell.com/twelve_point_investing_program.htm) or purchase *Investing Online For Dummies,* 5th Edition (Wiley)

What's Keeping You Up at Night?

At some point in people's lives, they worry about some aspect of their financial well-being. Everyone's financial circumstances are different. People who look like everything is financially under control often are shaking like leaves when they look at their checkbooks. You can use the Internet to stay away from temptation. For example, you can shop online to your heart's content and never spend a dime — unless, of course, you decide to buy something. The rewards of paying down a credit card can mean an extra $250 a month in your pocket instead of forking over that same amount in interest charges. You can invest that windfall in an IRA and be one more step closer to financial freedom.

Do you know where your dollars are?

If you don't know what you're doing with your money, you're probably not managing it well. Creating a budget is the best way to gain control of your finances. You need to plan for the expected and the unexpected to successfully prepare and use a budget. Budgets are never static; they're constantly monitored and adjusted as income and expenses change. Having a budget can help you determine whether you're living beyond your means or building wealth by increasing your net worth. Your budget is a tool, and you can use the Internet to help you improve your budgeting skills. For more information about online budgeting, see Chapter 4.

Many people view budgets as constraints on their lifestyles. However, when you think positively about your budget and focus on breaking old habits, you can stay on track. Online tools help you organize and keep track of your records right on the Web so you know exactly where you are. Being on top of your finances shows you in advance whether you're going to have problems paying bills and will need to make arrangements with creditors.

TIP

A word about financial advisors

Some do-it-yourself investors want a professional to review and assess their portfolios before they re-enter the market. Most financial advisors charge about 1 percent of the asset value of an account per year to custom design and manage a portfolio of stocks and mutual funds. Pay a visit to the Web sites of the Financial Planning Association at www.fpanet.org and the National Association of Personal Financial Advisors at www.napfa.org to find the names of financial planners and independent financial advisers in your area.

Debt is all the money you owe to others, including your mortgage, credit cards, car loans, and other bills. Debts are liabilities that reduce the amount of your net worth. The higher your debt is, the lower your personal wealth. What's more, increasing consumer debt has a debilitating effect on your overall net worth. Become aware of the 24/7 conveniences of online bill paying, various calculators, and worksheets so you can effectively manage your debt and so you don't incur late fees or otherwise damage your credit rating. For more about online bill paying, see Chapter 7.

Do you have more than you think?

A basic tenet of wealth building is setting money aside rather than spending it. Wealth building is not rocket science. You may remember your father owning blue-chip stocks and driving to the bank on payday to deposit funds in the family's checking and savings accounts. Although the world today seems much more complicated, one thing remains the same. If you want to be rich, you still need to accumulate assets.

Some individuals prefer safe low- or no-risk investments such as certificates of deposit (CDs) and Treasury bills. Others are more aggressive investors hoping to make more money in stocks and other financial instruments. Overall, building wealth is about careful strategy and planning. If you computerize all your financial activities, you can quickly respond to events in the stock market and take control of your money, regardless of your investing style. Find more information about developing a financial plan in Chapter 2.

Moving your money into cyberspace can be time-consuming. However, you soon find out that you're saving time and reducing your stress level because your computer automatically tracks the stock market's movements and your credit cards, brokerage accounts, and bank balances. Being able to watch over all these factors is a one-stop shopping style called *account aggregation*. Web sites that offer it can streamline your financial activities. Many of these Web sites are offered by your online bank or are free-standing online entities. You can also use personal finance software programs, such as *MS Money* or *Quicken*. Discover how you can consolidate all your accounts online in Chapter 4.

Protecting your assets

As you gradually accumulate assets, you want to protect and maximize them. Once again, the Internet offers assistance by providing you with state-of-the-art comparison shopping for the best insurance, savings and investment plans, and interest rates. Here's how:

- ✔ **Insurance premiums:** You can easily shop online with different companies and compare premiums of many types of policies. (See Chapter 18 for details.)

- ✔ **Savings and investments:** The Internet provides Web sites that show which financial institutions pay the best interest rates for savings, CDs, and other financial instruments. You also can find discount online brokerages that charge only a fraction of the fees charged by traditional brokers. (See Chapter 6 for more information.)

- ✔ **Lowering your interest rates:** You can comparison shop online for lower interest rates. Lower interest rates can make a big difference in how much you pay per month and how long you take to pay off the balance. Say, for example, that you charge $2,500 on a credit card with an annual percentage (interest) rate (APR) of 20 percent. The minimum monthly payment is $50. At that rate, you pay off in eight years and ten months. When the APR is 14 percent, the minimum monthly payment is $50, and you can pay off the balance in six years and two months. (See Chapter 3 for specifics.)

- ✔ **Dealing with debt:** The Web features a variety of online calculators that help you determine whether you have too much debt. (See Chapter 20 for the whole story.)

Chapter 2

What's the Plan Stan? Creating Your Online Strategy

Knowing where you're headed financially can make a big difference in how you plan to use your finances. Everyone has different incomes, spending patterns, and financial priorities, so making the effort to visualize where the money's coming from and where it's going is a great first step in managing your finances.

In this chapter, I explain some online tools and resources that can help you understand the importance of financial planning, assist you in creating your individual personal financial plan, and provide you with expert insights and advice about personal finance. In addition, I show you how to get a grip on your financial goals and objectives. Then I point you to an online test that tells you how much risk you can take. You'll also gain an understanding of the elements of your net worth statement. For example, you'll see how your net worth is equal to your personal wealth. You'll explore how to complete your personal net worth statement online and discover a Web-based calculator that compares your net worth to those of other people in your age group.

Planning to Use the Internet to Maximize Your Wealth

The three ways you can make a financial plan are hiring a financial planner or advisor, using financial planning software, or tapping into the Internet. Of the three options, I think the Internet is the best. Using the Internet for financial planning is less costly than hiring a financial advisor and more flexible than using personal finance software, and it gives you more control of your money. I don't mean to say that you'll never ask for professional advice nor ever use a software program such as *MS Money* or *Quicken,* but at the heart of the issue is the fact that no one cares more about your money than you do. Putting yourself in the driver's seat and taking control of your financial future by using the tools and resources on the Internet may be the best way to ensure that you achieve your financial goals and objectives.

The Internet can provide expert advice at little or no cost. With a little effort, you can use free (or inexpensive) online resources to maximize your personal wealth. Here are several online Web sites that offer free expert personal finance advice:

- **Andrew Tobias** (www.andrewtobias.com), author of *Manage Your Money,* offers insights in a daily online column.

- **Jonathan Pond's Web site** (jonathanpond.com) provides expert personal finance advice and links to other personal finance resources. Pond is a well-known TV host and author.

- **MSN Money** (moneycentral.msn.com/home.asp), illustrated in Figure 2-1, freely offers the expertise of a variety of columnists. Start by selecting a topic that's of the most interest to you.

You don't plan to fail, so don't fail to plan!

Many people believe that you have to be wealthy before you need a financial plan. The notion still lingers that saving as much as you can is the best thing you can do. Times have changed, however, and people who believe in this lackadaisical approach to financial planning don't have a financial strategy and are missing out on even the basics of maximizing what they have. Remember, investment tools and planning strategies used by the wealthy have as much value to high-income individuals as they do to the guy next door.

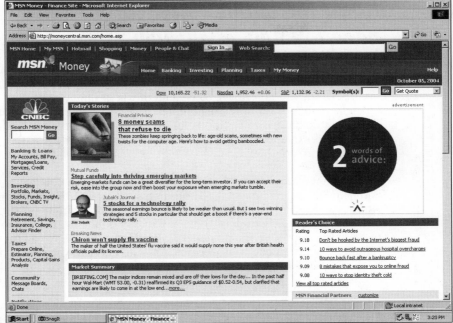

Figure 2-1:
Let the experts educate you about personal finance at MSN Money.

During the last 50 years, the complexity of financial planning required for the middle class has increased. Say, for example, that you just started to get ahead, and you're no longer living from one paycheck to the next thanks to that windfall gift you received or that inheritance from your rich Uncle Fred. And now all you want to do is save more money or make your money work harder for you. Fact is, you have only one way to reach those objectives, and that's by creating a financial strategy.

If you discover that you're having trouble developing a financial plan, you're not alone. Most people put off financial planning because it doesn't have a due date, but guess what: Now is the time to start making a financial plan, because doing so is the key to *your* financial independence. In other words, you need to take action, and this book is going to point the way to the best Internet tools and instructions to help you take control of your financial future — now.

What the online financial planners need to know about you

Two factors make online financial planning terrific. First, online financial planning is quick. Most online financial planners require only ten minutes of your time. Second, you don't have to be a math wiz or financial genius. Web-based financial planners simplify the complex process of financial planning by doing all the mathematical calculations for you. A wide variety of financial planners offer services online. Some Web-based financial planners are extremely simple, but others are complex.

In any event, your current financial position includes a number of variables, and using an online financial planner helps you structure your thinking about where you are and where you want to go with those variables. The list that follows includes 24 variables that are used by online financial planners to personalize your individual financial plan. If you don't have all the answers right now, you can use guesstimates now and enter the actual numbers later. Here's a sampling of some of the items you may use for your personalized financial plan:

- ✔ **Your age:** Your financial requirements change as your age changes. You may also be asked about the age at which you (and your spouse) plan to retire.

- ✔ **Marital status:** This factor is important for tax purposes.

- ✔ **Spouse's age:** Do you want to include your spouse in your financial plan? If you do, his or her age makes a difference.

- ✔ **Your goals:** Do you want to purchase a home, a vacation retreat, or a new car, or do you want to save for your children's educations?

- ✔ **Annual household income:** This amount is an important starting point. Annual income includes items such as salaries, wages, dividends, and interest.

- ✔ **Federal tax rate (as a percentage or as dollars):** You don't want to forget to include the taxman. To determine your Federal tax rate, see Yahoo! Finance located at `taxes.yahoo.com/rates.html`.

- ✔ **State of primary residency:** Some financial planning programs automatically include the state's tax rate. To determine your State tax rate, see Yahoo! Finance at `taxes.yahoo.com/statereport.html`.

- ✔ **State tax rates:** You can enter this amount as a percentage of taxable annual income.

- ✔ **Estimated inflation rate:** This amount has an impact on how much you have when you're ready to retire. For more information about how to estimate the rate of inflation, see the Federal Reserve Bank of Minneapolis at `woodrow.mpls.frb.fed.us/research/data/us/calc/hist1800.cfm`.

- ✔ **Anticipated changes in your annual income:** If you're starting out, you're likely to expect to make more money in the future. If you're nearing retirement and cutting back, you're likely to make less per year than you do now.

- ✔ **Total savings now in tax-deferred accounts (such as IRAs, 401(k)s, employee profit sharing, or stock ownership):** Have you been paying as much as you can into your tax-deferred savings plans for the last 20 years? How about the last year? For more information about tax-deferred accounts, see Gabelli Asset Management, Inc., located at www.gabelli.com/university/iradisc.html.

- ✔ **Annual savings you'll add (as a percentage of annual income or as dollars):** If you have a savings program that you follow, enter the amount you pay yourself each year. (For more about finding the best ways to save, see Chapter 6.)

- ✔ **Matching funds (if any) that your employer kicks in based on your contributions:** Enter the annual amount of matching funds your employer pays into your tax-deferred savings account (IRA, 401(k), and so on). For more information about tax-deferred savings accounts, see Chapter 10.

- ✔ **Total amount of your other taxable investments (set aside for retirement):** Are you receiving retirement benefits from another employer? Enter the taxable amount that's set aside each year.

- ✔ **Amount you expect to add annually to your investments:** Do you have an automatic investment plan? Do you regularly invest a certain amount each month? If so, see Chapter 8 to find out more details about choosing an online broker and making your first trade.

- ✔ **Estimated return on investments before retirement:** Using an online calculator (try the one at FinanCenter at www.financenter.com) determines the estimated amount of gain you can expect to realize on your investments before you retire.

- ✔ **Your life expectancy:** What is your life expectancy? Fill out this quick questionnaire at MSN Money (moneycentral.msn.com/investor/calcs/n_expect/main.asp) to find out.

- ✔ **Your desired annual income during retirement:** Keep in mind that if you want to travel, participate in leisure activities, or have a vacation home, the amount of income you need each year increases.

- ✔ **Federal tax rate during retirement:** The tax rate on your income is likely to change after you retire. Enter your best "guesstimate."

- ✔ **State tax rate during retirement:** Ditto for the State tax rate on your retirement funds.

- ✔ **Expected Social Security benefits:** To discover how much you can expect in Social Security benefits, see the Social Security Benefits Planner Web site at www.ssa.gov/planners/index.htm.

- ✔ **Pension benefits:** Your pension benefits can come in many forms. For more information, see Chapter 10.

- ✔ **Other income during retirement:** This kind of income can include annuities and so on.

- ✔ **Expected one-time payments:** Expected one-time payments may include a windfall from a distant relative or an inheritance from your parents.

The following are a few of the financial planning calculators you can find on the Internet. Don't worry about paying for the service; the online Net Worth Calculators listed below are free.

- ✔ **FinanCenter** (`www.financenter.com/financenter/plan/planner01.fcs`) offers an extensive financial planner that lets you know whether you're saving enough for your retirement years.

- ✔ **Quicken Retirement Planner** (`www.quicken.com/retirement/planner/personal`) can help you complete a basic retirement plan in about ten minutes. If you register with Quicken.com, you can save your plan for future retrieval and integrate it with other features of Quicken.com, such as its portfolio function, which tracks the gains and losses of your investments.

- ✔ **SmartMoney** (`www.smartmoney.com/retirement/planning/index.cfm?story=intro`) provides an in-depth retirement planner worksheet that lets you try out different scenarios. Scenarios can include beginning or delaying your retirement or how saving more money today impacts your lifestyle when you retire.

Being Where You'd Like to Be in Ten Years

Having a financial plan offers many benefits. With a little financial planning, you can get more from what you already have and reach your personal financial goals without penny-pinching or giving up luxuries. Your financial plans don't have to detail each and every financial activity on a day-by-day, dollar-by-dollar basis. The idea is to determine where you want to be in ten years. For example, the financial game plan for retiring before you reach the age of 55 and the plan for becoming the mother of eight children are different. Overall, financial planning takes into account these three primary elements:

- ✔ **Organizing and controlling your day-to-day finances.** Getting your finances organized and being smart about your expenses can help you have enough money to buy the things you really want during retirement.

✔ **Choosing and following a long-term course of action to achieve a financial goal.** A long-term goal can include items such as sending your children to college, buying a home, taking care of your parents, or living the good life in your retirement. Knowing exactly how much money you need to finance your goals and objectives can reduce stress and eliminate that feeling of always needing more money.

✔ **Building a financial safety net.** Safeguard yourself and your family so that emergencies, such as unemployment, illness, or disability, don't send you and your family into financial chaos.

Setting your financial goals

Take advantage of your dreams, goals, and aspirations to get a firm grasp on what you want your future to be like. You may have many ideas about what you want in your future life. Writing each goal on a piece of paper can help you get organized and assist you in finding out where you need to start. Answering these questions will give you several ideas:

✔ What are your financial goals and objectives? Do you want to own your own small business? Do you want to go to college? Do you want to own your own home? How about traveling around the world in a hot-air balloon? Write down each goal and objective no matter how big or small.

✔ How do you plan to reach your goals and objectives? What do you have to do to make your dreams a reality? What's the first step? What's the second step? For example, if you want to be a lawyer, it generally takes seven years of college and passing the bar exam. Break your goals down into short-term (one year or less), medium-term (one to five years), and long-term (five years or more) goals.

✔ Which goals and objectives are most important? Prioritize your goals and objectives. Work toward achieving the most important goals and objectives first.

✔ To achieve each financial goal, how much money do you need, where will you get the money, and how long will it take you to earn it? For example, my family wanted a vacation home without a mortgage. My father did the work himself during a ten-year period. Today the cabin is 30 years old and still doesn't have a mortgage.

After answering the questions in the list above, make sure that you go out and get an education about managing your personal finances. Read books like this one and surf the Internet's financial Web sites. Identify small, measurable steps you can take to achieve your financial goals. Start working on those steps and getting into the action.

Then, be sure to evaluate your progress on a monthly basis. Are things working out as planned? If not, make the appropriate adjustments to your plan. For example:

- ✔ If your financial goal is retirement and you receive an inheritance or your investment portfolio is reduced to a third of what is was three years ago, you may have to increase (or decrease) the time horizon for your financial goal.

- ✔ If your financial goal is to set aside one day's wages for savings each month, and after several months of trying to make ends meet you can only set aside four hours of wages per month, you may have to turn your hobby into a part-time job to reach your financial objective.

- ✔ If you've achieved one of your financial goals, you have to adjust your finances so you can start focusing on your next financial priority.

Devising your financial strategies

After you've determined your financial goals and objectives, you also need to determine the strategies you'll use to achieve them. As a general rule, younger people can take more risks than older people. If you're married with children or have older parents who may need your care, you need to take fewer risks than if you're not married or are unattached. If you're at the peak of your career and retirement is more than ten years away, you can take more risks. If you have a thin financial safety net and the amount of your savings are relatively small, you can't afford great amounts of risk. Finding out your *investment horizon* (the amount of time you can keep your money in investments) is important. Whether your time horizon is short or long term affects how much risk you can tolerate. Individuals with short-term horizons can only afford low risks. Investors with long-term horizons can tolerate higher risk levels.

Are you really a risk taker? Remember, aggressive investing has a bigger upside and a greater downside than standard investing. If you want more gains, you must also be prepared to risk higher losses. Don't fool yourself. Ask yourself this question: "If I achieve higher gains next month, will I invest more, or will I take my profits and invest in something safer?" If you tuck your profits away in an insured account, then you're not the risk taker you think you are.

Taking some risks (if you dare)

Risk often is represented by the volatility of prices. If the price of an investment frequently swings back and forth, then your investment is considered risky. When making investment decisions, you need to take your attitudes about risk into consideration. The amount of risk you can tolerate often depends on your knowledge of investments, your experience, and your personality. Each person has his or her own style and needs. Knowing exactly what your risk-tolerance level is helps you select investments that offer the highest return for the level of risk you're willing to take with your investments.

The Internet provides many online risk-tolerance tests. Here are a few examples:

- ✔ **Allstate** (`termlife.allstate.com/afs/aaAssetCalc01.asp`), shown in Figure 2-2, offers a survey of 12 questions. Enter your answers, and the online calculator will suggest an investment allocation strategy that suits your current needs and situation.

- ✔ **Charles Schwab** (`www.schwab.com`) offers an investor profile. At the Home Page, click "Planning" and then click "Tools," and finally, click "Investor Profile," to find out about your risk-tolerance level and to see a sample portfolio that best fits your unique needs.

- ✔ **Safeco Mutual Funds** (`www.webcalcs.com/cgi-bin/calcs/prod/risk.cgi?client=safecofunds`) has a questionnaire that helps you determine your personal comfort zone with regard to risk.

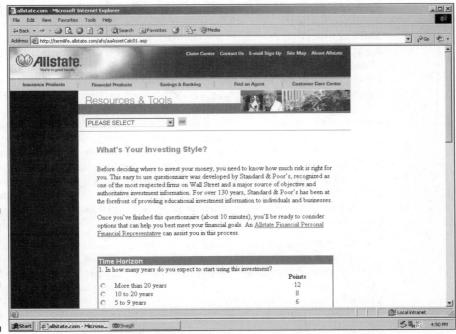

Figure 2-2:
Allstate provides an easy-to-use online risk toler-ance test.

What Are You Worth?

Many individuals don't know their net worth. Finding out your net worth is the starting point of your financial planning. Knowing your exact starting point enables you to determine how much you need to accumulate to achieve your financial goals. For most folks, increasing their net worth is the name of the game.

Before making plans for the future, you must know where you stand today. If you only know your bank balance, you're standing on shaky ground. To determine what you own, you need to add up all your assets. Next, you subtract everything you owe. The difference is your *net worth*.

Figuring your net worth isn't only the first step in financial planning, but it also comes in handy for many other financial situations. For example, mortgage lenders require a net worth statement, college financial aid is based on net worth, and personal loans and lines of credit require net worth statements for approval. Additionally, wealthy individuals use net worth statements of $1 million or more to qualify for high-risk investments.

Looking at the plus side of your finances

Most net worth calculators are divided into four parts: short- and long-term assets and short- and long-term liabilities. If you don't know the exact amount of any item, just use a guesstimate to estimate your net worth. You can always return to your net worth calculator with a more definite answer later on. The following are a couple of the categories used to calculate your net worth:

- ✔ **Short-term assets** are usually defined as items you can quickly sell. The most *liquid* of all your assets is cash because it doesn't usually lose any of its value when it's liquidated. Short-term assets can include cash in your checking and savings accounts or money market accounts; easy-to-sell investments like publicly traded mutual funds, stocks, bonds, or options; the cash value of your life insurance policies; money that is owed to you for work completed and items sold; or other easily sold items (think pawn shop).

- ✔ **Long-term assets** are sometimes called fixed assets and are often defined as items that can be liquidated in six months or more. Long-term assets are good examples of non-liquid assets. Long-term assets are frequently trickier to sell than short-term assets and may have penalties for early withdrawals. After you know more about your financial position, you'll know how much money to set aside as a safety cushion so you don't have to tap into these funds in case of an emergency.

Long-term assets can include certificates of deposit that carry early withdrawal penalties, IRAs, Roth IRAs, Keogh plans, tax-deferred annuities, funds in pension plans, employee stock options, or other stock options. See Chapter 10 for more details on these types of financial products.

Looking at the negative side of your financial picture

Your *liabilities* are amounts you owe to someone else. Here are some examples:

- All current unpaid bills, such as rent, utilities, telephone, and insurance premiums
- Outstanding balances on your gasoline credit card, Visa, MasterCard, or department-store credit cards
- Your car loan or other installment loans
- Your mortgage and other equity loans on your home
- Personal loans or other mortgages
- Margin loans against your investments
- The taxes that you owe, including property or income taxes that are due, taxes and penalties on any investments you may have sold, and taxes and penalties on retirement funds that you may have withdrawn

Summing up your net worth

To determine your net worth, subtract your liabilities from your assets. If the number is positive, you're already on your way to accumulating wealth. All you need to do is get organized and start maximizing what you have. If the number is negative, you need a game plan to change that negative number into a positive number.

If you're curious about how your net worth stacks up against others in your age group, check out the Expected Net Worth Calculator at www.banknorth. com/investment/calculators/networth.html. The Expected Net Worth Calculator is based on averages that divide individuals into different categories. It doesn't take extraordinary situations into consideration, so don't despair if find yourself in the "Under Accumulator of Wealth" category.

If you compute your net worth now and then again three months from now, you can tell whether your financial picture is improving or getting worse.

Valuing what you own

Keep in mind that some things may be valuable to you (such as the dirt you've collected from all the places you've traveled to during your vacations), but they don't have significant resale value the way cameras or video equipment does. Additionally, some long-term assets are difficult to sell at times. For example, try selling a large boat in the winter. No one is thinking about cruising and fishing when it's snowing, so not many people are in the market to purchase an expensive boat. Some long-term assets can take several months to several years to sell. These types of assets can include your home or other types of real estate, cars, artwork, antiques, collectibles, boats (as I mention earlier), motorcycles, airplanes, investments in privately held companies, or equity in a partnership or business.

All the Web-based net worth calculators listed below do all the math for you. That is, they subtract your liabilities from your assets and tally up the difference. Don't worry about cost; each Net Worth Calculator is free.

- ✔ **Altamira** (www.altamira.com/altamira_en/education-tools/ investment+calculators/net+worth+calculator.htm) has a net worth calculator that's designed to help users determine their current net worth and track changes in that value over time. Just input the relevant figures, and the calculator takes care of the rest.

- ✔ **CalculatorWeb** (www.calculatorweb.com/calculators/netwcalc. shtml) provides a variety of online calculators. Its net worth calculator is great for a quick snapshot of your financial position.

- ✔ **iVillage** (www.ivillage.com/money/tools/net_worth/) offers an easy-to-use net worth calculator. Simply fill in the values for each specific asset or liability. If you run out of boxes for any category, you can add the remaining values together and input the category subtotal.

- ✔ **MSNBC** (www.msnbc.com/news/358613.asp?cp1=1) supplies you with a form you can use to estimate your current net worth. Use the Tab key to move between fields. When you're finished, you can print or save your results.

- ✔ **Understanding and Controlling Your Finances** (www.bygpub.com/ finance/NetWorthCalc.htm) provides an online net worth calculator with detailed definitions of asset and liability categories that enable experienced individuals and financial newbies to easily walk through the process of calculating net worth at any given moment.

- ✔ **Young Money magazine** (www.youngmoney.com/java/calc_12.asp? source=overture) supplies a calculator that's designed to help you to take a snapshot of your current financial condition.

Chapter 3

Giving Yourself Credit

According to Experian (www.experian.com), the average debt held by credit-card-holding households is $4,663. In 2003, households in the United States charged $412 billion, a 185 percent increase from five years ago, according to Standard and Poor's. The increase in credit-card debt doesn't necessarily mean that American households are running deeper into the red ink, but it does point out the importance of knowing about your credit report. Many folks are taught that living in the United States is impossible without a credit card. Most people don't think much about their outstanding credit-card debt. For example, can you immediately write down how much you owe on your credit cards to within $100? If you don't know, you're not focusing on an item that can negatively impact your ability to make large purchases in the future.

This chapter shows how you can order your credit-card report online. You'll discover how to evaluate your credit report and correct any errors. This chapter explains how your credit score is derived and how it can affect the interest rates you have to pay when you borrow money. You'll discover how you can determine whether you've reached your debt limit and find suggestions for getting a credit card even when you have no credit history or you have damaged credit. This chapter explores how you can protect the quality of your credit and avoid tricks and scams. You'll become skilled at comparison shopping for the credit card that meets your individual financial situation. This chapter also looks into the features you want in a credit card and discusses the pros and cons of reward and affinity credit cards. Finally, this chapter reveals how you can apply online for a credit card, check your statement online, and even make payments online.

People Are Talking About You . . . in Your Credit Report

Thinking about applying for a credit card online? You may want to apply for your first credit card online, consolidate all your credit-card debt onto one card, take advantage of a low-interest credit card, or participate in all those credit-card rewards programs you keep hearing about. However, before you start shopping online for a credit card, you need to invest a few bucks (about $30) for an online credit report to find out exactly what your credit history looks like. You need to know what's on your credit report, your credit score, and if your credit report contains any errors. If you're married, don't forget to request a copy of your spouse's credit report.

The higher your credit score, the more creditworthy you are. Credit scores can vary by 30 to 50 points depending on which credit scoring program is used and differences in the credit data used to obtain your credit score. Keep in mind that card issuers are usually banks, thrifts, or credit unions. Like all loan officers, they look at your credit report and use that information to determine whether you're a good or poor credit risk. The three major online credit-reporting agencies are

✔ **Equifax** (www.equifax.com), which offers consumers online credit reports and credit scores that are called Beacon credit scores.

✔ **Experian** (www.experian.com), which provides consumers with online credit reports and credit scores called the Experian/Fair Isaac Risk Model.

✔ **TransUnion** (www.transunion.com), which supplies consumers with online credit reports and credit scores called Empirica.

Who gets your credit report?

A number of people are legally entitled to look at your credit report. Credit bureaus can provide information to the following entities:

✔ Creditors who are considering granting or have granted you credit.

✔ Employers considering you for employment, promotion, reassignment, or retention.

✔ Insurers considering you for an insurance policy or reviewing an existing policy.

✔ Government agencies reviewing your financial status or government benefits.

✔ Anyone else with a legitimate business need for the information, such as a potential landlord.

✔ Court orders, federal jury subpoenas, and any third-party you okay in writing.

Regulations in Colorado, Georgia, Maryland, Massachusetts, New Jersey, and Vermont enable you to receive a free credit report once a year. When you apply in writing you can get a free credit report in several other ways. For example, you can get a free report whenever you're turned down for a loan, but you need to ask for the report within 30 days of being denied the loan. You can also get a free credit report if you believe your credit file contains errors because of fraud, if you're receiving public welfare assistance, or if you're unemployed and are planning to apply for jobs within the next 60 days.

Understanding your credit report

Credit reports are frequently lengthy and confusing. Not understanding exactly what's in your credit report can be costly to your current and future financial health. Your credit report is divided into these four areas:

✔ **Identifying information:** Your full name, any known aliases, current and previous addresses, Social Security number, year of birth, current and past employers, and similar information about your spouse whenever applicable.

✔ **Credit information:** When accounts (with banks, retailers, credit-card issuers, utility companies, mortgage companies, student loans, and other lenders) were opened, your credit limit or the loan amount, any cosigners for the loan, and your payment pattern over a two-year time frame.

Your credit accounts are listed in several categories. Lenders look at these categories to make judgments about your creditworthiness:

Revolving credit: A good example of revolving credit is your credit-card debt. Lenders want to see that you have no payments that are 60 days or more past due and no payments that are more than 30 days past due.

Installment credit: A good example of installment credit is your car loan. Lenders want to see the same payment history here as on your credit cards.

Housing debt: A good example of housing debt is your mortgage or rent. Lenders want to see that you promptly pay your mortgage and that you have no late payments.

- ✔ **Public record information:** Federal, state, and county court records on bankruptcy, tax liens, or monetary judgments (some credit bureaus also list nonmonetary judgments).

- ✔ **Recent inquiries:** The names of the entities that have obtained copies of your credit report within the past year (two years for employment purposes).

For more information about credit reports and how they can assist or prevent you from reaching your financial objectives, see

- ✔ **About Credit/Debt** (`credit.about.com/index.htm?terms=credit`): Provides content, articles, and online resources for discovering the benefits and limitations of credit.

- ✔ **SmartMoney Debt Management** (`www.smartmoney.com/debt`): Supplies debt management worksheets, information about credit cards, and articles about dealing with debt.

- ✔ **Yahoo! Credit Center** (`loan.yahoo.com/c/`): Offers a wide variety of articles, links to credit bureaus, and answers to the most frequently asked questions about credit.

  A free online credit analyzer that can quickly determine your creditworthiness is also featured.

Correcting errors on your credit report

A recent Public Interest Research Group survey (`www.uspirg.com`) titled "Credit Bureau Errors Mean Consumers Lose" indicated that 25 percent of the credit reports surveyed included incorrect information that can clearly result in the denial of credit or other benefits. If you're turned down for a credit card, you can ask the credit bureau for a copy of your credit report. A copy of your credit report will be sent to you via U.S. Mail free of charge. Check to see whether the credit-reporting agency made any mistakes. Here are a few credit report errors that you may discover on your credit report:

- ✔ **Accounts that aren't yours:** Do you have a relative with the same name as you? His or her account may be on your credit report.

- ✔ **Late payments that actually were paid on time:** Some late payments stay on your credit history for years.

- ✔ **Debts that you paid off that are shown as outstanding:** If the debt has an outstanding balance, make sure that you get credit for repaying the lender.

- ✔ **Old debts that shouldn't be reported any longer:** These items add noise and confusion to what can otherwise be a clean credit report.

- ✔ **Outdated negative information:** Negatives should be deleted after seven years with the exception of bankruptcies, which can stay on your credit report for ten years.

Credit-reporting agencies are responsible for researching, changing, and removing any mistakes or incorrect information. Usually this process takes about 45 days. At your request, a corrected report is sent to the lenders who inquired about your credit during the past six months or to employers who have received it within the past two years.

If the credit bureau won't correct the mistakes on your credit report, you have a right to represent your side of the story in a brief 100-word statement that the credit bureau must attach to your file. Your statement can clarify inaccuracies and explain reasons for late payments. Anyone requesting your credit file automatically receives your statement (or a summary of it) unless the credit bureau decides it's irrelevant or frivolous.

The Internet offers more information about your rights as a credit holder. The following are a few examples:

- **Federal Trade Commission Consumer Web site** (`www.ftc.gov/bcp/conline/edcams/credit/index.html`) offers information about your rights as a credit holder and provides tips about resolving credit problems.

- **Federal Citizen Information Center** (`www.pueblo.gsa.gov/cic_text/money/fair-credit/fair-crd.htm`) supplies information about the Fair Credit Reporting Act and includes a link to a complaint form.

- **Consumer Action Web Site** (`www.consumeraction.gov/caw_money_general_tips.shtml`) provides information about your consumer rights as credit holders and provides suggestions about how to resolve credit problems.

Knowing the Score

Credit bureaus get their information from the financial entities that extend credit to you. Credit-reporting agencies collect and centralize this information to create your credit report. Your credit rating is drawn from your credit report. Your credit report details your borrowing, charging, and repayment habits. A good credit rating can help you achieve your financial goals; a bad credit rating limits your financial opportunities. Your credit score doesn't take into consideration any information regarding your ethnic group, religion, gender, marital status, or nationality.

The credit score provides a numerical representation of a consumer's credit at a specified point in time. Lenders use credit scores to indicate the likelihood of the borrower repaying the debt. A wide variety of credit-scoring programs are on the market. The most famous credit score is a FICO score created by Fair Isaac Corporation (`www.fairisaac.com`).

Your credit score is calculated by using a black-box algorithm. This black-box algorithm is a secret mathematical formula based on how others use credit. The algorithm is proprietary and not disclosed to the public. Credit scores measure the likelihood of default by looking at five factors. Your credit score is based on the following:

- **Payment history (35 percent):** This category includes repayment activities for all your accounts, your public records, and collection items, and details about missed or late payments. The focus is on how late you were, how much you owed, and how recently this activity happened. Major negatives in this category are having items sent to collections and bankruptcy.

- **Amounts owed (30 percent):** This category includes amounts owed on all accounts and on certain types of accounts, the number of accounts that are carrying balances, the total credit line you're using, and how much of an installment loan is still owed compared to the loan amount. In other words, if you have ten credit cards with credit lines of $8,000 each, you have $80,000 in available credit. The more credit the borrower has available to him or her, the greater the possibilities of increasing the debt load in a hurry.

- **Length of credit history (15 percent):** This category deals with how long your credit accounts have been established, how specific credit accounts were established, and how much time has passed since you used certain accounts.

- **Taking on more credit (10 percent):** This category takes into account how many new accounts you have, the length of time since you opened a new account, how many recent requests for credit you've made, the length of time since credit report inquiries were made by lenders, and where you have a good recent credit history.

- **Types of credit used (10 percent):** The types of credit accounts you have and the number of each type that you have make up this category. Lenders view having a variety of different types of credit accounts as good. It indicates that you know how to handle money.

Your credit score treats multiple inquiries during a 14-day period as only one inquiry and disregards all inquiries made within 30 days prior to the day the score is computed.

Assessing your credit score

Credit scores start at 450 and end at 850, but don't expect to have a perfect credit score of 850. According to Craig Watts, consumer affairs manager for Fair Isaac Corporation, obtaining a FICO score of even 800 is unrealistic. A FICO score in the mid-700s or higher is fine. Often your credit score is affected by lenders and credit-card issuers not reporting repayment activities in a timely manner, credit-bureau errors, or your applying for one too many credit cards.

Table 3-1 shows how your credit rating can affect your monthly payments. The first column is the credit scoring range. The second column shows the interest rates lenders are likely to charge based on your credit score. The third column indicates the monthly payment on a $150,000, 30-year, fixed-rate mortgage. The fourth column indicates how lenders view a certain numerical credit score.

Table 3-1   How Credit Scores Can Affect Your Monthly Payments

Your Credit Score	Your Interest Rate	Your Monthly Payment	Evaluation of Your Credit
720–850	5.74%	$875	Excellent credit. You'll get the best rates offered.
700–719	5.87%	$887	Good credit. You'll likely get the loan you desire.
675–699	6.41%	$939	According to the Experian Web site, the average credit score in the United States is 678.
620–674	7.56%	$1,054	Lender will take a closer look at your file.
560–619	8.53%	$1,157	Higher risk; you won't be eligible for the best rates.
500–559	9.29%	$1,238	Your credit options will be limited or not available.

Lenders take into consideration your credit reputation (your credit score and history), your collateral (the value of your loan amount in relation to your vehicle or home), and your capacity to pay (your current and future income, debt, and cash reserves). The Internet offers information about the relationship of credit risk and how much interest you'll have to pay. Here are a few examples:

- ✔ **Bankrate** (www.bankrate.com) offers the basics of credit scoring. See content titled "The Power of Credit Scores," and estimate your FICO score for free.

- ✔ **MSN Money** (http://moneycentral.msn.com/content/Banking/Yourcreditrating/P88401.asp) provides "How to Read Your Credit Report," an online calculator to determine your total debt load and more.

- ✔ **Pagewise** (www.essortment.com/in/Finance.Debt) supplies tips, articles, and hints about credit and staying out of debt. Check out "How to Read Your Credit Report Rating."

Boosting your credit score in a hurry

As shown in Table 3-1, your credit score, to a large degree, accounts for the amount of interest you have to pay for a credit card. The following are a few tips about how you can quickly increase your credit score.

- **Pay your bills on time.** If you paid bills late in the past, you can improve your credit score by starting to pay your bills on time.

- **Keep balances low on credit cards.** Next to correcting errors on your credit report, carrying smaller balances is the best way to increase your credit score. Within 60 days, paying down credit-card balances can increase your credit score by as much as 20 points.

- **Limit credit accounts to what you really need.** Any account that no longer is needed should be formally canceled because zero-balance accounts still can count against you.

- **Resist opening in-store credit cards.** Every time you apply for a retailer's credit card, your credit score gets dinged. Here's why: A department store credit card isn't good evidence of creditworthiness, and new credit cards reduce the age of your credit history.

- **Check your credit report information for accuracy.** Make certain that old negatives and paid-off debts are deleted.

- **Be conservative in applying for credit.** Make sure that your credit is checked only when necessary. Stay loyal to your credit-card issuer. Having at least one credit card that's more than two years old can help your score by 15 percent. The benefits of a card that's more than two years old taper off.

- **Don't close unused accounts that have outstanding balances.** If you're trying to boost your credit score, don't close unused accounts that have outstanding balances. Closing unused accounts without paying off the debt changes your *utilization ratio,* which is the amount of your total debt divided by your total available credit.

For more online information about improving your credit score see the following:

- **About.com** (`credit.about.com/cs/creditwise/a/blwosubarticle.htm`) offers a credit workshop to help you improve your credit score.

- **Fannie Mae Foundation** (`www.homebuyingguide.com`) provides a guide that can assist you in improving your credit score by explaining what credit is, how to establish good credit, how to repair credit problems, and how to take control of your credit. You can either download the guide or have it mailed to you.

Financial SOS: Online Help for Consumers with Overwhelming Debt

The average outstanding credit-card balance is around $6,000, and the average interest rate is about 18 percent. (Department and specialty store credit cards have interest rates of around 21 percent.) Here's an example that shows the true cost of credit-card debt. To calculate the amount of interest the average cardholder pays per year, multiply $6,000 times 18 percent. The total is $1,080 per year. An average cardholder who invests $1,000 per year and earns 8 percent per year on that investment will have a $14,487 portfolio after ten years — a tidy sum that shows how costly credit cards can be when you don't pay off your monthly balance.

Am I in trouble?

The percentage of delinquent credit-card payments has increased. The American Banker's Association reports that in the fourth quarter of 2003, 4.43 percent of card accounts were 30 or more days past due, surpassing an all-time high of 4.09 percent that was set during the third quarter of 2003. You know you're in credit-card trouble when

- You find yourself getting snagged by the same financial problems again and again.

- You observe yourself behaving in ways you know you shouldn't (you eat out when you know you should eat in or buy that new sweater, and so on).

- You're unable to reduce your debt, or when you do, your debt is back to its former level in no time.

A general rule about debt when you're just starting out is making sure that your outstanding credit balance never exceeds one month's wages. If your credit-card debt is more than you can pay off within three months (and you have three or four cards), you may want to consider paying off one or two of your credit cards and then destroying them.

How do your know whether you've reached your debt limit? The Internet features many tools that can help you evaluate your credit, including the following:

- **Lending Tree** (www.lendingtree.com) offers an online credit-assessment calculator. After entering your information, your credit is assessed as either good, fair, or needs improvement. Click on the report button for more information about what this assessment means to you.

> ✔ **Get Smart** (www.getsmart.com) supplies an online calculator that takes you step by step through your options to determine which type of credit card is best for you. (Check out "Plastic Perfection: Selecting the Right Credit Card," later in this chapter to find out the differences between credit cards.)
>
> ✔ **Bankrate** (www.bankrate.com) provides a Credit Score Estimator. The online calculator estimates your credit score instantly and free of charge.

Credit for the credit-challenged

This section of the chapter is geared toward people who have damaged credit. Personal bankruptcies reached 1.6 million in 2003. This amount is an 8 percent increase from the previous year. Outstanding consumer credit (no, not fabulous consumer credit but rather loans that consumers still owe), mortgage debt, and other debt totaled $9.3 trillion by April 2003, or an increase of $7 trillion in January 2000.

Most online banks, thrifts, and credit unions offer credit cards online. You can complete an application and receive credit immediately. Two types of credit cards are issued — unsecured and secured.

Unsecured credit cards are lines of credit extended to the cardholder up to a certain amount that often include limited cash advances. Cardholders don't have to put up any type of collateral to be issued an unsecured credit card.

Avoiding the hazards of debt consolidators

Be wary of credit consolidators that promise easy solutions to difficult situations. Here are two examples:

✔ Credit Debt Solutions is a nonprofit credit-counseling firm that advertises on the Internet that it can help debt-laden consumers. However, this firm makes "little or no attempt to lower consumer debt," and many clients find themselves contending with added late fees and over-the-limit penalties. In one situation, a client paid $2,375 to the credit-counseling firm, but the resulting payments never reached the client's creditors. After complaining to authorities, the money was refunded to the consumer. The firm had no business license to operate in its location and no license to offer credit-counseling services in the state where it was located.

✔ Debt counseling can actually harm your credit record. For example, your creditors may report you as late because you're not paying the originally agreed amounts that you owe or because the debt counselor is sending your payments late. Late payments affect your credit score.

Secured credit cards are lines of credit that require a security deposit or other form of collateral before they're issued. Obtaining a secured credit card is a good way to start restoring your damaged personal credit. In some cases, the credit card's limit is the amount of your security deposit. Other secured credit cards are more lenient, setting the card limit at 25 percent, 30 percent, or 50 percent beyond the cardholder's deposit. Secured credit cards reduce the card issuer's risk as they enable cardholders to rebuild their credit. After a period of time, if the cardholder makes timely payments online and stays within spending limits, the deposit is refunded with interest.

If your application for an unsecured credit card is declined by one credit-card issuer, don't be discouraged. Another credit-card issuer may have just the credit card you need and may approve your application. Many credit-card issuers specialize in dealing with folks who are considered poor-credit risks. When that's the case, you of course have to pay a higher interest rate and fees, but you'll have a credit card. When all else fails, you can try a secured credit card.

Secured credit cards sometimes include application fees, annual fees, and interest rates as high as 21 percent. The range of interest rates for credit cards varies from 9.72 percent to 21.90 percent, and annual fees vary from $18 to $90.

Don't forget to find out when your account will be reexamined to determine whether you qualify for an unsecured card. That reevaluation shouldn't be any longer than 18 months after you get your secured card. Don't forget to shop for the best deal on a secured credit card at these Web sites:

- **National Financial Planning Support Center** (www.fpanet.org/public/index.cfm): Offers learning tools that include online calculators, articles, checklists, and links.

- **Damaged/Bad Credit Cards** (creditcards.freestuffcentral.com/1-DamagedBadCredit.html): Provides links to credit-card issuers that provide credit cards for individuals with damaged credit.

  This site is a good place to start your comparison credit-card shopping.

- **Credit Card Network** (consumers.creditnet.com): Specializes in providing helpful information about repairing your credit, building a good credit history, and assisting you in locating the right credit card.

  At this site, you find credit discussions and other credit services. In addition to the ability to apply for a credit card online, you also uncover lists of credit cards that can help you reestablish your credit with cards that are geared for individuals who are ranked as subprime credit risks.

Protecting the Quality of Your Credit

Using your credit card wisely can help you protect the quality of your credit and save your money. A good example is someone who pays $5,397 for a computer that's worth only $1,750 — this situation happens! Say you charge that computer on a credit card at 18 percent APR interest and then pay only the minimum payment of $35 per month. At that rate, you pay off the computer in 264 months (that's 22 years) and end up paying $3,647 in finance charges, about three times more than what the computer was worth in the first place. See how not using credit correctly can cost you?

Most individuals need only two credit cards. Each card needs to come from a different credit-card issuer, but they can be the same brand (Visa, MasterCard, and so on). One card is for everyday use, and the second card is for backup. If your identity is stolen, or if processing problems occur with your primary credit card, you're less likely to encounter future credit problems when you only have two credit cards. The Internet can help you lighten your debt load by showing you how to make smart choices about spending. Here are a few examples:

- ✔ **Nolo** (www.nolo.com) offers numerous articles about how to avoid overspending, provides strategies for using credit and debit cards, and describes tactics for repaying debts. At the home page, click on Law Research Centers, and then under Why Do Further Legal Research, click on Legal Encyclopedia. On the next page, click on the Debt & Bankruptcy heading.

- ✔ **MSN Money Central** (moneycentral.msn.com/articles/banking/credit/contents.asp?p=2) provides useful suggestions for protecting your credit. Check out what's in your credit report, find out how to improve your credit score, and discover how you can preserve your good name.

- ✔ **Federal Trade Commission for the Consumer (FTC)** (www.ftc.gov/bcp/menu-credit.htm), shown in Figure 3-1, supplies a full menu of easy-to-understand articles about how to protect the quality of your credit. The articles are in English and Spanish. You can view articles in either text or PDF formats.

Many are the ways that the financially unaware can be fleeced, and when you're vulnerable and searching for a financial life preserver, be wary of compounding your credit woes by falling for

✔ **Advanced-fee credit-card scams:** Consumers are promised loans or credit cards regardless of their credit histories. After you pay the fee, the loan or credit card never arrives. A better use for money spent on an upfront fee is for a deposit on a secured credit card (I provide more information about secured and unsecured credit cards in "Credit for the credit-challenged," earlier in this chapter).

✔ **Bait and switch:** Card issuers may attract customers with a promise of no annual fees and then turn around and charge minimum monthly finance fees. Customers who have no balances still must pay a monthly finance fee.

✔ **Balance transfer fees:** Before transferring a credit-card balance, make certain you don't have to pay a balance transfer fee and find out how long the low rate on your new card will last. Your introductory teaser rate is usually good for only six months, and after that your new rate may be higher than your current rate.

✔ **Compounding fees:** Some credit-card companies triple dip their charges in the following manner: First you're charged for making a late payment (the late fee). Next you've exceeded your credit limit, so you're charged a second fee (the over-limit fee). Because you've exceeded your limit, the credit-card issuer increases your interest rate because you're a higher-risk customer.

✔ **Credit-card insurance:** Credit-card fraud and identity theft are everyday occurrences. New federal laws limit a consumer's liability to $50 for credit-card misuse. Just make sure that you notify your credit-card issuer as soon as you know about the problem.

✔ **Credit repairs:** You may have received a bogus e-mail suggesting you can eliminate your debt. No matter how desperate your financial situation, please disregard the e-mail. It's a scam. For an upfront fee as high as $2,500, you get a magical certificate that's supposed to convince your bank and other creditors to eliminate your obligation to repay your mortgage, credit cards, or other debts. The certificate is, of course, an entirely worthless document that adds more to your financial problems because you spent $2,500 you didn't have in the first place.

✔ **Reducing the grace period:** Card issuers can reduce the grace period from 31 days to 21 days or lower. If you're not on top of your credit-card statement, you may miss this change and end up paying additional interest and late fees.

To protect your credit card, never post your credit-card information in any form on a private Web site, and always check your online monthly statement for anything you didn't purchase.

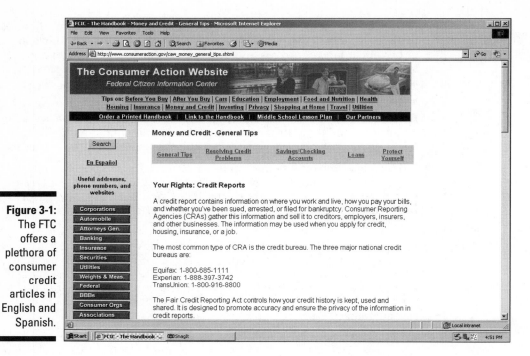

Figure 3-1:
The FTC
offers a
plethora of
consumer
credit
articles in
English and
Spanish.

Plastic Perfection: Selecting the Right Credit Card

The Internet provides many Web sites that specialize in assisting you with finding credit cards that meet your needs. The credit card that's right for you matches your current financial circumstances and helps you achieve your financial goals. Your search results can point you to several different kinds of credit cards, including

Lowest APR credit cards: If you don't pay off your credit-card balance every month, this card may be best for you.

No annual fee credit cards: If you have a high credit score, you shouldn't have to pay an annual fee for a credit card.

Best credit-card values overall: Individuals with excellent credit need to get the best credit-card deals available.

Secured credit cards: When you have no credit history or your credit history is damaged, a secured credit card probably works best.

Small-business credit cards: A great way to track and finance business expenses is with a small-business credit card.

The Web sites in the list that follows provide information about credit cards. These examples include credit-card search engines that can help you zero in on the card that's just right for you.

- ✔ **Credit Card Menu** (`www.creditcardmenu.com`) provides a complete listing of credit cards. Narrow your search by using the menu's search engine and indicating whether you want a credit card with a certain annual fee, interest rate, or introductory rate, and be sure to note what type and category of card (rewards of frequent flyer miles and so on) you want.
- ✔ **CardWeb.com** (`www.cardweb.com/cardlocator`) completes surveys of credit cards. You can automatically list the credit-card terms you want and search through the surveys. You can also apply for cards online and get a decision on your application within a few minutes on this site.

Locating great rates online

The Internet offers consumers three benefits: a wide variety of credit cards that are available, access to information about the latest credit-card features and choices, and online access to your credit-card statement and other management features, such as online bill paying.

The sections that follow are brief overviews of factors you can evaluate to help you discover which of those online credit-card deals is the best offer for you.

Checking out interest rates

If you don't pay off your credit card every month, you're charged interest on the unpaid balance. Card-issuing companies frequently offer *teaser rates* (low introductory interest usually for up to six months). After the introductory period, a higher fixed rate of interest takes effect. Keep in mind that when the fixed rate goes into effect, it also applies to charges that were made during the introductory time period but have remaining balances.

Uncovering the frustrations of fees

Some credit cards charge an annual or membership fee in addition to the interest they charge on your purchase balance. Individuals with high credit scores, however, usually don't encounter any problems going online and getting credit cards with low interest rates and no annual fees. Examples of other fees and charges that credit-card issuers assess are late fees, over-limit fees, charges for closing your account, charges for customer service, and charges for overseas transactions.

Grappling with grace periods

Credit-card issuers usually give you between 20 and 25 days' grace period each month when you're not charged interest on your credit-card purchase. In other words, if you pay off your credit-card bill within the grace period each month, you don't have to pay interest.

Competing through cash advances

Another way credit-card companies can compete is by offering cash advances. Many credit cards now are accompanied by a checkbook for limited cash advances. Keep in mind that cash advances are treated in several different ways. For example, cash advances from an automated teller machine (ATM) may not include a grace period.

Finding out what plan your credit-card company uses is important because the cash advance

- ✔ May not have a grace period and thus can be subject to a higher interest rate.
- ✔ May have a normal grace period but a higher interest rate.
- ✔ May have the normal grace period and interest rate.

Comparing credit cards on the Web

The following Web sites are great for credit-card comparison shopping:

- ✔ **CardWeb** (www.cardweb.com/cardtrak) offers useful, objective information to consumers seeking credit cards. You find news, statistics, and research. CardWeb is not affiliated with or sponsored by any credit-card issuer, financial institution, or consumer advocacy group.
- ✔ **Ask Bankrate** (www.bankrate.com) helps you find the best credit card for you. Fill out the questionnaire to see what type of credit card works best for your lifestyle. Using the right credit card lowers how much you pay in costly fees and interest. On the home page, click on "Credit cards," and then under Get the Best Credit Card, click on "Find the best credit card for you."

Selecting the features you want

Online comparison shopping for credit cards is great for saving time and money. When you comparison shop, you want to know about some of the numbers in advance so you can make the best decisions. Make sure you check out

- **Changing APRs:** Find out what happens when you're late with a payment. In some cases, your low interest rate doubles or even triples the first time you're late with a payment.

- **Costly cash advances:** Read the fine print about cash advances. If you get a cash advance, find out whether you have to pay a higher interest rate.

- **Fixed and variable interest rates:** Some credit-card issuers offer low, fixed-rate credit cards. Other credit-card issuers provide low, variable-rate credit cards. Which is best? Credit-card companies can raise their fixed-rate cards when interest rates increase. They only have to give you a 15-day notice of the rate change. With variable-rate credit cards, your interest rate changes regularly without any notification.

- **Teaser interest rates:** Credit cards with lower teaser rates, which often are in effect for only the first six months, are good, but be sure to check out the interest after the introductory period, and find out whether anything else changes.

- **Late fees:** If you know in advance that you're going to be late on several payments per year, compare late fees when evaluating credit cards. Your best deal may feature a slightly higher interest rate and a lower late fee.

- **Rewards:** Some cards offer rewards, perks, or cash-back incentives. You may want to consider one of these cards, even when it has a higher interest rate than your other credit cards and especially if you don't plan to carry a balance for a long period of time.

Racking up rewards by paying with plastic

Reward programs are defined as programs offered by credit-card issuers that give cardholders rewards for using their credit cards. Cardholders collect reward points every time they charge a purchase on their cards. Cardholders usually redeem these points for merchandise, travel, or cash, depending on the type of rewards program offered. According to SmartMoney.com (www.smartmoney.com), 55 percent of all card offers in April 2004 included rewards programs. Frequently, credit-card issuers use rewards programs to build customer loyalty.

Searching for affinity credit cards

Affinity credit cards clue everyone in on what your favorite charities, sports teams, hobbies, and activities are. For example, some sports teams issue affinity cards. Affinity credit cards are defined two ways — either as credit cards with a specific affiliation with a charitable cause or as credit cards that are associated with charities, sports teams, professional organizations, or universities.

The important thing to remember about affinity cards is that they provide you with an opportunity to support an organization. Whenever you charge a purchase to an affinity card and pay interest, the card issuer usually donates a predetermined amount to the organization pictured on the card.

You are, of course, likely to be charged a higher rate of interest (between 15 percent and 22 percent) for your affinity card; moreover, some affinity cards may have lower interest rates but include annual fees. If you pay off your balance each month, those factors shouldn't be an issue. The sponsored organization, in many cases, receives 50 basis points, or 0.50 percent of the total amount charged by the affinity cardholder. If you charge $100, the card issuer donates $0.50 to the organization you're supporting. However, no hard and fast rules apply.

Donations made through affinity cards, however, aren't tax-deductible because they're part of a contractual agreement you have with the card issuer and the charity. Regardless of the lack of a tax deduction, affinity cards are popular.

The Internet provides many sources for finding reward and affinity credit cards. A few examples include

- ✔ **Credit Card Catalog** (www.creditcardcatalog.com) offers a directory of affinity cards that you can apply for online. Reward cards offer incentives for cash-back payments, automobile purchases and gasoline, airline frequent flyer miles, entertainment, and hotels. Affinity cards can include organizations related to children, colleges and universities, environmental matters, gay and lesbian issues, Internet-related issues, and sports teams.

- ✔ **MBNA Corporation** (www.mbna.com/creditcards/index.html) enables you to apply online for credit cards that reflect your individuality. Select cards with travel and shopping rewards. Affiliation cards include sports teams, colleges and universities, environmental causes, and more.

Did you know that you can pay your taxes online with your credit card? Retailers like Official Payments (www.officialpayments.com) usually charge a service fee of 2.5 percent to 3.0 percent. (That's a $25 to $30 convenience fee for each $1,000 of taxes you pay.) The benefit of using your credit card to pay taxes online is convenience and more time to pay. In some cases, you may even maximize your credit card's rewards program, earning miles or points.

Applying online

Web-based credit-card applications are comparable to online bank account applications. Applying for a credit card online takes about ten minutes. The following example shows what steps you can expect when completing an online application:

1. **Select the credit-card issuer and card that's right for you.**

   You may go directly to the credit-card issuer's Web site or apply at one of the online credit-card comparison Web sites, such a Credit Card Menu (www.creditcardmenu.com).

2. **Check the applicant requirements.**

   You need to be at least 18 years of age or older and have a Social Security number.

3. **Provide your contact information.**

   Provide your personal contact information: name, address, e-mail address, and telephone number.

4. **Provide your residential status and related information.**

   State your residential status, years at your current residence, Social Security number, and birth date.

5. **Provide your employment information.**

   Include your current employer, contact information for your employer, number of years with the company, your occupation, annual income, and other household income. (Alimony, child support, and separate maintenance income don't need to be revealed if you don't want those amounts to be considered as bases for repaying your credit-card balance.)

6. **Provide your bank information.**

   State whether you have checking, savings, and/or money market accounts.

7. **Indicate your language preference.**

8. **Add the names of any additional users.**

9. **Read the terms and conditions of the credit card.**

   This fine print is about rates, fees, and other cost information. (You may want to print and file this information for future reference.)

10. **Click on the "Agreed to Terms" box, and then click the "Submit" button.**

11. **Review the data you have submitted to the credit-card issuer.**

12. **Click the "Submit" button again if the data is correct and you agree to the credit-card issuer's terms and conditions.**

Checking Out Your Online Statement

For people who travel or have tight budgets, online credit-card statements are a terrific way to keep tabs on what's happening with a credit card. Online statements indicate your current outstanding balance (what you owe), your credit limit (your total borrowing power), your available credit (recent charges may not be included), and your last payment amount. You'll also see an itemized list of transactions. Your online credit-card statement is updated every 24 hours, Monday through Friday.

There are usually three differing levels of access available for looking at archived past statements, including

- ✔ Unlimited access to all your past statements.

- ✔ Limited access as credit-card statements that remain on the Internet for two to six months.

- ✔ Current-only access to online statements. In this situation, you can't even see last month's statement.

One way to work around limited-access online statements is to print your statements immediately. You can file them or put your statements in a binder for bookkeeping purposes. *Note:* You also receive your monthly statement by the U.S. Mail.

Most online credit-card statements are divided into four areas:

Recent activity: Using your password and user ID, log on to the card issuer's Web site. The first page of your statement shows your recent activity, and you'll find an account summary indicating your total credit line, total credit balance, and total available credit. Next to your account summary, you'll discover a list that includes your current payment, credits, and any adjustments. Following that, you'll see your current transactions.

Your statement: Your statement is an online facsimile of your monthly paper statement, showing your previous balance, payments, transactions, finance charges, and your new balance. The minimum amount due is listed, as is your payment due date. Your total credit line, total available credit, credit line for cash, and available credit for cash are listed, and you'll find the APR that's applied to your balance for this time period.

Pay my bill: This section includes your account information, bank information, and a box for you to enter the amount you want to pay. Click to authorize the amount you want deducted from your account, and then print a copy of the confirmation form for your records.

Customer service: In addition to a section with answers to the most frequently asked questions (FAQs), the online Customer Service Center includes links to update your account information and contact the credit issuer.

Paying Your Credit-Card Bill Online

One of the most popular online activities is bill paying. The majority of major credit-card issuers, such as Citibank (www.citibank.com), CapitalOne (www.capitalone.com), Discover (www.discovercard.com), and American Express (www.americanexpress.com) accept online payments. The convenience can't be beat. You avoid writing a check, finding a stamp, going to the post office or mailbox, and hoping that your check arrives at its destination before you're charged a late fee. For more information on paying bills online, see Chapter 7.

If you're paying your bills from your bank account, you're usually limited to one online bill payment per 24-hour period, and you can make payments only for transactions that have been posted to your account.

Part II
Saving Time and Money Online

The 5th Wave   By Rich Tennant

"That reminds me - I have to figure out how to save for retirement _and_ send these two to college."

In this part . . .

In this part of the book, you discover how to save time and worries by using convenient online banking and bill paying services. You also establish how you can get the most out of what you have by purchasing savings bonds and Treasuries online.

Chapter 4

Almost Painless Online Budget Building

. . . .

In This Chapter

▶ Reviewing how the Internet saves time setting up a budget

▶ Partnering with the Internet for day-to-day control over your finances

▶ Identifying online tools and resources for tracking income and expenses

▶ Aggregating your accounts on the Web for one-stop access

▶ Spotting cash wasters and leaks with the Internet

. . . .

*E*xplore different ways to create a budget using online tools and resources so you can save time and effort when you're implementing a sensible budget. This chapter starts off with an explanation of the steps you need to follow to set up a budget. You'll discover the Web sites and pathways to online budget worksheets that can easily help you get started. You'll quickly grasp whether a weekly, monthly, or annual budget is right for you.

In this chapter, you'll find out just how your bank or a nonbank account aggregation Web site can track your personal finances with less hassle and more accuracy at no cost to you by allowing you to consolidate a range of accounts, bills, credit cards, and other financial information into one interface. Now that you're getting into the groove of online budgeting, you can start prioritizing your income and expenses so you gain an understanding of what regular net income is and how you need to deal with varying income and grasp what your everyday expenses are. You can also discover how online net cash flow calculators, such as those listed in Chapter 1, use information you provide to compute how much income you have or how far into debt you're going. After finding out how much money you're spending, you can create a realistic budget using online resources or a personal finance software program, such as *MS Money* or *Quicken*.

This chapter also details how to set up a budget using *MS Money 2004*. It compares the features of *MS Money* and *Quicken* and explores the benefits and liabilities of using both programs. As a result, you come away knowing how to use the Internet to compare your spending habits with those of other people who have similar net incomes. You even get tips on how to realign your expenses and discover why *budgets* (which actually are spending plans) can fail and what you can do to stop cash leakages. The chapter includes an examination of the top ten money wasters and discusses more online budgeting tutorials and Web sites that provide informative budgeting articles and insights.

Using the Internet for Your Budget Foundation

The difference between financial planning and setting your budget is that financial planning involves defining your financial goals and objectives, determining the best strategy to achieve those goals and objectives, and measuring your progress. Budgeting, on the other hand, starts with establishing the spending targets that help you stay within your means of paying your bills.

On average, most Americans spend about 10 percent more than they have, but that doesn't mean most Americans are spendthrifts or deadbeats. On the contrary, in most cases they overspend because they have only a vague idea of where their money goes. Often, the notion of living on a budget seems like punishment for hard work, when the better way to think about it is as a spending plan — nothing more or nothing less.

Creating a budget using a pencil and paper usually takes one to three hours, but if you've already started organizing information about your income and spending and make use of a *canned online budget* (a predetermined online budget based on your annual income), you can probably reduce the time required to build a budget to just several minutes. Now that you know how much time you don't need to spend establishing a budget, you can get started right away.

Your budget needs to be based on organization, not penny-pinching. Getting organized can show you how to save money without giving up the things you love. Your spending plan easily and instantly tells how much money you have to spend at any given time. This valuable information enables you to profit from opportunities and to react in a positive way to emergencies. FinanCenter.com offers three online budget calculators that get you pointed in the right direction by helping you answer these important questions:

✔ **How much am I spending?**

(www.financenter.com/consumer/calculate/us-eng/budget03.fcs)

✔ **How much should I set aside for emergencies?**

(www.financenter.com/consumer/calculate/us-eng/budget06.fcs)

✔ **What's it worth to reduce my spending?**

(www.financenter.com/consumer/calculate/us-eng/budget08.fcs)

Taking Control by Setting Up a Budget

One pretty tough call to make is determining what most people would do given a choice between getting pricked with a thousand needles and sitting down to set up a budget. Some folks are simply overwhelmed by the task (and may even consider the needles), while others simply have no idea where to begin. Luckily, the Internet and personal finance software programs have taken much of the drudgery (and pain) out of setting up a budget. In general, follow these steps to setting up a budget:

1. **List your income and expenses.**

   Everyone needs to start somewhere. List your income and expenses to determine how well you're doing. Several online net cash flow calculators are listed in "The rewards: Enjoying long-term luxuries" later in the chapter, so you can gain a quick view of your starting point.

2. **Determine the time frame of your budget.**

   Decide on the time period for your budget. If you're paid every two weeks, a two-week budget may work for you. If you pay bills monthly, a monthly budget may be more to your liking. Most people find an annual or semi-annual budget (that's based on real estate taxes and fees for annual insurance premiums) difficult to work with. There are no hard and fast rules about which time period is best.

3. **Choose a simple tracking technique.**

   You may want to track your expenses in a notebook or use a personal finance software program like *Quicken* (www.quicken.com) or *MS Money* (www.microsoft.com/money/default.mspx). On the other hand, tracking your expenses online at Quicken.com and downloading them to a spreadsheet application program may be easier for you. Choose the tracking method that you feel is the most comfortable for you to use.

4. **Determine general categories.**

You may want to start with general categories, such as housing, car, and food, and then add subcategories like house payment and home improvements, car payment and auto insurance, and groceries and dining out, thus fine-tuning your spending plan. Don't forget, you can always add categories you need or delete the ones you don't use.

5. **Establish income and spending amounts.**

   Tally up your income and deduct your expenses to find out whether you've been overspending, and then compare your spending habits to the averages for others with a similar net income at `www.msfinancial savvy.com/calculators/cal_bpc.html`. In what areas are you overspending or underspending?

6. **Monitor your inflows and outflows.**

   Closely track your expenses to prevent *spending leakages* (unaccounted dollars spent). If your cash purchases represent more than 5 percent of your budget, start collecting receipts so you can recall what you purchased and can realign your budget accordingly.

7. **Reevaluate and review your budget often.**

   Budgets aren't chiseled in stone, but as long as they're working, more power to you. However, you're always going to run into a reason for making an adjustment. Think about it; too many of them exist for you not to at least occasionally encounter them.

   Your reasons for budgeting change over time. Everyone wants a new car, right? And oops (or not), here come the kids draining the life out of the down payment on the house that people in their 20s often are saving for. Folks in their 30s and 40s frequently are concerned with paying for their children's college educations and living expenses, and after that, you're faced with funding your retirement years.

Here are several online budget worksheets that you may find helpful:

- ✔ **About.com's "Basic Budget Worksheet for Personal Budgets"** (`financial plan.about.com/library/blbudget.htm`), shown in Figure 4-1, uses preselected categories for budgeted amounts, actual amounts, and the differences. About.com also provides a budget worksheet for college students that's set up the same way.

- ✔ **Fidelity Investments** (`personal.fidelity.com/planning/investment/ content/budgetwork.html`) provides an annual personal budget. For your convenience, the Fidelity budget worksheet is printable.

- ✔ **NineMSN.com.au** (`finance.ninemsn.com.au/money/medic/budget planner/budgetplanner.asp`) has a five-step electronic budget sheet that enables you to develop weekly, monthly, and annual budgets. To create a budget using the *Money* Budget Planner, simply enter all of your expenses and your income. The planner then works out how much money you have left and provides you with a budget summary. You need to register (don't worry, its free) to save and update your budget.

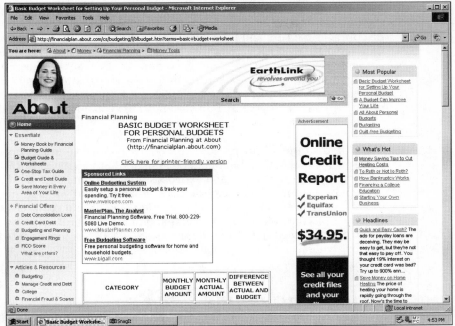

Figure 4-1:
About.com
provides a
great budget
worksheet.

Finding Online Resources to Track Your Income and Expenses

The best way to start your spending plan (or budget) is to track all your income and expense — everything. Use your income and expenses from now to six months ago. This will provide you with the latest information about what you're earning and spending. Don't forget: Keep your tracking method simple. Selecting a tracking method that's too complex makes your work too difficult, and you're likely to abandon your effort. Bear in mind that your spending plan is used as a communications tool. Difficult-to-explain spending plans won't win the support of others in your family.

The most difficult part of budgeting comes at the beginning when you must take a good, honest look at where you're spending your money. Sharing this information and having discussions about it with a spouse can be painful. Take heart in the fact that you're not alone. Many people have their own foibles about spending money.

If you don't yet have online access to your brokerage, bank, and credit-card statements, be sure to check out Chapters 3, 5, and 8, where you can find out how to immediately move these accounts to the Web. As you begin accessing your accounts online, you'll notice that you have to visit several Web sites to gather all the personal finance information you need. Some people like having their accounts scattered throughout cyberspace because they think doing so discourages hackers and impedes identity thieves. However, many people find having to deal with a plethora of passwords annoying. The solution is an *account aggregation service.* You can try any of the many free personal finance aggregation services that are available on the Internet. Aggregation services are essentially Web sites that consolidate all your online financial information so that it's easier to access. Two varieties are available — bank and nonbank aggregation services.

Note: On the other hand, if you're not ready to move your accounts online, write everything in a notebook. Keep in mind that you have to start making categories for your income and expenses. Any amounts of more than $25 need to be accounted for. Regardless of which method you use, make sure that it can be customized to suit your unique needs and requirements. Your spending plan can start out as a canned online calculator or software program, but you need to be able to quickly and easily customize it to reflect your individual needs, goals, and objectives.

Using your online bank's aggregation services

Many banks include account aggregation on their Web sites at no charge. Banks offer the service as a means of building customer loyalty and remaining competitive. With aggregation services, you can use your private online banking site to access your other Web-based accounts with brokerages, other banks, credit unions, credit-card companies, rewards programs, and individual retirement accounts. Essentially any personal account that can be viewed on the Web usually can be included in the aggregation, or collection, of accounts provided through your private online banking site.

The process is easy. Access your private online banking site. Next, enter the URL, user name, and password for each personal account you want to include in your aggregated accounts. Your bank automatically links the accounts to your private online banking site.

Keep in mind that setting up an aggregation account may take some time, especially if you've forgotten your password and have to have it sent through the mail. However, after your accounts are in place, your aggregation account becomes a convenient way for you to track all your income and expenses while you're at home, work, or play. Many online banks allow you to customize your personal Web page so you can view the information that's the most important to you first. The following are a few examples of financial institutions that provide account aggregation services for their customers:

- **Bank of America** (www.bankofamerica.com) provides online access to more than 3 million customers. In providing online access, Bank of America hopes to enable customers to do their banking whenever, wherever, and however they choose.

- **BC Centura Bank** (www.centura.com) offers a world-class array of financial solutions to individuals and businesses in North Carolina, South Carolina, and Virginia.

- **First Tennessee** (www.firsttennessee.com) is headquartered in Memphis, Tennessee. The firm is one of the 50 largest bank holding companies in the nation and provides banking and other financial services to its customers through various regional and national lines of business.

- **Harris Bank** (www.harrisbank.com) is one of the largest community banking networks in Illinois with $29 billion in assets. Harris has more than 140 locations throughout Chicago and additional affiliated offices in Arizona, Florida, and Washington.

- **Key Bank** (www.keybank.com) is based in Cleveland, Ohio. The company delivers its products and services through KeyCenters and offices and a network of approximately 2,400 ATMs, in addition to telephone banking and a Web site.

- **Wachovia Corporation** (www.wachovia.com) offers financial services to retail, brokerage, and corporate customers throughout the East Coast and the nation. The company operates full-service banking offices under First Union and Wachovia names in 11 East Coast states and Washington, D.C., and offers full-service brokerage services with offices in 49 of the 50 states. Online banking and brokerage products and services are available through the Web site.

Taking advantage of free nonbank online aggregation sites

Some nonbank Web sites offer the same services that bank or credit union Web sites provide. The following are a few of the more popular nonbank aggregation Web sites online:

- **AOL** (www.aol.com): This site offers a section devoted to information and tools related to many types of financial planning, but only AOL users have access to it. If you're an AOL user, you'll find an account aggregation section that streamlines your online account tracking.

- **MSN Money** (moneycentral.msn.com/banking/accounts/welcome.asp): This site provides free and easy navigation, personal finance research, and loan applications. You can create financial plans for retirement and college in addition to using account aggregation and bill-paying tools.

✔ **My Yodlee** (`www.yodlee.com/yodlee_index.html`): Many of the banks that offer account aggregation on their Web sites use technology from My Yodlee. If your bank or credit union doesn't have a Web site, you can still use My Yodlee at its corporate Web site. My Yodlee offers an informative demo, and the aggregation service is free.

✔ **Yahoo! Finance** (`finance.yahoo.com/accountaccess`): Yahoo! users can obtain and view their brokerage, banking, and credit-card account balances all in one place. This Yahoo! service is free and gives users the abili   to quickly get an online snapshot of their current financial situation,   abling them to stay on top of their personal finances more easily and   ke more informed decisions about their financial lives.

Prioritizing What Comes In and What Goes Out

Prioritizing your income and expenses can help you gain an understanding of what you must do to stop *cash leaks* — those annoying little outflows, such as spending an extra $50 or $100 for groceries or gifts that you didn't anticipate. In the sections that follow, I show you how to prioritize your inflows and outflows of money. After prioritizing your income and expenses, you can calculate the net cash flow for the time frame you've selected by using one of the online net cash flow calculators listed in "The rewards: Enjoying long-term luxuries," later in the chapter.

Reining in your income

An *inflow,* another word for income, is the amount of money you earn. Inflows include your monthly cash income that's your net pay from wages, salaries, or business activities. In other words, don't include the amount you paid to Social Security, the amount withheld for income taxes, or the amount that was deducted for your retirement plan.

Varying income and your budget

The number of people who are self-employed, working on contract, or are engaged in temporary positions has increased during the last several years. Consequently, many individuals think they can't develop a spending plan because they don't know how much money they'll be making. If you find yourself in this situation, make sure that you try to have an emergency fund that's equal to one to two months of your average monthly expenses. These funds need to be in an accessible, interest-bearing account for your leaner times.

Include other income that you may receive in cash (trust distributions, bonuses, dividends, retirement payments, Social Security payments, and miscellaneous regular income). Don't include irregular income such as tax refunds or your winnings at the racetrack.

Shelling the nut: Core expenses

The first step in creating your budget is determining the time period you want to measure. Most bills (home mortgage, utility, telephone, and so on) are monthly, so establishing a monthly budget often is a good time frame to measure.

Total your monthly bills, such as mortgage or rent payment, homeowner's association or condominium fees, utilities, transportation expenses, alimony, automobile gas, food (don't forget those restaurant bills), car loan and other installment loan payments, Visa or MasterCard payments, and department store credit-card payments. Include your monthly outlays for medical and auto insurance, and depending on your occupation, you may want to include what you pay for clothing and dry cleaning and laundry services.

Don't forget to add real estate and income taxes, homeowner's insurance, and other annual bills. Just divide the annual total by 12, and then add the average monthly amounts due whenever you're preparing a monthly cash flow statement. Last but not least, don't forget to pay yourself and enter the amount you'll save or invest each month.

Calculating real-life everyday expenses

Sometimes what you pay per month goes beyond basics, including your monthly health-care, charity, or child-care expenses. You may also be paying for your children's school or living expenses, cable TV, an Internet service provider, home and auto repairs, pets and pet care, medical and dental expenses, and unexpected expenses for emergencies and such. Discretionary costs can include holidays, travel, and entertainment. Keep an eye on the cash you pay for different everyday items. These expenses can show you that your walking-around money is much higher than you expected.

The rewards: Enjoying long-term luxuries

Deduct your outflows (your core and everyday expenses) from your inflows (your regular income). The difference is your personal net cash flow. Whenever the number is positive (everyone hopes it is), you have money to save or invest. Your savings can help you reach important financial goals, such as a down payment on a house, paying off debt, and enjoying a financially comfortable retirement.

Inflows – Outflows = Net Cash Flow

Whenever the difference between your income and expenses is a negative number, you're going into debt. Overall, a negative number indicates that you need to increase your income or analyze your expenses to see how you can reduce them. Don't cut back on insurance, but you may want to find out whether you can lower your rates.

You may want to consider cutting down on expensive restaurants, take-out food, gambling, cosmetics, and alcohol (in no particular order). What you remove from your expense list reduces your debt or adds to your savings. Track what you're saving, and you're bound to be pleased. Seeing positive results makes following a spending plan much easier.

Several online net cash flow calculators that you may find useful are found at the following Web sites:

- ✔ **iVillage** (`www.ivillage.com/money/tools/cash_flow`) provides an online net cash flow calculator to assist you in determining where all your money goes.

- ✔ **Raymond James Financial, Inc.** (`www.raymondjames.com/calc_budget.htm`) offers an online worksheet that tracks your income and expenses. After your totals are calculated, print out the form and compare your income and expenses with your budget to ensure you're not overspending.

- ✔ **Tomorrow's Money** (`www.tomorrowsmoney.org/section.cfm/387/429`) offers this online net cash flow calculator to assist you in determining your typical monthly and annual expenses. By subtracting those expenses from your income, you see where you can begin creating additional savings and how much you have to invest for your future. All you need is your checkbook, your most recent bank statement, and a pay stub to get started.

- ✔ **Visa** (`usa.visa.com/personal/practical_money_skills/budget_worksheet.html`) helps you to estimate your budget, entering amounts from your core income and everyday expenses. You can use the "Tab" key on your keyboard to move from one box to the next. After filling in all the applicable boxes, click the "Calculate Form" button at the bottom to total your monthly income and expenses and determine your discretionary income.

Customizing Your Budget with MS Money or Quicken

The two more popular personal-finance software applications available are *MS Money* and *Quicken*. Each product has several levels of features from bare-bones to deluxe versions. These two personal finance software packages are available for less than $100, and each has over-the-top features that are almost unimaginable, such as *MS Money*'s ability to automatically create budgets and *Quicken*'s tool that automatically collects tax data for export to *Quicken*'s *Turbo Tax* software program. During the last eight years, these fierce competitors have battled for the hearts and minds of personal finance users. Table 4-1 highlights some of the features of *Quicken Premier* and *MS Money Premium*. Each sells for about $80. If you're thinking about buying a personal finance software package, check out Chapter 12 to find out how to get the best price online.

These two personal finance software applications are designed for Windows platforms (*Quicken* for Macintosh has been discontinued) and come equipped with income and expense categories already set up. You simply enter the figures, and the programs do all the calculations. Each program saves you time and paperwork and provides you a way to customize your budget. For example, you can forecast changes in your expenses or create special budgets to determine how they affect your net cash flow.

Creating a budget using MS Money

Before you start, consider watching *MS Money*'s budget video. Click on "Instructional Videos," and then click "Create a Budget." The video is a demonstration that gives you a better understanding of how to get started. Keep in mind that budgeting for everyday (variable) expenses is difficult. When you have several months of transactions to work with, click "Autobudget" at the bottom of the "Enter Your Expenses" page. The program calculates an average of your past spending to help you determine how much to budget in specific categories. To create a budget using *MS Money*

1. **Click "Budget Planner" on the Planner menu.**

2. **Click on "Create a Budget."**

   This step takes you to the "Learn About the Budget" page.

3. **On the "Learn About the Budget" page, decide whether you want *MS Money* to prefill your budget with amounts and categories for you or start your budget with only recurring transactions and default categories.**

   Click "Next," which takes you to the "Enter Your Income" page.

4. **On the "Enter Your Income" page, enter or edit the income you want to include in your budget and delete any budget groups or categories you don't want to include.**

   Click "Next," which takes you to the "Enter Your Expenses" page.

5. **At the "Enter Your Expenses" page, enter the spending limits you want to set for your expenses, and delete any budget groups or categories that you don't want to include.**

   At this point, *MS Money* calculates how much you have in unbudgeted funds.

6. **Select where you want to spend or save any unbudgeted income.**

   You can select either "Spend All Excess Income" or "Save Some or All Excess Income." Enter the name of your savings goal and the amount you want to allocate. If you have multiple goals, click on "Add Another Goal," and when you're finished, click "Next."

7. **Review your budget summary, and if it meets your requirements, click "Finish."**

8. **Return to the "Review Your Current Budget Status" page at least once a month to check on your progress and enter updates.**

Downloading information to keep it simple

Whenever you can download as much of your financial information as possible to your personal finance software, you're better able to keep the process simple and reduce the likelihood of making errors. Information that you can download comes from your brokerage, bank, credit card, and other accounts that you can set up online. Although getting all your information online may take awhile, you won't regret it.

Table 4-1 compares *Quicken* and *MS Money* personal finance application programs. Both *Quicken* and *MS Money* provide ample graphics, charts, and reports. For example, you can print a report of work-related expenses, which, as you know, is very useful when you're preparing your tax returns. Neither of the personal finance software programs deals with cash expenditures very well. You have to split them into separate categories so they can be included in your budget.

On the negative side, *MS Money* requires manual data entry when you begin creating a budget; however, it makes up for that drawback by offering free online bill-paying services for two years (see Chapter 7 for more on online bill paying).

If you're tired of financial surprises, have variable income, or plan to become a one-income family, you may want to run several what-if scenarios with *MS Money* or *Quicken*. This will enable you to discuss spending trade-offs, such as not purchasing a new car this year, in a reasonable way.

Table 4-1	A Comparison of Quicken Premier and MS Money Premium	
Description	**Quicken Premier 2004**	**MS Money 2004 Premium**
Manage your personal finances.		
Balance your checkbook.	X	X
Reports & graphs show where your money goes.	X	X
Pay bills — write or print checks or pay online.	X	X
Create & manage budgets, forecast cash flow.	X	X
Download bank & credit-card transactions.	X	X
Track tax data and transfer to *Turbo Tax*.	X	
Find ways to reduce debt.	X	
Monitor your total net worth.	X	X
Download & track investments, 401(k) & IRA.	X	X
Monitor your asset allocation.	X	X
Unlimited product support for 3 years.		X
Online services for 3 years.		X
Plan for retirement, college, or a new home.	X	X
Do long-term financial planning.		X
Find hidden tax deductions.	X	X
Create what-if scenarios.	X	X

(continued)

Table 4-1 *(continued)*

Description	Quicken Premier 2004	MS Money 2004 Premium
Optimize your investments and taxes.		
Analyze your portfolio.	X	X
See a consolidated report of investing activity.	X	X
Compare investments to market indexes.	X	X
Get investing insights to help improve performance.	X	X
Compare the Morningstar Rating on your funds.	X	
Generate Schedules A & B.	X	
Generate Schedule D tax reports.	X	X
Estimate tax withholding.		X
Learn from step-by-step investments tutorials.	X	
Receive Advisor FYI financial guidance.		X
Find ways to minimize capital gains taxes.	X	X
Automatically calculate capital gains/losses.		X

Comparing Your Spending with Others'

The goal of an effective spending plan is to save. Savings are for emergencies, major expenditures, and your financial independence, which usually happens — like it or not — around the time of your retirement. After you've established your spending patterns, you can compare what you're actually spending to what your budget says you can spend.

If you don't already have a budget, you can start with one of the Internet's canned budgets and customize it over time. For example, Figure 4-2 shows the canned budget at Bankrate (www.Bankrate.com/brm/calc/worksheet.asp). Simply enter your income and expenses and click on "Calculate" to compare your income and expenses to the national average. Your results show the national average by indicating the difference between your budget amounts and the average.

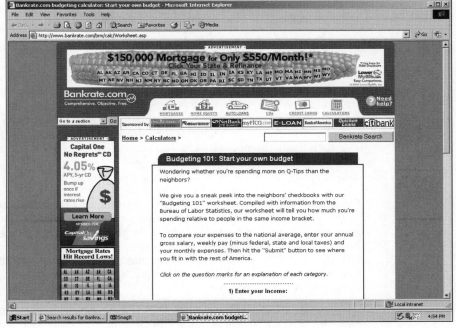

Positive numbers show you spending less than most people like you.
Negative numbers indicate that you're spending more than people like
you. A check mark in any category indicates relatively high spending on
your part. Click on a check mark for a comment about your spending. Print
your results, and then repeat the process for your next time frame. It's as
simple as that.

You need to maintain records of several budgeting periods. If, for example,
you have 12 budgets, you can create an annual budget. Compare your actual
annual budget to your budgeted spending. The difference, which is called the
variance, shows the areas that need more control or adjustment.

Overall, staying within your budget requires more than a little work. Monitoring
and reviewing your budget enables you to determine the good along with the
bad. For example, if you're spending less than expected, you may have identified one or more sources for saving and investing.

What to Do If Your Budget Doesn't Balance: Don't Panic!

As you track your expenses and budget, you begin to understand exactly where your money is going. Your spending plan may not balance for one or more reasons. In many cases, a review of your expenses and budget can reveal where you're spending money on items you don't really need. This, in turn, gives you an opportunity to realign your expenses and make other adjustments. Timely adjustments can help you steer clear of financial disasters.

The following are the top four reasons why your budget isn't working:

- **Budgeting to the last penny.** Budgeting to the last penny is a sure path to failure. Unexpected expenses always pop up. As a result, you need to keep your budget as flexible as possible. You really don't have to account for the two tacos you ate at lunch; however, even if you can save only $5 a month, make absolutely certain that you put that fiver in the bank. Doing so puts you in the habit of saving, so that when you have more money to save, you save it.

- **Underestimating your expenses.** Don't be surprised if at first you underestimate how much you spend by 10 percent or even 20 percent. Budgets often don't balance because the actual cost of items such as gifts, pets, servicing the car, entertainment, and food are higher than expected. In contrast, you may also have overestimated your income. People with variable incomes often overestimate how much they make. Double-check, right now, because you may actually be making less than you thought.

- **Quitting before you get started.** A frequent source of spending-plan failure is quitting before you really get started. The old axiom "If at first you don't succeed, try and try again" applies here. Don't get frustrated. Make the appropriate adjustments and move on.

- **Not understanding the rewards of staying within a budget.** Spending plans aren't meant to punish and constrain you. You don't have to justify spending each and every dime. Spending plans help you get the most from your money. In other words, knowing where you spend your money makes it possible for you to spend your money on the things that give you the most enjoyment.

If you need a little more help in this area, check out *Frugal Living For Dummies* by Deborah Taylor-Hough (Wiley), which shows you how to live the good life with less.

Avoiding money wasters

Discovering where you're wasting your precious dollars doesn't sound like much fun, does it? But you're bound to like the results. In a few years, you can change your entire lifestyle for the better merely by avoiding a few money wasters. To get started, check out these top money wasters:

- **Paying credit-card late fees:** As soon as you receive your monthly credit-card bill, pay the amount due (more if possible). Doing so ensures that you don't have to pay any late fees. Check out Chapter 7 to find out how you can pay your credit-card bills online.

- **Letting your insurance costs ride:** During the last five years, the term rates for life insurance policies have fallen. If you haven't gotten any recent quotes on your insurance needs, you need to go shopping online to find out whether you can reduce your insurance expenses. (For more information about insurance issues, see Chapter 18.)

- **Owning more house than you need:** Is your house more than you need? If you're spending more than 25 percent of your income on your home, it may be time to downsize and purchase something smaller (see Chapter 13).

- **Buying a new car every year:** Today's cars are made better and last longer than in the past. Choose a car that you like, take good care of the car, and keep it for two years longer than usual. You may even want to check out a certified preowned model. If you work at home, you may not need a car for long commutes. If you and your spouse work in the same city (and keep about the same hours), you may want to consider commuting together and purchasing just one car. (For more information about purchasing a car online, see Chapter 15.)

Look sharp! Using the Internet to keep your eye on the ball

Revisit your budget regularly and watch for something I call *expense creep*. That's when your expenses slowly increase while your income remains the same. Always keep your eye on several categories where you know you spend the most money, and you may even want to consider tracking your personal money-waster categories in detail. The following are online Web sites that provide additional insights and tutorials on budgeting:

- ✔ **About.com** (`financialplan.about.com/cs/budgeting/ht/set%20up%20budget.htm`) provides step-by-step suggestions for setting up a budget and links you to a basic budget worksheet at `financialplan.about.com/library1budget.htm`. Starting with this canned budget, go through your checkbook and credit-card statements adding needed or deleting unnecessary budget categories. Don't try to squeeze your expenses into someone else's categories. Try creating a personalized budget that reflects how you spend your money, and don't forget to use enough detail to give you the information you need to make intelligent decisions about your budget.

- ✔ **CNNMoney** (`money.cnn.com/pf/101/lessons/2`) offers a short online tutorial about building a budget at "Money 101." Read suggestions about how you can free up money for use elsewhere. The tutorial concludes with a short quiz that tests your understanding of budget-making.

- ✔ **Junior Achievement Personal Finance** (`www.japersonalfinance.com/gsjapf/activities/act_index.jsp`) offers a short online tutorial about how to separate needs from wants when organizing your budget and a budget worksheet.

- ✔ **Wife.org** (`www.wife.org/columnists/foreman/foreman.002.htm`) provides information on budgets and planning. You're bound to enjoy "The Ten Secrets to Attracting Money."

Chapter 5

Here's the Deal: Online Banking

• •

In This Chapter

▶ Discovering two types of online banks

▶ Deciding what types of banking accounts you need

▶ Locating the online bank that matches your individual requirements

▶ Opening an online banking account

• •

Recently, comScore Networks (www.comscore.com), a firm located in Reston, Virginia, which specializes in consumer behavior and attitudes, released a study about online banking trends. The results indicate that in the first quarter of 2004, more than 22 million Internet users used online banking at the nation's top ten banks. That amount represents more than a 29 percent increase for the same time period in 2003 and makes online banking one of the fastest growing activities on the Internet.

The Tower Group (www.towergroup.com), based in Needham, Massachusetts, anticipates that by the end of 2007 about 42.5 million households (that's around 37 percent of all households in the United States) will be registered to bank online. By 2011, Banking Online Report (www.onlinebankingreport.com) expects this number to increase to more than 50 million American households and more than 300 million households worldwide.

One of the main attractions of online banking is the 24/7 convenience. Online banks additionally are making user interfaces friendlier and easier to navigate. Transactions also are faster as Internet users convert to cable modem or DSL access. In this chapter, I help you get started in online banking by showing you the differences between online banks and explaining the benefits and limitations of traditional banks. I help you define what type of banking services you already have, and I review the types of banking services that are available so you can decide what you need. Finally, I make it easier for you to assess which bank is the right fit for your user profile and explain how to open an online checking account.

Online Banks: What They Are and How They Work

Online banks are divided into two categories: Web-only (or virtual) banks and bricks-and-mortar banks with online services.

- ✔ **Virtual banks:** Virtual banks don't have any physical branch offices, so no tellers are available to answer your questions. Virtual banks, as far as customers are concerned, exist only on the Internet and are governed by the same rules and regulations as traditional banks. As a general rule, the money that's saved on overhead, reduced bank personnel costs, and branch office facilities is passed on from the virtual bank to customers in the form of higher yields on interest-bearing savings accounts, checking accounts, certificates of deposit (CDs), and money market funds. (See Chapter 6 for more about these types of accounts.)

- ✔ **Real-world banks with online services:** A regular bank that has a Web site, branch offices, and offers online services is what I call a *click-and-brick* bank. Today, most national banks, many regional banks, and even some smaller banks offer online banking. These online banking services frequently have names that make the service seem more familiar to the customer, such as PC banking, home banking, Internet banking, or electronic banking. Click-and-brick banks (as they're affectionately known) offer a variety of services. Generally, national banks offer fully functional online banking either for free or for a small fee. Smaller banks offer limited online access. Some, for example, may only have read-only access to your account.

REMEMBER

Paying the cost of online banking

According to a study by Bankrate (www.bankrate.com), it costs more to open a virtual checking account than a traditional checking account; however, you can expect to earn more interest and pay lower fees at a virtual bank than you do at a traditional bank. Although service fees are also higher with virtual banks, they require less than half of the minimum balance that traditional banks require to avoid having to pay service fees. Virtual banks again far outstrip traditional banks when it comes to yield paid on interest-bearing checking accounts.

Bear in mind, however, that traditional banks provide many services for free that virtual banks charge their customers for. Many click-and-brick banks (banks that have branch offices and Web-based services) don't charge for checks and bill paying. Additionally, many national click-and-brick banks don't charge any fees for debit cards, traveler's checks, or notary services.

Overall, the differences between online banks and traditional banks are many. The following sections offer short summaries of some of the advantages and limitations of the online banks compared to traditional banks.

The advantages of online banks

Most online banks make opening an online account easy. Customers can always access their accounts 24/7/365. If you're traveling in the U.S. or overseas, you still can log on to your account to take care of a banking problem from virtually anywhere. Online banks generally process and confirm transactions faster than offline banks. Many online banks now offer *account aggregation* (an online service provided to individuals, allowing them to consolidate a range of accounts, bills, credit cards, and other financial information into one interface in order to simplify the managing of personal finances), stock quotes, rate alerts (a notification, often by e-mail or pager, of a market event such as interest-rate changes), and portfolio management programs so you can manage your personal finances more effectively than with a traditional bank. Online banks enable customers to complete routine transactions online (account transfers, balance inquiries, bill payments, and stop-payment orders) whenever and wherever they want to. Account information usually can be downloaded to personal software programs, such as *MS Money* or Intuit's *Quicken* for easy bookkeeping. Fees are often comparable to traditional banks and in some cases are even lower.

The benefits of traditional banks

Setting up accounts and getting used to online banking takes time. Sometimes navigating an online banking site is difficult and requires you to read tutorials about your private Web-based banking site. Online banking can be limited to certain geographical areas. All deposits made to online-only banks still must be mailed. Traditional banks accept deposits at branch offices, night deposit drops, and by mail. Online bank account information can be accessed anytime, day or night, and can be done from anywhere. Only a few online banks update information in real time, while others do it daily. Payment requests must be made as much as two weeks in advance for online banks. If you're an online banking customer at a virtual bank, you can't ask a teller a question. Finding out whether a transaction was processed often is difficult to tell. Traditional banks, on the other hand, usually have more-extensive networks of automated teller machines (ATMs) than virtual banks. If you bank with a virtual bank, you usually don't have access to traveler's or cashier's checks.

How you access online banks

Online banks can be *vertical* (Web-based only) or *click-and-brick* (branch offices and Web-based services). The three ways to access an online banking account, in order of increasing popularity, are

- ✔ **Personal finance software packages:** The leading personal finance software packages are *MS Money* and Intuit's *Quicken.* Account information is downloaded in seconds for both programs. Quick downloads enable you to track, verify, and categorize the income and expenses for your brokerage, checking, credit card, and other accounts. At some banks, this specialized type of connection service is free. For other banks, you pay a fee of around $6 per month.

- ✔ **Your bank's proprietary software:** Some banks offer proprietary software to customers — the programs the banks use. This software enables customers to track and categorize income and expenses and transfer funds to, from, and between different accounts. With your bank's software, you can download information for more-difficult personal finance tasks, such as tax reports, budget making, and cash flow forecasting. Prices of these services vary from free to several dollars per month.

- ✔ **Your bank's Web site:** When you travel, a bank's Web site often is the best way to keep tabs on your accounts. This approach is frequently ideal for individuals who want the functionality of a click-and-brick bank. You can check your income and expenses online, and in some cases, download them onto an *MS Excel* spreadsheet, and yet still retain the convenience of accessing branch offices and frequent use of your bank card at a national (or even international) ATM network. The fee for PC banking is around $6 per month.

Finding out whether online banking is right for you means a visit with Bankrate at `www.bankrate.com/brm/news/emoney/equiz1`. Answer the five-question quiz to determine whether you're likely to enjoy using a virtual bank. If possible, take the test right now. The answer may surprise you.

Accounting for Your Accounts

Banks offer a wide variety of accounts, but you generally can boil them down into the five types that I describe in the sections that follow. The Federal Deposit Insurance Corporation (FDIC) usually insures each type of account for up to $100,000. Most banks offer all five kinds of accounts, so you can select one or more at the same location or elsewhere. Review each overview of the accounts listed below to determine what types you have.

Savings accounts

Savings accounts are designed to encourage individuals to save by paying them interest on the funds they maintain in the account. Generally speaking, the amount of interest paid for a savings account is more than for an interest-bearing checking account but less than for an MMDA or CD. Some savings accounts make use of a *passbook,* or a small pamphlet in which tellers record your transactions. Banks often charge a fee whenever the account balance falls below a specified minimum. Savings account information often can be viewed on your bank's Web site. If you use a personal software program like *MS Money* or *Quicken,* you also can download your savings account information to the program. Additionally, if you want to transfer funds from your savings account to another account at the same bank, you can use your personal financial software to do so. Keep in mind that a transfer or other similar transaction usually is completed by the beginning of the next business day. (See Chapter 6 for more information.)

Your basic checking account

Basic checking accounts have a limited set of features. The average minimum initial deposit for opening a basic checking account is about $50. With it, you can write checks, download information, and receive monthly statements. However, these bare-bones accounts don't pay interest on account balances and may restrict the number of checks you can write per month or charge fees when you write more than a certain number of checks per month. Additionally, you may have to pay a PC banking fee whenever you want to view or download your checking account information. The convenience of using a basic checking account often costs upward of $200 a year in banking fees when you fail to maintain the minimum balance in your account.

Interest-bearing checking accounts

The features of *interest-bearing checking accounts* are usually in opposition to the features offered with basic checking accounts. You earn interest on your account balance, can write an unlimited number of checks, and have access to the convenience of using a debit card. Interest-bearing checking accounts sometimes are called NOW accounts, or *negotiable order of withdrawal accounts*. The amount of interest you receive is based on your account balance. The amount required to open an interest-bearing checking account often is $500, and the bank usually sets a minimum balance, frequently $2,000 or more for maintaining the account without a service charge. Fall below that amount, and you'll be dinged with the fee. The amount of interest that you earn in an interest-bearing checking account frequently isn't as much as you'd otherwise earn by investing the minimum balance in equally insured financial products. Although the debit card looks like a credit card, it actually is connected to your bank account. In other words, no credit is involved in debit-card transactions (see Chapter 3 for details about credit cards). Keep in mind that inflation usually outpaces what banks pay in their interest-bearing accounts, so it may actually cause the interest you earn to disappear.

Money market deposit accounts

In a *money market deposit account* (MMDA), your balance is invested in short-term Treasury bills, commercial debt, or certificates of deposit. Interest rates, in general, are higher for MMDAs than they are for interest-bearing checking accounts, but the balance in an MMDA usually has to be higher than an interest-bearing checking account before it begins earning interest. In addition, you're usually limited in terms of the number of transfers and checks you can make and write each month, and you're charged a service fee whenever your account balance falls below a specified amount. (For details, see Chapter 6.)

Certificates of deposit

Certificates of deposit actually are geared to specific times. Basically, you have to agree to keep all of your CD-invested money in the account for a set period of time that can range from three months to six years. The longer the time period, the higher the interest rate you earn. Heavy penalties are leveled for early withdrawals, so longer-term CDs are not a terrific place for parking your emergency funds. (To find out how CDs can maximize your savings, see Chapter 6.)

The Right Fit: Locating an Online Bank That's Right for You

Before even thinking about opening an account, you need to determine what your user profile is and what types of accounts and services you need to be able to take control of your personal finances. Ask yourself, for example, whether the online bank that offers the highest yield on an interest-bearing checking account also offers account aggregation. *Account aggregation* is an online service that allows individuals to consolidate a range of accounts, bills, credit cards, and other financial information into one personal Web page. What about charges and fees? Sometimes access is free for a certain number of times per month or during a free trial period, so shop around and read the fine print before you sign on the dotted line. You may need to set up more than one account.

Your user profile

Every person has an individual profile that can be used to help determine what type of online banking and bank is best for you. Your user profile can be classified as

- ✔ **Experienced Internet user:** You have more than two years of online experience and regularly surf the Internet and use e-mail.

- ✔ **All-in-one-stop shopper:** You have more than five years of experience on the Internet, regularly pay bills online, track your investments online, and don't want to travel from one Web site to another to complete your financial housekeeping.

- ✔ **Saver:** You're interested in protecting your savings and looking for the online bank offering the highest interest rates and the lowest fees.

- ✔ **Borrower:** You seek low interest rates on your loan, the ability to track your loan payments online, and the ability to talk to someone if something goes wrong.

Comparing a bank's attributes to your user profile can help determine exactly which bank best fits your user profile. Here are the attributes that can affect your decision-making:

- ✔ **Overall cost:** How much does the bank charge for usual services? Are there additional handling fees or a required minimum balance? What are the interest rates?

- ✔ **Customer service:** Can you make a service request or inquiry or get advice online? Can you personalize your data or reuse your data for future transactions? Does the online bank have a customer loyalty program?

- ✔ **Online resources:** Does your online bank offer a menu of services and financial products? Can you complete transactions (originating your mortgage online is one example) for each service or product online?

- ✔ **Confidence:** How reliable is your online bank's Web site? Will your bank protect your privacy? Does your online bank provide security guarantees?

- ✔ **Ease of navigation:** How simple is it to open an account? Is there an easy pathway to the Web site? Can you access your data easily?

Exercising your rights as an online banking customer

Whenever you have a dispute about a transaction, contact your bank immediately. You have 60 days from the date of your bank statement to notify your bank of an error. You can notify your online bank in person, by telephone, or in writing. This kind of problem needs to be resolved within ten business days of your notification. To be on the safe side, keep a paper trail of all your transactions and payments. To find out how you can pursue a dispute with your bank, become an educated consumer at the FDIC Consumer Protection Web site located at `www.fdic.gov/consumers/index.html`.

These distinct attributes of online banking appeal to different user profiles. For example, experienced Internet users may be more concerned about online costs and resources than savers, who rarely visit the Web site. Confidence and receiving the highest interest rate possible are issues that may be of concern to savers. The ease of navigation may be more important to an online all-in-one-stop shopper than it is to a borrower. A borrower may be more concerned about low interest rates and customer service than the saver. Table 5-1 shows which online banks may be appropriate for your user profile.

Table 5-1	Potential Online Banks for Different User Profiles
User Profiles	*Potential Online Banks*
Experienced Internet user	Citibank (`www.citibank.com`), Charter One Bank (`www.charteronebank.com`), Bank of America (`www.bankofamerica.com`)
All-in-one-stop shopper	Citibank (`www.citibank.com`), Wells Fargo (`www.wellsfargo.com`), Charter One Bank (`www.charterone.com`)
Saver	Charter One Bank (`www.charteronebank.com`), Citibank (`www.citibank.com`), eTrade Bank (`www.etradebank.com`)
Borrower	Wells Fargo (`www.wellsfargo.com`), Citibank (`www.citibank.com`), Bank of America (`www.bankofamercia.com`), Charter One Bank (`www.charterone.com`)

How the banks stack up

As a means of assessing how the online banks listed in Table 5-1 compare with each other, I've prepared the following list of reviews:

- ✔ **Bank of America** (www.bankofamerica.com) provides easy navigation and a hassle-free Web site for setting up and managing an account. The MyAccess checking account is free when you use direct deposit and limit yourself to three visits to a teller per month. Bank of America offers many features that appeal to all-in-one-stop shoppers. For example, bill paying is free, and you have access to IRA accounts and the ability to apply for mortgages or other loans over the Internet, trade stocks, and obtain investment advice online.

- ✔ **Charter One Bank** (www.charterone.com) offers non-interest-bearing "Totally Free Checking" and VIP interest-bearing checking with an annual percentage yield (APY) of 0.50 percent. APY is the rate of return on an investment, such as an interest-bearing checking account or savings account, for one year. You can open a checking account for $50. Overdraft protection is available, but you pay $29.50 for a check that's returned for having nonsufficient funds (NSF). At the Charter One Web site, you can set up alerts, get advice, enjoy the rewards of your debit card, or apply for a loan, all in English or Spanish.

- ✔ **Citibank** (www.citibankonline.com), at this time, has one of the most functional yet simple Web sites around. Citibank's online banking includes the ability to customize the color of your page layout and account alerts. One of the account aggregation features lets you check out your Citibank and non-Citibank accounts online. Citibank also includes insurance and brokerage services. Spanish speakers can complete their online banking in Spanish.

- ✔ **E*TRADE Bank** (www.etradebank.com) offers free online bill paying with unlimited payments when you maintain at least a $2,000 balance. If your account balance falls below the $2,000 minimum, you pay a $6.95 per-month fee. To open an account, you need $1,000. All deposits must be made by mail, so expect time delays. If you maintain a $5,000 balance, E*TRADE refunds the fees for all your ATM deposits. One of E*TRADE's best features is its online access. You can call up an account history for the past year.

- ✔ **Wells Fargo Bank** (www.wellsfargo.com) offers customers a financial portal for access to banking, brokerage, bill paying, and online applications for credit cards, mortgages, and other types of loans. A number of online tools at Wells Fargo help you determine whether you're on track to reach your personal financial goals.

If your favorite bank isn't listed above, don't despair, just check out *InvestorGuide.* It offers an extensive directory of hyperlinks to online banks at www.investorguide.com/banklist.html.

Don't forget the fees when you shop

The following checklist outlines the fees you need to evaluate so you can determine exactly what you need from an online banking account:

- ✔ **Foreign ATM fees:** ATM fees include the amount of money other banks charge you for using their ATM machines to access your bank. Frequently, account holders must pay fees to their own bank and the other bank for using an ATM that's "foreign" to their home banks.

- ✔ **ATM surcharges:** *ATM surcharges* are what your bank charges you every time you use its ATM machines. Some banks charge as much as $5 per transaction. Today, banks make more than $2 billion per year on ATM fees.

- ✔ **Call-center charges:** The fee that you're charged when you contact customer service is referred to as a As part of being competitive, most banks don't charge for this service; however, some banks may offer this service for free during a trial period and then start charging you a fee after a predetermined period of time. So watch out.

- ✔ **Debit card fees:** Fees that your bank charges you for using a debit card can be assessed on a monthly or a per-transaction basis. Banks additionally and frequently have the option of increasing the monthly fees or changing when you pay the fees for debit card usage.

- ✔ **Fee for printing checks and deposit slips:** Gone are the days of seeing copies of your checks and deposit slips for free — to say nothing of the Real McCoy actually getting them back. This fee is the amount your bank charges you when you have checks, deposit slips, or other paperwork printed.

- ✔ **Low-balance penalties:** If your account sinks below a minimum balance, the bank charges a penalty fee. For example, if your balance goes below the minimum for just one day, you may lose more than a month's worth of earned interest.

- ✔ **Money order fees:** Banks make you pay for money orders. Bear in mind that Internet-only banks may not offer money orders at any price.

- ✔ **Monthly maintenance fees:** These fees are what your bank charges you for physically maintaining your account or accounts. Some online banks have the option of increasing monthly maintenance fees at any time.

- ✔ **Other bank fees:** Banks find other ways to get money out of you. Miscellaneous other bank fees can include bank analysis fees when you want a particular transaction to be investigated.

- ✔ **Overdraft charges:** Who doesn't know about these fees? An overdraft charge is the amount of money your bank charges for covering one of your checks when you don't have enough money in your account to do so. Overdraft charges vary from one bank to another, and your bank has the option of increasing its overdraft charges.

- ✔ **Per-check charges:** With some basic checking accounts, you're required to pay a fee for each check you write. You also may be charged a fee for each check that you write that's more than the number of checks you're allowed to write from your interest-bearing checking account without being socked with this fee.

- ✔ **Returned-check/NSF fees:** NSF fees are the money the bank orders you to pay when it's forced to reverse a transaction and return a check to you via U.S. Mail for insufficient funds. Remember, you owe not only the NSF fee but also the amount of the check.

- ✔ **Traveler's check fees:** This amount is what your bank charges for issuing you traveler's checks. Keep in mind that your Internet-only bank may not offer traveler's checks.

Beware of boozing and banking. According to BBC News (news.bbc.co.uk), on Sunday mornings, the helpdesks of many banks are overwhelmed with calls from customers who made transactions they regret. These transactions often occur after midnight and are fueled by alcohol consumption. Customers sometimes sign up for online services, buy products they really didn't want, or occasionally make a transaction they can't remember.

Banking online: Unplugged

Just imagine that you're taking your business associates out to lunch when your pager goes off. It's your online bank sending you an alert that your deposit was just credited to your business account. Now you can confidently use your business debit card to pay for lunch. That's the beauty of mobile banking. In the U.S., online bank users have been slow to adopt mobile banking. However, banks will likely begin using wireless banking to build customer loyalty and lower service costs. The economics of customers using wireless devices can't be ignored and are likely to force banks into offering wireless customer service, alerts, and other related services.

The first banks in this market should achieve a competitive advantage (like Amazon.com) that other banks will envy in the future. At this time, Harris Bankcorp (www.harrisdirect.com/pre/wc1_whatisit.htm and www.harris direct.com/wc1_features.htm) is your best bet for mobile banking. Harris Bank started its wireless banking service in 2000. Today, you can receive your account balances, holdings, and order status via your Web-enabled cell phone, PDA, or RIM 2-Way Pager. Other mobile information that you can receive includes trading quotes, news, charts, market summaries, and model portfolio information.

Laughing all the way to your online bank

You don't have to go beyond your keyboard to find special deals for Web-based banks. A few good deals that are geared just for Internet shoppers are included in the list that follows, where you also find the APY and minimum deposit required to open an account. Don't forget to go to the bank's Web site to check for any additional deals or changes, and, of course, remember to read the small print.

American Bank (www.pcbanker.com) offers an interest-bearing e-checking account that bears 1.5 percent interest. The minimum deposit needed to open an account is $100.

Bank of InternetUSA (www.bankofinternet.com) offers something called "Boomer Checking" with an interest rate of 1.5 percent APY (must be at least 40 years old) and "Senior Checking" (must be at least 50 years old), which pays an interest rate of 1.75 percent APY. You can open either account for a minimum deposit of $50.

E*TRADE Bank (www.etradebank.com) offers "Value Checking" with an interest rate of 0.65 percent APY. The minimum to open a Value Checking account is $2,000.

NetBank (www.netbank.com) offers a "Net Value Checking" account with a 1 percent APY. The minimum needed to open this account is $50.

Step Right Up! Opening Your Online Bank Account

For many online banks you need to be 18 years or older and have a U.S. address, a Social Security number, a driver's license or state ID, and a second form of identification, such as a U.S. passport, military ID, or major bank or credit card. Some banks may ask for the address of your employer and may even check your credit history (for more information about this topic, see Chapter 3).

Go to the Web site of the bank of your choice. (You may want to check out the online banks listed in "How the banks stack up," earlier in this chapter.) Complete the online application form. Figure 5-1 shows how new NetBank customers (www.netbank.com) can select the type of bank accounts they want when they open their online bank accounts.

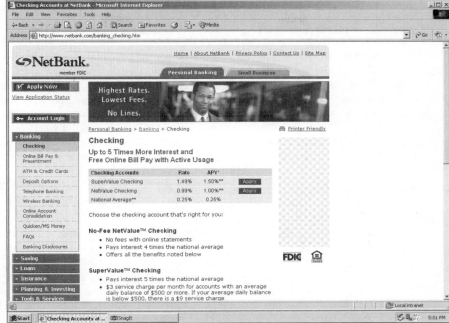

Figure 5-1:
Select the
types of
accounts
you want to
open when
you start
banking
online.

For example, you may want to start with just a basic checking account, or you may want to open several different types of accounts (like an account for your college fund or a special vacation). After completing the account application, you receive a new customer package usually within five business days. (Some online banks can complete this process within the same day.)

The new customer package includes your user identification number, password instructions, and step-by-step instructions about how to get started. If your bank is in a different state, reread the fine print about fees and charges. Because of state banking regulations, the fee structure may be different than you expected.

One easy way to get started is by opening an online checking account with your current bank. Even if the branch office is just in the next block, you'll have to wait for the user identification number and password instructions to be sent to you via the U.S. Mail.

Using PayPal, the non-online bank

According to the Federal Deposit Insurance Corporation (FDIC), PayPal (www.paypal.com) isn't a bank or savings association. PayPal is designed to do only one thing — transfer money. The transfer is immediate and guaranteed. PayPal doesn't transfer funds unless the buyer has a credit line or the required amount needed to complete the transaction in his or her bank account.

PayPal is a peer-to-peer payment service that secures transactions when paying for goods and services via e-mail. Basic PayPal accounts are free for consumers, with no hidden expenses or monthly fees. At this time, PayPal has about 40 million registered users in more than 45 countries. With PayPal, you can send money to anyone in the U.S. with an e-mail address. PayPal also can be used on a Web-enabled cell phone. In the future, PayPal will be available on Web-enabled pagers, PDAs, and other handheld devices.

When you enroll for your PayPal account, you need to add a funding source for your payments. For immediate payments, you need a credit card or debit card. You can also use PayPal Buyer Credit (click at the bottom of the home page for the online application) if you've already been approved. To pay for a purchase, click on the "Send Money" tab and then enter the recipient's e-mail address and the amount of your payment. Remember, you can fund your PayPal account using your PayPal balance or your U.S. checking account (which usually takes two or three days).

PayPal may become like a fifth credit card. Fearful of credit-card fraud and identity theft, many online shoppers prefer using PayPal in place of credit cards to complete their online transactions. Consequently, PayPal has released a new application program that plugs into e-commerce sites so that online shoppers can pay for purchases using Visa, MasterCard, American Express, Discover credit cards, and PayPal.

If you encounter a problem downloading bank information to your personal finance program, you may be batted back and forth between your online bank and software vendor. Don't let these organizations wear you down! If you're persistent, at some point everything will work out, and you won't ever have to worry about getting timely, accurate information again.

Chapter 6

Saving Money (Yes!): Finding the Best Rates Online

In This Chapter

▶ Finding the best savings rates online

▶ Evaluating short-term Web investments

▶ Recognizing different types of money market accounts

▶ Choosing the best certificates of deposit online

▶ Buying savings bonds and Treasuries online and without a broker

Saving money is one of the most important things you can do in life. Although watching your savings grow may not be exciting, it's necessary to ensure your financial independence. An advantage of saving is that you're better able to accumulate enough money for large purchases, such as cars and houses. Additionally, savings help you through tough times by providing you with an emergency fund.

In this chapter, I show you how to find the best savings rates online and determine which accounts are paying you the best returns. This chapter suggests the best places to stash your short-term savings and explains the joys of compound interest. I also clear up the confusion between money market deposit accounts and money market funds (a difference that's important to your financial well-being) and show you why shopping for the best rates is important to your pocketbook and what factors to consider when evaluating a short-term investment.

Furthermore, this chapter explains the ins and outs of savings bonds so you don't end up with an unexpected tax bill. I also describe how you can open an online trading account with the U.S. government so you never have to pay a brokerage to buy or sell Treasury securities. I also discuss a new type of online hybrid that saves you time and money and provides you with information about how you can get into the action by opening a high-yielding account.

Using the Internet to Find the Best Savings Rates

Differences exist between saving and investing. The primary difference is that saving is putting away money for emergencies or other short-term goals. All banks have savings plans where your money can earn interest and be safe. Savings accounts are the most common type of accounts in the U.S. You can open a savings account without a minimum initial deposit and for as little as $25.

What makes savings accounts safer and better than stashing your cash under your mattress is that the Federal Deposit Insurance Corporation (FDIC) insures them for up to $100,000, and you earn money on your money. The balance in your savings account earns interest because the bank uses your money to fund loans to other people. In other words, the bank pays you to use your money. The interest you receive from your savings account balance usually is compounded daily. And to top it all off, you can withdraw your money anytime you want and not incur any penalties or fees. For more online information about savings accounts see these Web sites:

- ✔ **Bankrate.com** (www.bankrate.com): The best part of this Web site is its rate comparisons for mortgages, credit cards, and money market accounts. However, Bankrate.com also provides information on a wide range of personal finance topics, savings accounts, money market accounts, and certificates of deposit (CDs). Phone numbers and links to 4,000 institutions offering savings accounts and other short-term financial products also are provided.

- ✔ **Treasury Direct** (www.publicdebt.treas.gov): This government Web site offers detailed information about marketable U.S. Treasury securities. This information includes auction dates and how to purchase Series EE and Series I savings bonds online. The yield on current inflation-adjusted Series I bonds is higher than five-year Treasury Inflation Protected Securities (TIPS).

- ✔ **SmartMoney.com** (www.smartmoney.com/shortterm/index.cfm?story=setyouws): SmartMoney.com offers an online calculator that assists you with setting your short-term goals. Say, for example, that you want to purchase a new car or house. Although you know how much it costs now, using this calculator helps determine how much you need to set aside so that you have enough money when the time comes to make your purchase.

Getting a grip on rates and yields

Calculating interest can seem complex, especially when the terms "rate" and "yield" are involved. Right next to the annual percentage rate (APR) you often find the annual percentage yield (APY). The APY always is a higher percentage rate than the APR.

Computing the Annual Percentage Rate (APR)

Computing simple interest (see "The joys of compounding interest," later in this chapter) is easy when using the following formula with these abbreviations and values: simple interest (I) = 5 percent, principal (P — your investment), APR (R) interest expressed as a decimal. In this case R = 0.12, P = $10,000, and Time (T) = 1 year.

Using the formula $I = R \times P \times T$, the simple interest for the amounts in the example are:

I = $10,000 \times 0.12 \times 1$

Therefore, I = $1,200

Computing the Annual Percentage Yield (APY)

When analyzing which of several savings investments is best, you need to compare their annual rates of yield (APY). A higher APY usually offers the greater yield for investing. Interest can be compounded daily, monthly, or annually. How interest is compounded affects your APY (the amount of your return). APY takes into account the compounding of interest on already compounded interest. The following example shows the APY when interest is compounded monthly. APY is calculated by taking one plus the periodic rate and raising it to the number of periods in a year.

For example, using a standard compound sum of an annuity table, a 1 percent per month rate has an APY of 12.68 percent per year. Now your $10,000 investment is multiplied by the APY of 12.68 percent. Your investor's return for the year is $1,268. The formula looks like this:

APY = $10,000 \times .1268 = $1,268

Finding where to stash your cash

Short-term investing means putting your money where it can make more money by earning interest. Unfortunately, to be able to get the reward of more interest, you must either take on more risk or invest for a longer period of time. Table 6-1 compares different types of investments and indicates the range of interest rates they earn. When looking at these general guidelines, keep in mind that interest rates constantly fluctuate, and your personal tax situation affects how much your investments actually gain.

Table 6-1	Comparing Savings Options	
Time Frame for Savings	**Investment Type**	**APY (Annual Percentage Yield)**
Less than a year	MMDAs, money market funds, CDs, and Treasuries that mature in less than one year	0.02 to 1.7 percent
One to three years	MMDAs, money market funds, one- to three-year CDs, and Treasury securities	1.7 to 3.0 percent
Three to five years	Three- to five-year CDs and Treasury securities	3.0 to 4.3 percent
Five to seven years	Series EE savings bonds and Treasury securities	3.9 to 4.3 percent

The joys of compounding interest

The most powerful investments have stable, compounded returns. Regardless of what's happening in the economy or stock market, you can always count on the magic of compounding. Over time, a modest-but-steady rate of compound interest can build into a sizable nest egg.

Simple interest is a return that your financial institution pays you based on a certain percentage of every dollar you put aside in your savings account. For example, if you have $1,000 in your account (called *principal*), and the bank pays 2.5 percent annual interest, then you receive 2.5 cents for every dollar that was in your savings account for the entire year. After 12 months, you accrue an additional $25 in your savings account.

Savings accounts are the most familiar type of fixed-income investment, and they provide

✔ Substantial safety for the principal balance

✔ Low probability of failure to receive earned interest

✔ High liquidity

One drawback to savings accounts is that returns (the amount of money you earn for giving up the immediate use of your money) often are the lowest available. A savings account is a classic example of a low-risk and low-return investment. Want to check out how much and how fast your savings can grow? Try the calculators at these Web sites:

FinanCenter (www.financenter.com) features an online calculator that determines how much your money can earn. You can use this calculator to figure out how much money you'll have at some future date or how long it will take to reach a predetermined savings goal. On this Web site's home page, click on "Our Products," then "Calculators," then (under "Calculator Categories") on "Savings," and then on "What will it take to become a millionaire?"

CNN Money (money.cnn.com). Use the savings calculator at CNN Money to determine how fast your savings can grow depending on an interest rate, initial deposit, and additional payments. Go to CNN Money home page and click on "Calculators" in the left margin. Select the "Savings Calculator."

Okay, so now you're wondering just how long it takes to double your money. The *Rule of 72* is a quick and dirty way to calculate your rate of return without using an online savings calculator. Simply divide the rate of return (interest rate) on your savings into 72. That gives you an estimate of how long it takes for your investment to double in value. An investment earning 6 percent annually, for example, doubles in 12 years (72 ÷ 6).

How much should you be saving?

Table 6-2 provides examples of how much you need to save each month to reach specific financial goals. For example, assume that you need $10,000 for your investment nest egg (retirement fund, house down-payment fund, college expenses fund, or some other large financial goal). If you save $147.05 per month for five years at a 5 percent rate of return, you'll have the money you need. Table 6-3 shows that if you put away only $139.68 a month for five years at a 7 percent rate of return, you'll have $10,000. That's the magic of compounding.

Table 6-2	Monthly Dollar Savings Needed to Achieve Goal (with a 5 Percent Rate of Return)		
Savings Goals	*5 Years*	*10 Years*	*20 Years*
$5,000	$73.52	$32.20	$12.16
$10,000	$147.05	$64.40	$24.33
$20,000	$294.09	$128.80	$48.66
$50,000	$735.23	$321.90	$121.64
$300,000	$4,411.37	$1,931.97	$729.87

Table 6-3	Monthly Dollar Savings Needed to Achieve Goal (with a 7 Percent Rate of Return)		
Savings Goals	5 Years	10 Years	20 Years
$5,000	$69.84	$28.89	$9.60
$10,000	$139.68	$57.78	$19.20
$20,000	$279.36	$115.56	$38.40
$50,000	$698.40	$288.90	$96.00
$300,000	$4,190.40	$1,733.40	$576.00

The Internet provides many online calculators to help you figure compound interest. All you need to know to use these calculators is the amount you want to save, the average rate of interest you expect to receive, the frequency of compounding (monthly, weekly, and so on), and how long you plan to save. The following Web sites can help you get started:

✔ **AARP** (www.aarp.org.) provides information on different types of interest and links you to a variety of online interest calculators.

✔ **Federal Reserve Bank of Chicago** (www.chicagofed.org/consumer_information/abcs_of_figuring_interest.cfm) provides consumer education about how the interest you pay or receive is calculated.

Tricks and tips for saving more money

Everyone seems to want your money. Who to pay first and how to prioritize your finances can quickly become complicated when you haven't determined your short-term investment goals — whether you should invest for one year, three years, or five years.

Regardless of your savings targets, here are a few guidelines that you need to follow:

✔ Take advantage of information that the government has compiled about people who can't budget, and set up several automatic deductions from your paycheck. For example, you need to set aside one hour of each day's wages for your retirement. If you don't have an emergency fund, set aside 30 minutes of each day's wages for your emergency fund. If you didn't catch on to the theory behind this strategy, it's called "paying yourself first."

✔ As your salary grows, make sure that the weekly amounts you set aside for your retirement and emergency funds also increase. As you keep saving the same or increased amounts, you'll soon see that when interest rates are low, you earn less on your savings, and when interest rates are high, you earn more. Comparing your results with others, you soon discover how this "dollar cost averaging" results in great return.

✔ If you're paid every two weeks you receive four extra paychecks per year. (There are 13 weeks in each quarter of the year.) If you're paid weekly, several times a year you receive five paychecks in one month. You may want to consider using direct deposit to bank your "extra" paychecks in a savings account.

✔ Calculate how much you'll pay in taxes at the beginning of the year so you can check out how far ahead you'll be when you save your money in a tax-free Individual Retirement Account (IRA) instead of paying it to the taxman. For more information about IRAs, see Chapter 10.

Here are some online sources of additional savings information:

✔ **DollarStretcher.com** (www.stretcher.com/index.cfm) is a weekly online resource for simple living that offers ways to save money and time. More than 200,000 individuals subscribe to the free newsletter.

✔ **Cheapskate Monthly** (www.cheapskatemonthly.com) is a 12-page newsletter for individuals who are serious about stretching their dollars. You can receive the newsletter via U.S. Mail or online. Online subscriptions are $18 per year, and offline subscriptions with online member access are $22.95 per year.

✔ **Better Budgeting** (www.betterbudgeting.com) offers a free newsletter, a debt e-book, and a budget worksheet. You'll find this Web site's articles a good resource for personal budgeting, money-saving information, and advice on family budgeting, getting out of debt, and living the frugal life.

Another Savings Option: Money Market Deposit Accounts (MMDAs)

A *money market deposit account* (MMDA) is a savings account with an attitude (in other words, unique features). MMDAs are savings accounts offered by financial institutions that pay a slightly higher rate of interest than savings accounts. Interest paid on these accounts can range from 2 percent to 5 percent. Like savings accounts, MMDAs are FDIC insured up to $100,000, and you usually can make as many deposits as you want without any charges or fees. The primary advantage of MMDA accounts is their liquidity; often you can make withdrawals at any time, anywhere. You can, for example, use checks, transfers, and automated teller machines (ATMs).

How money market funds work

Money market funds (MMFs) are mutual funds offered by investment trust companies in short-term (no more than 90 days), safe investment opportunities, such as bonds. In contrast to MMDAs, MMFs are a type of mutual fund that isn't insured by the FDIC. However, regulations require these funds to be invested in high-quality, short-term corporate loans, Treasuries, or government-agency bonds. Returns on MMFs are higher than on MMDAs because investors pay a premium for FDIC insurance.

Returns on MMFs often average 5 percent, but you may find an even better return if you shop around before investing. Initial minimum deposits range from $1,000 to $5,000. One of the more attractive features of a money market fund is that you can withdraw funds at any time by writing a check drawn on your account. No sales commissions or brokerage fees are assessed. Fund managers determine which money market instruments to buy and sell and charge about a 1 percent management fee. The three types of money market funds are

- ✔ **General-purpose funds:** These funds invest in short-term debt instruments such as CDs, Treasury securities, and short-term corporate IOUs.

- ✔ **Government funds:** These funds usually invest in U.S. Treasury securities.

- ✔ **Tax-exempt funds:** These funds invest in short-term municipal bonds that are federally tax-exempt and sometimes state tax-exempt.

Money market funds are subject to two kinds of risks. The first is the risk of default. Since the inception of money market funds in 1972, no investors have lost even a cent of their principal investment. However, there's always a first time for everything, even if default seems unlikely. The second area of danger is interest-rate risk, or a sudden increase in the interest rate. When the average maturity of the funds is relatively long at the time of the spike, then the risk to the fund becomes greater.

The following online sources provide information about MMDAs.

- ✔ **Bankrate** (www.bankrate.com) includes a listing of financial institutions that offer special deals on MMDAs. Some of the offers are available only to Internet shoppers, so read the fine print.

- ✔ **Instruments of the Money Market** (www.rich.frb.org/pubs/instruments) is the seventh edition of a book that's no longer in print. Because of the importance of this topic, the Federal Reserve Bank of Richmond provides the book online. Each chapter can be read independently.

- ✔ **Investopedia** (`www.investopedia.com`) offers several tutorials. Check out the "Money Market Tutorial." After you've completed the tutorial, take the quiz to test your money market knowledge.

- ✔ **Money Fund Basics** (`www.ibcdata.com/basic.htm`) can assist you in discovering all the ins and outs of money market funds with its IBC Financial Data tutorial.

What to look for in money market funds

MMDAs often require a higher initial minimum balance than savings accounts. Check-writing privileges frequently are limited to three checks per month, and you probably have to maintain a certain minimum balance in the account. As long as you maintain the minimum balance, you earn the money market rate of interest. Whenever the balance falls below the required minimum, you're likely to earn only the current interest-bearing checking account rate, and you may get dinged with a service charge (usually about $5).

When shopping for an MMDA account, you want to investigate the following:

- ✔ **Annual percentage yield:** APYs are the amount of return you can expect from your investment in the MMDA.

- ✔ **Minimum deposits:** Minimum initial deposits can vary from a few dollars to thousands of dollars.

- ✔ **Minimum balance requirements:** Although some financial institutions may require low initial deposits, they may also require you to maintain a larger minimum balance.

- ✔ **Check-writing limitations:** Most MMDAs have limited check-writing privileges. Don't be surprised if you can write only three checks per month.

- ✔ **Other fees and penalties:** Make certain you read the fine print when investing in an MMDA. Fees for excess withdrawals and for not maintaining the minimum balance can wipe out your profits.

Shopping Online for the Best CD Rates

Certificates of deposit are considered to be as safe as savings accounts for amounts below $100,000. The advantage of CDs over savings accounts is that they pay more interest. CDs, however, are not as liquid as savings accounts because in return for receiving more interest, you agree to put off using the money you've invested for a specific period of time. CDs are *timed deposits* that can be purchased from banks, brokerages, or bankerages (see "Taking Advantage of Bankerages," later in this chapter). CDs reach maturity in as little as one month up to as long as five years. Each CD has a set interest rate (what the CD pays), yield (what the investor receives), and can be issued in almost any denomination.

As a general rule, CDs offer higher returns than Treasury bills because CDs have a slightly higher risk. *Treasury bills* are negotiable debt obligation issued by the U.S. government, having a maturity of one year or less. Treasury bills, called *T-bills,* are exempt from state and local taxes. The rate of return on Treasury bills is an *investor benchmark*. Returns that are greater than Treasury bills are considered good. Returns that are less than Treasury bills are considered poor returns for the amount of risk the investor takes on with an investment that wasn't backed by the full faith and credit of the U.S. government.

CDs are issued by large financial institutions, such as commercial banks, savings and loans, and other thrift institutions that aren't in any danger of bankruptcy. Interest paid to CD holders depends on the current prime interest rate and the amount of the CD. How competitive the financial institutions are in the CD market makes a big difference in the APYs they offer. That's why shopping around for the best CD rates is so important.

Corporations generally purchase large CDs that can be sold on the secondary markets of the National Association of Securities Dealers Automated Quotation System (NASDAQ) and New York Stock Exchange (NYSE).

When small investors want to redeem a CD before it matures, they have to go to the issuing financial institution and suffer a loss-of-interest penalty.

Whenever you redeem your CD before it matures and interest rates have increased during the life of your CD, the market value of your CD is less than what you paid for it. On the other hand, whenever you redeem your CD early and interest rates have declined during the life of your CD, the market value of your CD increases. If you're able to sell your CD in the secondary market before it matures, you can make a profit.

Evaluating CDs before taking the plunge

Don't forget to thoroughly investigate a CD before purchasing it. The following are a few things you need to consider when making your decision:

✔ **Terms and disclosures:** Understand the terms and read the disclosure statement. I know it's boring, but you really do need to read the fine print before you invest. For more about what to look for in the fine print, see Bankrate FAQs about CDs at http://www.bankrate.com/brm/news/sav/20020805a.asp.

✔ **Maturity date:** Understand how long it takes for the CD you're buying to mature, and make sure you know the maturity date of the CD you purchase. You don't want to purchase a CD that matures in 20 years when you can only invest for 5 years. Conversely, you don't want to forget to renew your two-year CD when it matures. For more information about this topic, see Bankrate at www.bankrate.com/brm/news/sav/20020104a.asp?print=on.

✔ **Find out who the issuer is:** Knowing who issued your CD and verifying that your deposit is insured by the FDIC are important factors. For example, if the aggregate amount of your CDs is over $100,000 at one FDIC-insured financial institution, you may not be insured for your total investment. For more information on this topic, see the SEC Web site at www.sec.gov/investor/pubs/certific.htm.

✔ **Call features:** Find out whether the issuer has any rights to terminate *(call)* the CD after a certain period of time. Don't automatically assume that a "one-year non-callable" CD matures in one year. It doesn't. This disclaimer means that the CD issuer can't redeem the CD during the first year, but the disclaimer has nothing to do with the CD's maturity date. A "one-year non-callable" CD may still have a maturity date 15 or 20 years in the future.

✔ **Penalties for selling a CD before maturity:** Find out how much you'll have to pay if you cash your CD before maturity. You can expect the penalty to be the loss of three to six months' worth of interest income. For more details on early withdrawal penalties, see Bankrate at www.bankrate.com/brm/news/sav/20010820a.asp.

✔ **Confirm the interest rate:** Find out whether your CD's interest rate is fixed or variable. The latter is called *rising rate CD*. Be sure to ask how often interest is paid because the frequency of interest payments affects your APY. Last but not least, find out how you'll be paid. Ask whether you'll receive interest payments by check or by an electronic transfer of funds.

For more information about CDs, or to discover where you can file a complaint, contact the FDIC Central Call Center at 877-275-3342, or go online at www.fdic.gov.

Finding banks that offer competitive CDs

You can find which banks offer competitive rates on CDs by checking out the following online resources:

- ✔ **The Bank-CD Rate Scanner** (www.bankcd.com) guarantees e-mail reports on the best CD rates, MMDAs, savings accounts, checking accounts, and IRAs. The Bank-CD Rate Scanner is a subscription service that offers a list of the top CD rates from more than 3,000 financial institutions, indicates minimum deposit requirements, and provides contact information for the financial institutions. Information is e-mailed daily. A particular rate costs you $9.95. The information that you request is e-mailed to you. Your request doubles as an invoice that's due within 15 days.

- ✔ **Bankrate.com** (www.bankrate.com) is the grandfather of interest rate comparisons for mortgages, credit cards, MMFs, and CDs. You can check rates daily, find out who's offering the best rates in your neck of the woods, and get e-mail alerts to update you on changes in CD rates and other banking issues. You discover online links and telephone numbers for more than 4,000 institutions.

- ✔ **RateService** (www.rateservice.com) is free with your registration if you're a corporation. It provides e-mailed alerts and portfolio tracking. Discover the highest yields for CDs and other coupon financial products at RateService.

Now for something different: EverBank (www.everbank.com) offers savings and CDs in foreign-currency denominations. These financial instruments frequently offer higher yields and opportunities for higher returns whenever the dollar declines. However, extra profits aren't guaranteed. FDIC-insured euro-denominated CDs can lose whenever the dollar rises.

Trying a Little Bondage: Savings Bonds and the Internet

Savings bonds are issued by the U.S. government. New bond rates are announced every May and November. Savings bonds are a near-cash investment because you can cash them anytime six months after the date of purchase. Following the events of September 11, 2001, the U.S. government introduced the Patriot Bond, which is exactly like the Series EE bond.

For many folks, the only way they can save money is by purchasing savings bonds. In the past, the United States Treasury Department offered three types of bonds. The Series HH bonds were discontinued in August 2004. The following describes the different types of savings bonds:

✔ **Patriot Bonds (Series EE):** You pay half the face value of a Series EE bond at the time of purchase, and you receive the face value when the bond matures. The interest rate isn't fixed, so the length or term of maturity is variable. The minimum denomination is $50, and the maximum denomination is $10,000. Interest rates for Series EE bonds are 90 percent of the average interest rate on five-year Treasury securities. Currently the yield on Series EE bonds is about 2.66 percent.

✔ **Series HH:** A Series HH bond pays interest directly to your account at a financial institution every six months. These bonds have fixed interest rates for 10 years and earn interest up to 20 years. Series HH bonds were available in denominations of $500, $1,000, $5,000, and $10,000.

On August 31, 2004, the U.S. government discontinued Series H and Series HH bonds. This action may create an enormous tax bill for investors if they don't immediately reinvest. To determine whether you need to convert your Series H or Series HH bonds, go to www.savingsbond.gov to determine your tax liability. The form for converting your bonds, Form PDF 3253, is available at the Treasury Web site (www.savings-bonds-alert.com/support-files/sav3253.pdf).

✔ **Series I:** Series I bonds are inflation-indexed savings bonds. The U.S. government adjusts the amount of I bonds semiannually to keep up with inflation and protect the purchasing power of the bondholders. The current yield on I bonds is 4.66 percent. The first part of the rate is a 1.1 percent component that applies to the 30-year life of the bond. The second component is a variable rate that's set annually and is currently at 3.5 percent. The variable component reflects the Consumer Price Index and the buying power of investors who own the bond. A noteworthy comparison: The current yield on T-bills (see "Shopping Online for the Best CD Rates," earlier in the chapter) is about half what it is for I bonds.

If you have a bunch of old bonds and wonder whether they're still earning interest, see the Bureau of Public Debt Web site at www.publicdebt.treas.gov/sav/savstop.htm.

What's good and what's bad about savings bonds

Returns on savings bonds are so low that they'll never make you rich. In fact, returns are so low that large pension funds and other big investors don't purchase savings bonds. However, for many individuals, savings bonds are the best approach for saving money.

Factors favoring savings bond are that you can

✔ **Save automatically.** Employers who sponsor savings bond programs can automatically deduct amounts you designate from your paychecks to purchase bonds. For many people, this program is a painless way to save. In other words, if you never see the money, you never spend it.

✔ **Diversify your risk.** If you already have investments in stocks and bonds, you may want to invest in savings bonds. Doing so adds a no-risk element to your investment portfolio.

✔ **End up with a safe investment.** In exchange for a low return, savings bonds offer absolute safety for the principal investment; they're absolutely no-risk investments.

✔ **Avoid paying any sales commission.** Investing in saving bonds doesn't require the services of a broker to help you purchase them. That's right — no brokerage fees or sales commissions are assessed.

✔ **Invest minimal amounts.** The minimum investment in a savings bond is $25. If you subscribe to an employer-sponsored program, the minimum amount you pay each week can be even lower.

✔ **Pay no or low taxes.** The difference between the purchase price and the redemption value of Series EE bonds and the payment made on HH bonds comes in the form of interest. Interest income is subject to federal income tax but not state or local income taxes. You can defer paying federal income tax on the interest until you cash in the bonds.

✔ **Gain educational tax benefits.** The Education Bond Program allows interest to be completely or partially excluded from federal income tax when the bond owner pays for qualified higher education expenses at an eligible institution or state tuition plan in the same calendar year the bonds are redeemed. For details, see Treasury Direct at `www.publicdebt.treas.gov/sav/saveduca.htm#eligbds`.

Factors at odds with savings bonds are that you

✔ **Face penalties for early redemption.** If you cash in your Series EE bonds after you've held them for six months, you'll pay three months' worth of interest — ouch! Series EE and Series I bonds cease paying interest after 30 years.

✔ **Need to be careful when you redeem your bonds.** Make sure that you know when interest is posted. If you redeem a bond right before interest is posted, you won't reap your interest payment. If you redeem your bond early on in the same month that interest is posted, you may lose six months' worth of interest.

Sometimes you can spend and save at the same time. At BondRewards (`www.bondrewards.com`), you can shop online at your favorite stores (more than 150 online stores participate in the program) and receive a small percentage of your purchase price in the form of a U.S. Savings Bond.

You can get additional information about savings bonds from the following Internet sources:

- **Savings Bond-Alert** (`www.savings-bonds-alert.com/united-states-savings-bonds.html`): An expert provides you with a market analysis of short- and long-term interest rates for savings bonds at this Web site.

- **The Bureau of Public Debt** (`www.publicdebt.treas.gov/sav/savbene.htm`): This Web site provides information on the benefits of savings bonds and covers interest rates and maturity periods.

Check in your safe-deposit box or among the papers of elderly relatives for old bonds. More than $2 billion in savings bonds never have been redeemed.

Where you can purchase savings bonds

You can purchase savings bonds online at TreasuryDirect (`www.treasurydirect.gov`). Keep in mind that TreasuryDirect is the most cost-efficient way to purchase these savings instruments. It takes only about ten minutes to set up and manage an account. You can even find information about the savings bonds you already own. The Web site provides tutorials about purchasing and redeeming Treasuries. TreasuryDirect is an online way to buy and sell U.S. Treasuries in a paperless, electronic form.

Among the several other ways and places that you can purchase savings bonds are

- **Federal Reserve banks:** If you write to your local Federal Reserve Bank and ask for an application, you can purchase savings bonds by mail. The Federal Reserve Bank of New York (`www.federalreserve.gov/otherfrb.htm`) provides the address of the 12 regional Federal Reserve banks.

- **Many financial institutions:** Most banks are qualified as savings bond agents. These agents accept the payment and the purchase orders for the Series EE bonds and forward the orders to a Federal Reserve Bank, where the bonds are inscribed and mailed. Allow 15 days for delivery.

- **Employer-sponsored payroll savings plans:** You can purchase savings bonds through your employer under these plans. Almost 50,000 employers participate in employer-sponsored payroll savings plans, and some banks offer EE bonds through bond-a-month plans.

If for some reason you must purchase your Treasuries in the secondary market, you have to go through a broker. Brokers often sell investors the latest issue of Treasuries, which means you pay an extra premium for the liquidity of these current securities.

Valuing your savings bonds

In May 1997, Series EE savings bonds were radically changed. Series EE bonds purchased before May 1997 aren't affected by these changes. The Bureau of Public Debt suggests that purchasers of Series EE savings bonds understand these changes:

- ✔ **Interest rates are calculated in a new way.** The earnings of Series EE bonds issued in May 1997 or thereafter are based on the five-year Treasury security yield. New rates for Series EE bonds are calculated at 90 percent of the average yields for five-year Treasury securities (for details, see "Investing with Uncle Sam (T-Bills)" in the next section) during the preceding six months.

- ✔ **You pay a penalty for cashing bonds before five years.** You can cash in a Series EE bond after six months, but if you cash one before holding it for at least five years, you give up the last three months' interest as a penalty fee.

Series EE bonds, regardless of when they were issued, don't pay out accrued interest in periodic cash increments the way Series HH bonds did. An alternative investment exists for people who are about to retire and want an investment that pays interest in cash: Sell the savings bonds, pay the tax, and use the proceeds to purchase a 20-year Treasury security. Treasury securities pay interest in cash so that retirees can use the interest payments for living expenses. *Note:* If selling your Series EE bonds puts you in a higher tax bracket, try selling them during a two-year period.

For more info about managing your savings bonds, check out

- ✔ **The Savings Bond Wizard:** This savings bond tool helps you manage your inventory of savings bonds on your personal computer. The downloadable program is free and enables you to determine the exact redemption value of each savings bond. You'll know how much interest each bond is earning and be able to maintain a bond inventory. Your bond inventory can be an important record whenever you need to replace any of your savings bonds. The free Savings Bond Wizard is designed for Windows and is downloadable at www.publicdebt.treas.gov/sav/savwizar.htm.

- ✔ **The Savings Bond Calculator:** This online calculator, provided by the U.S. government, can assist you with quickly calculating the values of your savings bonds. Access it at www.publicdebt.treas.gov/sav/savcalc.htm.

If you think you may have lost some savings bonds, complete the Claim for Lost Bond form. Fill out the form with as much information as possible, including old addresses and whether the bonds were purchased through a payroll deduction plan. Don't forget to include many different forms of your name. Searches usually take between three and six weeks. The Bureau of Public Debt's new Treasury Hunt (`www.publicdebt.treas.gov/sav/sbtdhunt.htm`) feature can help you find bonds that never were delivered.

Investing with Uncle Sam (T-Bills)

For short-term investing, Treasury bills (called T-bills) are the Nation's most marketable security. T-bills are issued with 3-, 6- or 12-month maturities. When you purchase a T-bill, you pay less than the face (or par) value. When the T-bill matures, you receive par value of the T-bill. T-bills aren't like coupon bonds, which pay interest in increments. If you purchase a three-month T-bill with a par value of $10,000 for $9,800 and hold it until maturity, you receive $200 in interest.

Treasury bills are sold to the public at an auction every Monday at the New York City Federal Reserve Bank. T-bills are issued through competitive bidding (tendering an offer) at these auctions. Bids of more than $1 million are considered competitive bids. Bids of less than $1 million are always classified as noncompetitive bids. T-bills are sold first through competitive bids. Remaining T-bills are then sold noncompetitively for the average price of the winning bids. Individual and institutional investors alike can bid on T-bills. T-bills also are sold on the secondary market by broker-dealers who buy and sell them.

T-bills, which are issued in denominations of $1,000, $5,000, $10,000, $25,000, $50,000, $100,000, and $1 million, are considered *risk-free* because they're backed by the full faith and credit of the U.S. government. T-bills additionally are free from state and local taxes. However, federal taxes are due on earned interest.

The two primary limitations of T-bills are their lower rates of return and early cash outs that can be less than your original investment. Rates of return for T-bills are lower than money market funds or CDs because of their lack of risk, and cashing out a T-bill before it matures may mean not getting all your cash back. For example, if you're forced to sell your T-bill when interest rates have increased during the term of the T-bill, the resale value of your T-bill will likely decrease.

Determining the value of a T-bill

Interest rates on T-bills are listed online and in most major daily newspapers. T-bills that mature in a year or less are listed at the *discount rate,* which is the rate that takes into consideration the time value of money. The discount rate is shown as the "Bid/Offer" rate. The "Yield" column is expressed in a way that lets you compare the equivalent yields of one Treasury security with another. In other words, you don't need to do any additional math to compare a T-bill that matures in a month with one that matures in six months.

As an example, a $10,000 Treasury bill with a one-year maturity that's quoted at a rate of 2.5 percent provides $250 in interest and sells at a discount of $9,750. The effective yield is $250 ÷ $9,750, or 2.56 percent. The same 2.5 percent T-bill with six months to maturity provides $125 in interest ($250 ÷ 2) and sells for $9,875. The effective yield is ($125 ÷ $9,875) × 2, or 2.53 percent.

Checking out Treasury notes

Treasury notes are negotiable debt obligations issued by the U.S. government and backed by its full faith and credit. Treasury notes mature in 2, 3, 5, or 10 years. Treasuries that mature in more than ten years are called *Treasury bonds.* Treasury notes are in electronic form (they don't come in paper form).

You can purchase Treasury securities online directly from the government by using the online *Treasury Direct* program. If you want to open a free trading account, check out www.treasurydirect.gov for instructions and information about Treasuries. For more Web-based information about evaluating Treasury securities, see

- ✔ **InvestingInBonds.com** (www.investinginbonds.com), which offers tutorials about purchasing Treasury securities and explains how to read bond tables. The Bond Market Association sponsors it.

- ✔ **Key Bank** (www.key.com/templates/t-ca3.jhtml?nodeID=H-3.32), which offers 11 online bond calculators so you can analyze your bonds any way you desire.

- ✔ **SmartMoney.com** (www.smartmoney.com/bondmarketup/?nav=DropTabs), which provides the latest information about the bond market and what's happening with key interest rates.

Purchasing Treasury notes without a broker

The Treasury Direct program (www.treasurydirect.gov) enables investors to participate in regularly scheduled auctions. Minimum investments are $10,000 for bills, $5,000 for notes maturing in less than five years, and $1,000 for securities that mature in five or more years. Here's an overview of how you can purchase Treasury securities online:

- ✔ You can buy Treasuries with or without a broker. To buy T-notes (Treasury notes) without a broker, you need to open a Treasury Direct account and deposit the funds to pay for your purchase in your account.

- ✔ You can purchase Treasury notes electronically by placing a bid in an auction. If you're an individual investor, you'll likely place a noncompetitive bid to ensure that you receive the number of securities and the amount of securities you want.

- ✔ A *noncompetitive bid* specifies only a quantity (limited to some specified maximum amount) and your agreement to pay the average accepted competitive bid.

- ✔ At the time of your bid for a T-note, you don't know what its interest rate will be. Your rate of return will be equal to the average accepted for the T-notes sold in the competitive bidding.

- ✔ The minimum purchase amount is $1,000. Bids must be placed in multiples of $1,000.

- ✔ After you buy a T-note, the federal government will pay interest to you every six months until your note matures. Your interest payments are paid into your Treasury Direct account, as is the security's principal value at maturity.

- ✔ After you buy a note, you can hold your Treasury note until maturity or until you sell it. For a fee (less than $50) and at your request, Treasury Direct will sell your T-note for you.

- ✔ When a fixed-principal note matures, you can reinvest its principal into another note, or Treasury Direct can redeem the note and deposit the proceeds into your checking or savings account.

If you prefer not to buy directly from the U.S. Treasury (Treasury Direct), you may buy through your financial institution, broker, or dealer. These securities are recorded and held in what's known as the commercial book-entry system. Contact your local financial institution, broker, or dealer for more information on this method of purchasing Treasury securities. Expect to pay a commission for this service.

See the Bureau of Public Debt's Web page at `www.publicdebt.treas.gov/bpd/bpdsignup.htm` for more information about Treasuries and to subscribe to the mailing list for important information about dates and rates.

Taking Advantage of Bankerages

In the past, doing all your banking at one bank was common practice. The consolidation and deregulation of the banking industry and the Internet have changed all that. Traditional banks are now competitive with virtual banks, brick-and-mortar banks, and online brokerages. One online financial institution may have the best checking account, another may have the best rates on CDs, and still another may have the lowest brokerage commissions, and so on. Today, there are new hybrids emerging that can simplify the task of tracking down the best rates for all your personal finance needs.

Kiplinger.com, located at `www.kiplinger.com`, has coined a new name for these hybrid financial institutions. It calls them *bankerages,* primarily because at many online banks you can open brokerage, savings, and money market deposit accounts. Conversely, brokerages are now offering car loans, mortgages, and other bank products, in addition to enabling investors to trade mutual funds, stocks, bonds, Treasuries, and other securities. Through it all, the FDIC insures your banking account up to $100,000, and the Securities Investor Protection Corporation (SIPC) insures brokerage accounts for up to $500,000, with not more than $100,000 of that coverage in cash.

SIPC insurance isn't the same as FDIC insurance. SIPC insurance doesn't insure you against the loss of your money caused by poor investment decisions or investment scams. The SIPC only insures you against your brokerage going out of business.

What to look for in a bankerage

Having a bankerage account can help you keep tabs on your savings and investments. You can easily rebalance your investment portfolio on your own to maintain your target allocations and results. In other words, the online combination helps you to save time and money and gain flexibility and convenience that can't be achieved with services that are otherwise scattered throughout the Internet. The following lists several of the attributes you should look for in a bankerage.

✔ **Account aggregation:** This trait enables you to see all the different types of investments and accounts you have with one financial institution at the same time.

✔ **Low brokerage charges:** Some bankerages offer low-cost commissions for sales personnel. Mutual fund management and brokerage fees charged by bankerages are also low.

✔ **Wide range of services:** Some bankerages offer incredible amounts of high-quality research. Other online bankerages provide cost-basis information, so you can easily determine your taxable gains or losses.

✔ **Bill-payment services:** Some online bankerages provide free bill-payment services. (For more about online bill-payment services, see Chapter 7.)

✔ **Low banking fees:** Banking fees charged by bankerages can vary widely. Some online bankerages offer free or low-fee ATM costs. Some bankerages have *sweep account programs* that automatically transfer funds above (or below) a certain amount to higher-interest-earning accounts at the close of each business day.

✔ **Good rates:** Some bankerages offer higher yields on CDs than others. Additionally, some bankerages offer higher rates on interest-bearing checking accounts than others.

The following are a few examples of bankerages:

✔ **Fidelity** (www.fidelity.com) states that applying online takes approximately 10 to 15 minutes. If necessary, you can save your application and return it within 30 days. Fidelity is a winner when it comes to low banking fees, low brokerage fees for index mutual funds, and research.

✔ **NetBank** (www.netbank.com) offers an online application. If you don't like online applications, you can always download its paper application. Applicants need a U.S. Social Security number to apply for an account.

✔ **Citibank** (www.citibank.com) requires U.S. citizenship with a U.S. address to open an account. A driver's license or state ID and a second form of identification, such as a U.S. passport, credit card, or U.S. military ID, also are required. All applicants must be at least 18 years old and provide a valid Social Security number, mother's maiden name, and employment address. If you're not a U.S. citizen, try calling 800-374-9700.

✔ **Charles Schwab** (www.schwab.com) is changing from a premium discount brokerage to a bankerage by offering mortgages, refinancing, and equity lines of credit. You can even pay your bills online.

✔ **Wells Fargo Bank** (www.wellsfargo.com) allows you to get greater control of your finances with just one password. With Wells Fargo OneLook you can securely manage your Wells Fargo and non–Wells Fargo accounts. You have online access to your bill-paying services, checking, savings, credit card, mortgage, loans, and investment accounts.

Opening a high-yield account

After you find a great interest rate for an MMDA, an MMF, or a CD, how do you open an account? Don't worry — it's easy. Just follow these simple instructions:

1. **Contact the bankerage online to complete an online application.**

   Download a complete application or call the bank's toll-free number to open an account. Expect to provide more information than in the past because of the Patriot Act.

2. **If you call the bankerage, ask for the person who supervises personal accounts.**

   Some banks have a national desk for out-of-town customers like you.

3. **Tell the contact person how much you have to invest and the type of account in which you're interested.**

4. **Ask for the latest interest rate and annual percentage yield (your return).**

5. **Find out when you'll begin earning interest and when you can first withdraw funds.**

6. **Ask for an application to open an account.**

7. **Complete the application forms and signature cards; make copies for your records.**

8. **Send the completed bank forms and your check by U.S mail.**

   The bank confirms your deposit by return mail.

Chapter 7

Stampless Bill Management: Paying Your Bills Online

*I*f you're tired of getting bills in the mail, constantly being unable to get to your mailbox while traveling, or spending a good portion of the year at your retirement retreat, or if you're simply fed up with paying late fees, then what you need is an online payment service that takes the burden of paying bills off your shoulders and serves as a new middleman.

In this chapter, I explain the different levels of online bill-payment services and help you decide which works best for you. I also give you an in-depth look at the advantages and limitations of paying your bills online, profile a number of online bill-paying services, and show you a comparison of the basic features of the two industry leaders, StatusFactory and PayTrust.

In the process of discovering more about paying your bills online, you'll also discover the differences between online bill-paying, paying bills using your personal finance software program (such as *MS Money* or *Quicken*), and paying through your online bank.

Paying your bills online takes much of the worry out of, well, paying your bills, as long as you're not overdrawn! Dive into this new world and see how your personal finance software can become your budget's best friend. And you can save money whenever you take advantage of free check payment services at online payment centers and banks.

Look, Ma, No More Stamps!

Convenience is the primary benefit or value of paying bills online. For computer users, the convenience factor is fairly obvious, but if you're an individual who rarely uses the Internet, you may have a harder time accepting that it's more convenient. To ease any anxieties you may be experiencing about paying your bills online, here are some collateral advantages you may not have considered:

- **You get organized.** Electronic bill presentment is the process of delivering billing statements to customers electronically over the Internet or other online network. Because your bills are presented to you online, you're forced to be more organized about paying your bills.

- **Online bill-presentment programs are getting better and smarter every day.** With some programs, you can get your bills, sort charges by category, break out travel and entertainment expenses on your credit card, or sort telephone charges by area code for tax purposes or reimbursement by your employer.

- **Bills don't get lost in the mail.** Okay, so you won't be able to use this as an excuse any longer, but bills sometimes are left unopened, get lost in the pages of a magazine, or just fall off the kitchen table and end up who knows where. Lost bills can lead to late fees and dings against your credit rating. Online payment services send you alerts before the due date of each bill. Additionally, if your online bill-paying center doesn't receive an expected bill, the service lets you know that something isn't right.

How Online Bill-Paying Works

One of the top concerns of individuals paying bills online is security and the protection of their personal information. Online bill-paying services are password-protected in a manner similar to ATMs. Your personal identification number (PIN) is required for all transactions. Unlike normal Internet communications, all the information you send to and receive from your bill-paying service is encrypted using the maximum level of security supported by your browser and 128-bit RC4 encryption. This type of encryption means that messages can't be redirected, read, or tampered with.

Full-service online bill management is the crème de la crème of the online bill-paying world, but you have a variety of other ways to use the Web for paying your bills — from no frills to full service. The following sections talk about all of them. Here are the basic ways you can use the Web for bill- paying:

✔ **Level 1:** Having your bills presented electronically

✔ **Level 2:** Using electronic payments and electronic checks

✔ **Level 3:** Paying bills through your online bank

✔ **Level 4:** Using an online payment-management service

Level 1: Receiving bills electronically

After you begin your online bill-paying service, you'll register your payees and create payee accounts. *Payees* can be anyone who bills you, such as your insurance carrier, phone company, or credit card issuer. A *payee account* is an account for any company, service, or individual you make payments to. With *electronic bill presentment* (a scanned electronic copy of your bill), you'll probably receive your bill via e-mail. Some bill-paying services enable their consumers to pay right within an e-mail response via an account reduction (think eBay's PayPal invoices), but other types of bills are static and for information purposes only (think of your car loan and the payment that's due).

Online bills can also arrive at your online doorstep in other ways. Sometimes you may receive a Web alert in your e-mail inbox or on your private Web banking site (or both). If your online banking site aggregates your accounts and you've registered the payee account, you may be able to receive an alert when the *e-bill* (electronic bill that may not have a hard copy) is issued, pull up the bill, and pay it — all from your private bank Web site. For more information, see "Setting up your online bill-paying account," later in this chapter.

Level 2: Checking out electronic payments

Electronic payments (or e-payments) are transfers of funds to pay a bill or bills that are almost instantaneous. Your online bill-pay services company or online bank can initiate electronic payments, but there's one glitch. If the payee (the entity getting paid) isn't set up to accept and receive electronic payments, you have to send an electronic check, and doing so takes more time.

Electronic checks look just like normal paper checks. Your online bill-pay service or bank can initiate an electronic check and mail it. Sending a check by snail mail, however, takes much more time and can cost more money (if you have to pay bank checking fees) than an electronic payment. However, more companies are catching on to the new trend toward paying bills online because they receive their money faster than usual and have started accepting electronic payments.

Most credit-card, telephone, and utility companies allow you to pay your account at their Web sites for free, and other billing agencies are following suite. If you have several accounts with the same biller, you can pay all your accounts at the same Web site. For example, say you have three credit cards with one credit card issuer. Frequently, your credit card issuer will notify you via e-mail that you have a new statement. You can go to your credit card issuers' Web site and immediately pay your bill. If you have other accounts with the same credit card issuer, you can also pay those accounts at the same time. Many online billers even allow you to set up automated payments so that your monthly bill is paid through a checking account or credit card without any additional user intervention.

A quick and easy way to get started with online bill-paying is to pay your bill at a Web site. If you want to try paying a few bills or even just one bill online, Web sites can be a good starting point.

Level 3: Using your online bank

Paying bills through your online bank is an alternative that's often free and more convenient. You still receive your bills in the mail, but you can pay them at one site. For more about online bill-paying through your bank, see "Paying Bills with Your Online Bank," later in this chapter.

Level 4: Getting the full-service treatment

Individuals with full-service online bill-pay management use their services to receive their bills, present them online, and have online access to at least one bank account. Overall, the full treatment provides the following perks:

- ✔ **You receive your bills.** Frequently, bills are for utilities, credit cards, tuition, or insurance.
- ✔ **Your bills are scanned into your database.** The online bill-pay service scans your bills into your database. Your bills are shredded after they're scanned.
- ✔ **You're notified when your bills have been received.** An automatic alert is sent to your e-mail inbox. This is your notification to visit your bill-pay management service's Web site to view your bills.
- ✔ **Your bills are presented online.** Online bill-presentment enables you to review copies of your scanned bills via the Internet 24 hours a day, 7 days a week.
- ✔ **You can be flexible in your bill-paying.** You decide how much to pay and when to pay. You can schedule payments for your regular bills and wait to pay others on demand. Or you may want to send one-time payments or large semiannual payments from different bank accounts.

✓ **You can leave your computer at home.** To pay your bills online, you don't need to lug your desktop to a vacation spot or business location. All you need is access to a computer that supports your browser, 128-bit encryption (so that no one can eavesdrop on your activities), and your personal identification number (PIN). Log on to your account 24/7/365 and take care of business.

Paperless online bill management is often used by utilities, telephone companies, and others who want you to pay your debts electronically. Consequently, some online bill-management companies offer a partial-service that accepts only electronic payments for bills. Electronic payments are identical to online payments with one difference. As a general rule, no paper checks are ever used. As a result, the online bill management service doesn't have to print checks and use the post office. Here's how they work: Your bill payment service sends you a notice that a bill is due via an e-mail message. You're directed to your online bill management Web site where you can view the bill and directly pay the bill online.

You need to know the big difference between an automatic debit and online bill-paying. A *debit* is the deduction from a bank account. Debits can be check payments, finance charges, or other withdrawals that reduce the balance of your bank account. For example, suppose that you authorize your bank to automatically deduct your loan payment from your checking account every month. Your account is reduced by the amount of the payment, and if you're not careful, you can easily become overdrawn. *Online bill-paying* is like a debit, but it's more flexible, as you'll see in the section that follows. You can change the date or amount of the payment whenever you desire, giving you more control over when transactions occur in your checking account.

Limitations of Online Bill-Payment Services

Like all things, online bill-paying services have limitations that sometimes counteract their advantages. The following is a short list of some drawbacks to using online bill-paying services.

✓ **There's no free lunch.** Although many national online banks provide free online bill-paying to be competitive in their markets, as a general rule, these freebie services don't include bill presentment. (For selected examples of online banks that offer bill-paying privileges, see "Bill-paying through your online bank," later in this chapter.) In other words, you're still responsible for finding the bill and paying it before it's due.

✓ **Setup times are lengthy.** In the business of online bill payment, generally speaking, the longer the setup time, the better the service. Setup times can vary from a few minutes to several hours. However, one exception is that many online payment services now provide information about payees that's coded into their systems. Figure 7-1 shows how you can add a new payee with just a few clicks. In contrast, if your payees aren't already included in your service's database, the time required to set up your new account may be much longer than you anticipate.

✔ **You have one more thing to memorize.** If you use a full-treatment service, you have to memorize the physical address of your online bill-payment service to be able to make any online credit-card purchases that use your personal billing address as a confirmation tool.

✔ **Some billers simply won't switch your account to your online bill-paying service.** Sometimes, billers just don't understand that, as much as possible, you want to live in a paperless world. In other words, creditors are reluctant to switch accounts from residential to commercial addresses.

Today, many online bill-paying services have taken steps to speed up the address-changing process. All you have to do is click on your billers from a list provided by your service and enter your account number. The service soon thereafter begins receiving your bills. If you're new to online bill-paying, you can't immediately start ignoring your snail-mailed statements. The change in billing location can take a cycle or two before your bills actually are sent to your service.

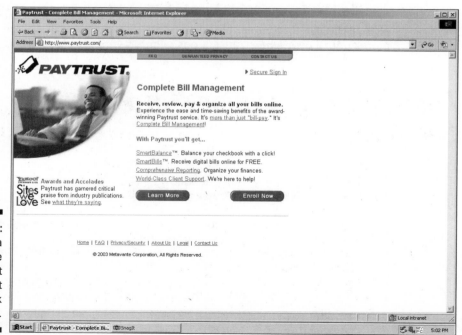

Figure 7-1:
Adding a
new payee
at PayTrust
often is just
a click
away.

Even after you begin using an online bill-payment service, you still want to keep a paper record of the bills you selected for online payment and on what day they were to be paid. That way, when you receive notice that your bills have been paid, you can compare your online status report to your paper receipt.

Don't feel discouraged that you still have to keep a paper receipt. These paper receipts are from your own printer and merely summarize your transactions. You'll soon discover that the weight and size of these receipts are much less than your old system.

Choosing an Online Bill-Paying Service

You need to consider many factors when deciding which online bill-paying service is best for you. When evaluating an online bill-paying service, find answers to these questions:

- **Can the service you select interface well with your bills?**

    Finding any mismatches means you're still paying those bills by hand. For example, these types of mismatches can include housecleaning or janitorial services, landscaping, day-care services, or pool cleaning.

- **Do you have to complete the forms or other paperwork to set up each individual vendor?**

    Another way to ask: Does the service have a database of vendors from which you can select to speed up setup time? Figure 7-2 shows you how to easily add billers that already are coded into the service's system.

- **Can you make automatic or recurring payments in advance?**

- **Does the service automatically notify you when a bill arrives?**

- **After a bill arrives, if you haven't authorized payment, does the service notify you of the due date so you can avoid late fees?**

- **Can you access the history of your payments online?**

    Find out whether additional information is archived, and if so, how much it costs you to access it.

- **What types of reports (tables, charts, or graphs) will you receive?**

- **Does the bill-paying service offer a free trial period or any discounts (like the first month free)?**

    Often services offer multiple levels of service for increased fees by providing options that differ by the number of payments or services you use.

Figure 7-2:
To shorten your setup time, match your payees to the billers that already are coded into the service's database.

Comparing online bill-payment services

As online bill-pay services grow easier to navigate, provide more pages of answers to frequently asked questions (FAQs), and offer online help and more toll-free customer service by phone, they're better enabling their customers to pay their bills electronically. The profiles of online bill-pay services in the list that follows can help you define the kind of online bill-payment service that meets your individual needs:

✔ **CheckFree** (www.checkfree.com) (see Figure 7-3) is an Internet solution that keeps more than 400 online-payment services up and running. In other words, CheckFree is the bill-management service through which banks, credit unions, brokerages, and Web portals often provide their respective online bill-paying services. CheckFree offers two levels of service. Its paid service ranges in cost between $4.95 and $12.95 per month, depending upon which of the 400 payment-service providers you select. The free service is "private-labeled" through your bank, Yahoo! Bill Pay, MS Money, Quicken, and so on. The best part of the CheckFree's cost-free service is that it includes a long list of utility, telephone, insurance, credit-card, and other financial companies.

✔ **PayTrust** (www.PayTrust.com) is an Internet solution for bill delivery, payment, and management. It works with any bank and any payee you may have. Although many banks offer the ability to issue payments online, you're still required to track and manage all paper bills that come to your house. By receiving your bills and managing the process online, PayTrust lightens the burden of handling monthly bill payments. PayTrust enables you to make payments to anyone — even someone who doesn't normally send you a bill. For details about its two levels of service, see Table 7-1.

✔ **StatusFactory** (`www.statusfactory.com`) offers a menu of three levels of service, archives bills online for 12 months, and offers the option of purchasing a CD of scanned bills for $29.95. Whenever you contact customer service, however, expect to pay for the call. StatusFactory has two features that make it stand out from the crowd. First, StatusFactory guarantees that your payments are sent as scheduled, or the company pays any penalties or late fees. (Some, but not all, online bill-payment services offer this guarantee.) Second, whenever you find yourself in what you define as an emergency situation, StatusFactory can send a payment to a biller overnight via Federal Express for $20. For more details, refer to Table 7-1.

✔ **Yahoo! Bill Pay** (`finance.yahoo.com/bp`), through an affiliation with CheckFree, offers two levels of service. The Premium Plan enables you to pay anyone at any time. You can receive bills electronically from more than 200 billers. The first three months are free; after that, you pay $4.95 per month for the first 12 payments with a 40¢ fee for each additional transaction. The Basic Plan is free for payments to more than 100 billers and can receive bills electronically from up to 85 billers at no charge.

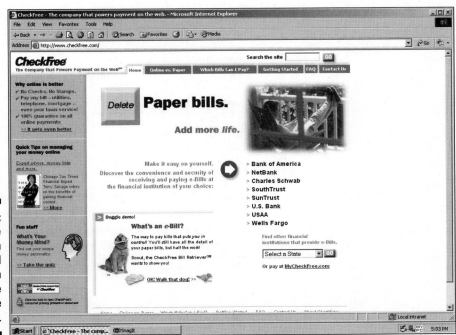

Figure 7-3:
CheckFree provides an animated demo with Scout, the CheckFree bill retriever.

Table 7-1 compares the full-service online payment plans offered through StatusFactory and PayTrust.

Table 7-1	Comparison of Two Online Bill-Payment Services	
Service Description	*StatusFactory*	*PayTrust*
Menu of services	Yes	Yes
Cost per month	$5.95 up to 5 payees $11.30 up to 15 payees $17.30 up to 25 payees	$4.95 per month plus 50¢ per transaction $12.95 per month for first 30 transactions plus 50¢ per additional transaction
Shreds paper bills immediately after scanning	Yes	Does not shred immediately
Permits you to view bill online	Yes	Yes
Sends you e-mail alerts	Upon receipt Prior to payment After payment is made Expected bill not received	Upon receipt Prior to payment After payment is made Expected bill not received
Provides online archive	24 months	12 months
Includes a pay-anyone feature	Yes	Yes
Permits you to schedule automatic or recurring payments	Yes	Yes

Consider these differences between StatusFactory and PayTrust:

- ✔ StatusFactory has three payment levels, and PayTrust only has two.
- ✔ StatusFactory immediately shreds your bills after they're scanned into your personal database.
- ✔ StatusFactory provides a 24-month online archive of your bills, but PayTrust provides only a 12-month online archive.
- ✔ Customer service at PayTrust is limited, but the StatusFactory's toll-free customer service line is staffed 24/7.
- ✔ An optional year-end CD review of paid bills is $29.95 at StatusFactory and $25.00 at PayTrust.

Although the companies that offer full-service bill-paying basically are alike, noting their differences may prove critical when determining which one you choose.

Setting up your online bill-paying account

After you decide which company best meets your needs, you need to set up an account. Here's how:

1. **Collect all your bills.**

   Collect all your bills so you have the account numbers of your billers or payees. You may want to arrange them alphabetically so you can enter them into the online payment system faster.

2. **Locate your checkbook.**

   Sometimes this step isn't as easy as you think, right? Grab your checkbook so that you have the name of your bank and the account number of the checking account you plan to use for bill-paying.

3. **Open your online bill-paying account.**

   To open your account, fill out the online account application form for the bill-management provider you've chosen. Enter your name, address, phone number, e-mail address, and other vital information like your Social Security number, driver's license number, and sometimes even your mother's maiden name. You'll also be asked to select a user name and password.

4. **Activate your account.**

   After you register, go to the payment Web page. Activate your payment privileges by filling out an authorization form that indicates which account funds you want to use for bill-paying. Print the form, sign it, and send it with a voided check from your account via U.S. Mail to the online bill-paying service.

5. **Determine which bills you want to pay online.**

   Referring to the bills you collected in Step 1, decide which ones you want to pay using the online bill-paying system. If you have online bill presentment, after a month or two of transactions, billers send their invoices directly to your online bill-paying service. Even when the address of the invoice doesn't change, you nevertheless need to register the bill for online bill-paying.

Online bill-paying services frequently try to help customers register billers by encoding *common billers* (the ones everybody has to pay) into their systems in advance. Extensive lists of more than 200 common billers aren't uncommon — hurrah! Additionally, full-service online bill-payment services often handle the *address switch* — the change of address from yours to theirs — for you. Whenever a service doesn't handle the address switch for you, you guessed it . . . you have to do it yourself.

You register billers not listed as common billers by adding their names, account numbers, and payment addresses to your register.

6. **Schedule automatic or recurring payments.**

   Scheduling your regular payments is easy. You know the ones I'm talking about: car loans, credit cards, mortgages, utilities, automatic payments, and other recurring bills.

7. **Select which account to pay bills from.**

   Point your online bill-paying service in the right direction when you pay bills from different accounts. For example, although you use your checking account to pay monthly bills, you may want to point your online bill-paying service toward your savings account when paying semiannual real estate taxes.

   Full-service online bill-paying companies include online bill presentment and payment services. When the service receives your bill, it notifies you via e-mail and posts the bill online. You can then log into your bill-paying account and view the scanned version of your invoice.

   When you're not using a bill presentment service, you still must open your mail at home. You then log into your online bill-paying service account, enter the bills' information online, and arrange payment of the bills just as though you received them over the Internet.

8. **Watch for online alerts.**

   Online full-service payment companies tell you when your bills arrive (and when an expected bill hasn't been received). Your service will notify you when your payments are due in a few days. What's more, scheduling bills — the ones you automatically pay — makes generating alerts unnecessary, so you won't receive 50 or 60 alerts every month.

9. **Pay unscheduled bills.**

   For all levels of online bill-payment services, you need to log onto your account to order payments for unscheduled bills. This step usually takes only a few minutes. To authorize payment, all you have to do is point and click. Although the process is easy for you, it's next to impossible for someone else to do, because no one else has access to your account.

10. **Verify that your bills are paid.**

    Your service pays your bills using the funds from the accounts you select. When you order payment, or a scheduled bill comes due, the service either sends an electronic transfer directly to the biller or cuts a check.

    Check payments can be withdrawn immediately from your account, but your online bill-payment service always verifies that funds are available before sending one.

Paying Bills with Your Online Bank

The primary reason for the rapid increase in online banking is the ability it gives you to manage your finances more quickly and efficiently. If you're willing to break the habit of paying bills by mail, you're ready to start using your bank to pay bills online. Most online banks make opening accounts online easy. Customers can always access their accounts 24/7/365. When you're traveling in the United States, outside the country, or even overseas, you still can log on to your account to pay your bills.

Online banks generally process and confirm transactions faster than traditional banking methods. Many online banks now offer account aggregation. *Account aggregation* is an online service provided to individuals that allows them to consolidate a range of accounts, bills, credit cards, and other financial information into one personal Web page. Account aggregation allows you to manage your personal finances more effectively than with traditional banks. Online banks permit customers to complete routine transactions (account transfers, balance inquiries, bill payments, and stop-payment requests) whenever and wherever they want while online. Additionally, you usually can download account information to personal finance software programs such as *MS Money* or Intuit's *Quicken* for easy bookkeeping.

Letting your fingers do the walking

In the past, many people avoided paying bills online because they feared identity theft and loss of their personal information. Today, however, computer users think of online bill-paying as the natural thing to do. If you're new to computers, you may want to wait until you're more comfortable with the technology before trying to pay bills online, just to make sure you understand when, what, and where to click. One of the bigger enticements of paying bills through an online bank is that it's usually free. Web-based bill-paying is offered by *virtual banks* (online-only banks) and *click-and-brick banks* (traditional banks with online banking), which I discuss at length in Chapter 5. Table 7-2 compares bill-paying through a full-service online bill-management service with bill-paying through an online bank.

Table 7-2	Comparison of Online Bill-Pay Services Systems and Online Banks	
Service Description	*Online Payment Systems*	*Bill-Paying with Your Online Bank*
Who gets the bill?	Bills are sent directly to online payment service.	Bills are sent to you via U.S. Mail.
Are bills scanned into your personal database?	Optional-bill-presentment services receive your bills, scan them into your personal database, and shred the original bill.	No.
Do you receive e-mail alerts?	E-mail alerts are sent: 1. Upon receipt 2. Prior to payment 3. After payment is made 4. When expected bill is not received	No, but you don't need them because you already have the bills.
Can you see your bills online?	Scanned bills are presented online.	No, but you don't need to; you already have them.
Can you pay anyone?	Yes.	Yes.
Can you schedule automatic or recurring payments?	Yes.	Yes.
Do you usually have to pay for the service?	Yes.	No.

Bill-paying through your online bank

After selecting an online bank and registering the accounts you want to use online, your next step is scheduling when you'll make a payment. Doing so means

1. **Selecting the account from which you want to pay a certain bill.**

   For example, you may have family and business bank accounts from which you can pay monthly expenses. Or you may want to pay large or annual bills from an interest-bearing checking account.

2. **Indicating the amount you want to pay and the date you want the payee (the biller) to receive payment.**

   Your bank usually tells you how many days in advance you must schedule a payment so that it reaches the biller on or before the due date.

3. **Determining whether you want to schedule recurring bills.**

   When paying bills online, you normally are able to schedule recurring bills so that you don't have to go through the same steps every month. You frequently have options of making multiple payments at one time or automatically paying electronic bills (called e-bills) you receive.

Your payments are made either electronically or with electronic checks. If the payee is set up to receive electronic payments, your bank account is immediately reduced when you issue a payment, and the payee's account is credited. Companies that don't accept online payments are issued an electronic check; however, a four- to five-day notice usually is needed for the processing of electronic checks.

Bill-paying with your personal software program

You can use a personal finance software program such as *MS Money* or *Quicken*. In doing so, you may be downloading your bank statement every day (see Chapter 5 for details on how to set up this online service). Check with your bank to see whether it provides bill-paying services. If it does, you don't need to sign up for bill-paying in *MS Money* or *Quicken*. Your bank already has enrolled you. If your bank doesn't support electronic bill-payment services, follow the set-up procedures detailed in your personal finance program for an online bill-payment service.

When you're using *MS Money* and your bank supports online bill-paying, follow these easy-to-use steps to make your first online payment:

1. **Set up an account for online bill-paying.**

   After you set up an account for online bill-paying, you can create an electronic payment.

2. **Click on the "Account List."**

   It's located in the "Account & Bills" menu.

3. **Select the correct account.**

   Click the account in which you want to prepare an electronic payment (Epay).

4. **Make an electronic payment.**

   In the left margin of your screen, click on "Make an electronic payment" or "Transfer." Then click again to prepare an electronic payment.

5. **Enter the payment information.**

   Asterisks mark the fields that must be completed. If you don't have an account number for the biller, type your name in the Account number box.

6. **Send your payment immediately.**

   To send the payment immediately, click "Submit payment." Don't forget that you must be connected to the Internet to send an immediate payment.

7. Save an electronic payment for later.

Click on "Save Draft" to save your payment for later, and don't forget to submit your completed transaction for payment later. Otherwise your electronic payment sits in your Save Draft file forever.

Note: If your financial institution can't process and deliver your payment by the date you entered, MS Money asks you whether you want to accept a later date.

Following the money trail

You need to create a money trail to determine whether your online billing payments are being processed correctly and on time. Most bill-payment Web sites include a payment activity page that lists your payments and their current status. An online bill-paying activity page indicates whether a payment is scheduled, pending, or processed. Remember that in addition to scheduling the payment four to five days in advance, the recipient of the payment also may take a few days to apply your payment to your account.

Whenever you're anxious about paying certain bills, you can ask your online bank to send an e-mail message or a wireless alert to your personal digital assistant (PDA). You may want to print the completed transaction or receipt page when you pay your bills online to verify account transfers. You can use these printouts as reminders to make sure that transactions you complete are posted on your private Web banking site or are included in your next statement.

Sometimes companies change their billing addresses or your account number without providing you with any warning. As a result, when you set up your payments, always verify these details. Doing so is a good way to avoid late fees caused by your payment going to the wrong company or the wrong account.

Reviewing banks that have online bill-paying

Some people find paying bills a mind-numbing chore and a race against the calendar. Online bill-paying through your bank has changed what used to be a two-hour chore to a mere 15-minute interruption in work, travel, or play. Several national banks offer online bill-paying. Profiles of some of them follow:

- ✔ **Bank of America** (www.bankofamerica.com) serves customers with more than 15 million active checking accounts, 4 million of which are actively accessed over the Internet. According to Bank of America executives, the number of people paying their bills online in 2003 increased by 1.3 million in fewer than ten months — about a 50 percent increase. In May 2003, Bank of America dropped its bill-payment charge for online payments. Today, all bill-payment services are free. You can view bills from 130 different companies and access your IRA accounts. One of the more innovative features that Bank of America offers is the ability to view images of canceled checks online. Additionally, you can personalize your private bank Web site.

- ✔ **Citibank** (www.Citibank.com) provides free bill-payment privileges if you have a checking account with Citigroup. Additionally, you can easily personalize your private Citibank Web site. At your personalized page, you can pay bills, get news, see your account balances, transfer funds, review your bank statements, and even stop payments on checks. Citibank's bill-payment services include an account aggregation feature that enables you to view the balances of accounts that have Web sites, such as your cell phone provider, the miles you've acquired on your frequent flyer programs, and brokerage accounts. You can even view your Hotmail or AOL e-mail accounts.

- ✔ **Wells Fargo** (www.wellsfargo.com) has about 10 million checking accounts with about 3.3 million active online users. Wells Fargo offers a great account aggregation service that includes banking, brokerage services, and online bill-paying. Bill-paying is free for the first two months and remains free of monthly service charges during any month in which the combined balances in your qualifying personal accounts total at least $5,000. Otherwise, Wells Fargo's bill-paying service is $6.95 per month. This fee includes up to 25 payments per month. Each additional payment is 40¢. You can view a year's worth of bill payments online at Wells Fargo's Web site.

Part III
Investing and Planning for the Future

The 5th Wave   By Rich Tennant

Being Dracula's slave didn't pay much, but Renfield always found extra money to invest.

In this part . . .

1n this section of the book, you discover how to select the online broker that's right for you. You also become aware of how to use online tools that can help you plan for a comfortable retirement and settle your estate.

Chapter 8

Selecting an Online Broker and Making Your First Trade

During the peak of the market in March 2000, there were 12 to 15 million online brokerages accounts, and about a third of all trading on the New York Stock Exchange and NASDAQ systems was attributed to online investors. Since that time, according to Gomez (www.gomez.com), an Internet research company, trading volume has plunged 40 percent, but online brokerages are still going strong. In December 2001, 19.7 million online investor accounts were active — a slight increase from 2000.

Today, according to the Pew Internet and American Life Project, about one out of every ten Internet users has bought or sold stocks online. However, you may be intimidated by the thought of do-it-yourself investing because you're either new to the Internet, new to investing, or both. Actually, the Internet is a great place to learn the basics.

In this chapter, I show you how to select the online broker that's best for you. I explain what to look for when selecting a broker and compare the industry leaders. You find out where to look online for brokerage ratings and how to open your own brokerage account. Finally, I show you how to use online simulations to practice online trading and show you how to make your first trade. I conclude this chapter by discussing how to know when to hold and when to fold.

Sorting Them Out: Selecting an Online Broker

These days, securities brokers come in a wide variety of shapes and sizes. It's up to you to decide for yourself how much assistance you need in selecting your investments and how much you're willing to pay for it. Because of the rabid competition among brokers, you can count on better customer service today than what was available five years ago. Discount and online brokerages have increased their customer service and added more servers so that customer trades are executed rapidly. Full-service brokers are increasing the capabilities of their Web sites and charging less for their services. The following are a few guidelines for selecting a broker that's right for you:

- **Full-service brokers:** Full-service brokers usually charge higher commissions and fees than discount brokers, but they also offer services that aren't available through discount brokers. Full-service brokerages offer expert advice and good ideas that are especially helpful and needed when the stock market is gyrating. Other services include ways of establishing personal financial profiles, estate planning, and tax advice.

- **Discount and online brokers:** If you know what you want, why not use a discount or online broker to purchase securities as inexpensively as you can? Full-service discount brokerages like Charles Schwab (the first discount brokerage) and TD Waterhouse have added a huge amount of advisory and account management services. The research available to account holders is staggering, but each firm currently charges hefty commissions for infrequent trades and a maintenance fee whenever your account balance falls below a certain minimum. In contrast, discount brokerage E*TRADE still offers trades with low commissions and few frills. The only problem: You can't visit a branch office to talk to someone or make a quick deposit.

  One of the drawbacks to discount and online brokers is server down time when markets are experiencing high-volume trading. This problem can be compounded by checks being lost in the mail, orders going unfilled, and other types of financial horrors.

- **Buying mutual funds:** Mutual fund buyers have the choice of purchasing a fund through a broker or directly from the fund company. Many brokerages offer only a limited number of funds and may charge you a brokerage commission. However, if you buy a fund that's owned and managed by your brokerage, the trading commission usually is waived.

What to look for in brokers

Some discount brokerages simply aren't suited to the needs of certain types of online investors. As a general rule, online investors who use discount brokerages aren't seeking advice. They just want low-cost trades and excellent customer service. Individuals who are new to investing or online investing may want more of the bells and whistles of traditional brokerages. For example, premium discount (full-service) online brokerages may be a better match for infrequent traders, affluent investors, and individuals who want access to in-depth research resources and tools. The following is a list of some of the elements you may want to consider when evaluating an online brokerage.

- ✔ **Account information:** You want information about your cash balances, your order status, and your portfolio's value. You also want a historical view of your trades and easy-to-understand statements for your taxes.

- ✔ **Analytical and research tools:** When offered by your online broker, real-time quotes, reports on insider trading, economic forecasts, company profiles, breaking news, and earnings forecasts are real timesavers and often cost savers, especially when your broker automatically sends end-of-the-day prices to you.

- ✔ **Fees:** Commission structures change radically from one broker to the next. One reason for the wide range is that some online brokerages include special or additional features for your cash account — for example, low or no fees for account maintenance, account closing fees, no IRA inactivity fees, or fees for retirement account maintenance. You probably want a low required-minimum amount to open an account, a debit card, interest earned on cash balances, and unlimited check-writing privileges, in addition to no fees for postage and handling or for accepting wire transfers.

- ✔ **Securities traded:** Ascertain which types of investments the broker enables you to trade, for example: stocks (foreign and domestic), options, bonds (corporate and agency), Treasury securities, zero-coupon bonds, certificates of deposit, precious metals, mutual funds, and unit investment trusts.

Considering costs

Many brokerages advertise terrific deals for new accounts. However, you may get tapped for extra fees if you don't read the fine print. The following are a few examples:

✔ **Higher fees for limit orders:** *Market orders* (which direct your broker to buy or sell shares at the best price currently available) may be cheaper than *limit orders* (which direct the broker to buy or sell shares only at a specified maximum or minimum price). The lower market-order fee may be the commission fee that's advertised by the brokerage.

✔ **Higher fees for different kinds of securities:** Some brokerages charge higher fees for trading over-the-counter (OTC) stocks than they do for trading listed stocks. *Listed stocks* are traded on all of the major exchanges. Stocks that aren't listed are referred to as *OTC stocks.* OTC stocks often are traded on the NASDAQ or American Stock Exchange.

✔ **Higher fees for trading a certain number of shares at one time:** Some brokerages charge additional fees for trading more than 1,000 shares at one time. You may also discover additional fees for trading fewer than 100 shares, an amount that's called *an odd lot.*

✔ **Higher fees for closing your account or for withdrawing funds from your account:** Some brokerages don't charge for transferring some or all of the funds from your IRA account but do charge for withdrawing or transferring funds from your trading account. Several brokerages charge as much as $50 per account.

Comparing industry leaders

Table 8-1 provides a quick overview of several top-rated online brokerages. Ameritrade and TD Waterhouse are considered discount brokerages. As a general rule, the discount brokerages are geared toward investors who have a few to tens of thousands of dollars to invest. Discount brokerages usually offer lower fees, less customer service, and fewer banking amenities than their premium discount brokerage brethren. Charles Schwab and Fidelity Investments are considered *full-service discount brokerages.* Full-service discount brokerages often are customer-service oriented online businesses that target investors with several thousands of dollars to invest.

Table 8-1	**Comparisons of Several Top-Ranked Online Brokerages**			
Account Minimum Information	*Ameritrade*	*TD Waterhouse*	*Charles Schwab*	*Fidelity Investments*
Cash account	$2,000	$1,000	$5,000	$2,500
Margin account	$2,000	$2,000	$10,000	$2,000

Account Minimum Information	Ameritrade	TD Waterhouse	Charles Schwab	Fidelity Investments
Retirement account (IRA)	$1,000	No minimum	No minimum	No minimum
Commission Structure — Online Trades				
Standard commission*	$10.99 (Reduced commission: None)	$17.95** ($12 with 18 trades quarter or $250,000 in assets)	$32.95 ($19.95 with $100,000 in per assets or 9 trades per quarter)	$32.95** ($14.95 with $100,000 in assets or $30,000 in assets plus 36 trades per year)
Fee Schedule				
Account maintenance fees	$50 per annum (waived if $2,000 in assets or 4 trades per 6 months	$100 per annum (waived if $35,000 in assets or 2 trades per 6 months	$45 per quarter (if balance is below $25,000) $30 per quarter (if balance is below $75,000) $0 per quarter (if balance is above $75,000)	$50 per annum (waived if trader agrees to electronic statements, balance is above $30,000, or 2 trades per year) $2 per annum deducted from each mutual fund per month if balance is below $2,000
Other Attributes				
Compatible with Quicken/ MS Money	Yes	Yes	Yes	Yes
ATM and Checking	Yes	Yes	Yes	Yes
Local offices	No	Yes	Yes	Yes
Dividend reinvestment	Yes	Yes	Yes	Yes

* For online market orders
** Higher for limit orders

Here are more details about the online brokerages in Table 8-1:

✔ **Ameritrade** (`www.ameritrade.com`) is the most utilitarian of the brokerage Web sites analyzed in Table 8-1. Ameritrade is geared for active traders because it offers time and sales data, complex charting, and streaming news. You'll find streaming Level II quotes and complex options trading. To lower costs, trade confirmations and statements are presented online. You can track your online history for a year and a half, so don't be concerned about having to immediately print your monthly statement. Unlike full-service discount brokerages that provide statements that are ready for your CPA, with Ameritrade, you're on your own when it comes to the tax man.

✔ **Charles Schwab** (`www.schwab.com`) recently expanded the mutual fund research area on its Web site. The public side of the Web site offers investor education called "Market Insight." Individuals with trading accounts have access to content that Schwab can generate on the fly to meet an individual investor's needs and desires. Expect to see more Chinese language in the Web site in coming months. Charles Schwab recently increased the "Bankerage" part of the business by offering mortgages, home equity, and margin loans. (See Chapter 6 for more information about bankerages.)

✔ **Fidelity Investments** (`www.fidelity.com`), at this time, is the most popular online brokerage on the Web, according to the Pew Internet and American Life Project. The steady, slow-moving Fidelity of the past is long gone. Today, Fidelity has beefed up its retirement planning tools and zeroed in on the needs of active traders. Fidelity's next initiative is to launch a new look and feel to its Web site. Additionally, you'll find improvements in trading capabilities and options and margin trading. Other improvements include better screening, research, and analytics.

✔ **TD Waterhouse** (`www.tdwaterhouse.com`) has made it easier than ever to open a trading account. New additions for TD Waterhouse include more content for fundamentals and charting analytics. Coming soon are online tools to assist you with developing a financial plan and more focus on the needs of options traders.

Checking online brokerage ratings

Some companies provide speedy trades, whereas others are ranked for their customer service and commission costs. To gain an idea of which companies stand out from the crowd and meet your individual requirements, see the following online brokerage-ranking services.

✔ **J.D. Power** (`www.jdpower.com/cc/finance/index.jsp`) states that online investors' priorities are shifting when dealing with online brokerage firms. Lower commission costs, customer service, and the integrity of the firm now are the focus, according to the J.D. Power and Associates

2004 Online Trading Investor Satisfaction Study. Visit the Web site for the top-to-bottom rankings study and the press release.

✔ **Keynote** (www.keynote.com/solutions/performance_indices/ broker_index/broker_trading.html) provides the Keynote Web Broker Trading Index. Rankings include average response times and success rates for creating a standard stock-order transaction on selected brokerage Web sites. The sites that appear in the weekly Index are selected based on publicly available market-share information published in *The Wall Street Journal* and other reliable industry sources.

✔ **Smart Money** (www.smartmoney.com/brokers/index.cfm?story= 2004-intro) offers rankings of 24 brokerages. Elements of the rankings include stock picking and customer service.

Opening Your Online Brokerage Account

If you're uncertain about what information a brokerage firm needs or the requirements for opening a trading account, try the online simulation at InvestingOnline.org (investingonline.org). This interactive tutorial clearly explains what you need to know when you complete an online application form to open an account with an online brokerage.

Brokerage firms are responsible for executing your trades, maintaining your account records, providing updates and information about markets, mutual funds, and supplying other related services. The brokerage you select needs to be insured by the Securities Investor Protection Corporation (SIPC). The SIPC insures securities and cash in a brokerage account for up to $500,000 (with no more than $100,000 in cash).

Nothing is stopping you from having more than one online brokerage or trading account. For example, you may have an account with a mutual fund company. Another account may be for short- to mid-term positions at a brokerage that's well-known for low trading fees. Finally, you may have a brokerage account for your long-term investments, such as your child's college fund or your Individual Retirement Account (IRA). Varying your trading styles with each account or brokerage can help you smooth out your returns in a bumpy market. Keep in mind that you can open a trading account with a brokerage firm by completing an application via telephone, through the U.S. Mail or online. Here are the steps to follow when you're opening an account online:

1. **Provide personal contact information.**

   Because of the Patriot Act, when you open your account, you'll be asked for more personal information than in the past. Brokerages ask for your name, address, date of birth, and other information that enables them to identify you. The brokerages also may ask to see your driver's license or other identifying documents. (Often copies of these items can be faxed to brokerages.)

2. **Determine the type of account you want to open.**

   Both online and offline brokerages offer several types of accounts. The type of account you open depends on how you want to use your trading account. Examples of brokerage accounts include taxable, tax-deferred, individual, or for you and another person.

3. **Determine whether you want a cash or margin account.**

   A *cash-only account* means that you can only place trades that you can cover with money in your account. A *margin account* includes a line of credit from your brokerage (for which you pay interest on outstanding balances) to fund your trades. Trading on margin isn't recommended for beginning investors.

4. **Fund your new account.**

   Many brokerages require a minimum initial deposit. To fund your account, you can make an automatic transfer from your bank account or send a check to the brokerage. You can also open the account by transferring existing securities from another brokerage, bank, or mutual fund company or by presenting existing stock or bond certificates.

5. **Take the last steps.**

   If you're funding your trading account from your bank account, make sure that you have sufficient funds in the account. After the brokerage receives the minimum required initial deposit, you receive your account number and password by U.S. mail or electronically. This information enables you to log in to your trading account. You're now good to go for your first trade.

Ready, Set, Go! Making Your First Online Trade

Before you trade your first dime, you may want to try out your trading strategies using an investing game. The following are a couple of the Internet's more interesting trading simulations and games.

- ✔ **Fantasy Stock Market** (www.fantasystockmarket.com) enables you to discover the basics by investing $10,000 in fantasy money. The Fantasy Stock Market game includes ranking the top performing players every month and listing the most actively traded stocks. The seven-day trial is free. Subscriptions are $19.95 per year.

✔ **Virtual Stock Exchange** (www.virtualstockexchange.com) is a service of CBS MarketWatch and is absolutely free. With your free registration, you receive $1,000,000 in virtual money that you can trade on any stock exchange. You can even sign up for a public competition to see how your investment strategies stack up against other Virtual Stock Exchange investors.

Using the right buying technique to increase profits

Smart online investors are informed investors. To get a real-time quote, check with your online brokerage. Each brokerage quotes securities in a different format. To find a stock, bond, or mutual fund, you need to know the security's ticker symbol. Your brokerage should provide a ticker symbol look-up feature. If you don't want to use your brokerage, one of the financial news services, such as Bloomberg.com (www.bloomberg.com), Yahoo! Finance (finance.yahoo.com), or CNN Money (money.cnn.com/markets/xstream), offers online ticker symbol look-ups.

Online investors can be their own brokers. In other words, online investors must specify the type of order to execute for their own stock orders. Knowing how to designate the terms of your order can increase the chances of your order being executed at the price you want. When you look at your online brokerage's order form, you'll notice several ways to buy or sell securities. In the past, a full-service broker decided which type of order was best. Today, you select the method that you think is best. Here are the four most frequently used ways to specify a trade:

✔ **Limit orders:** You set a maximum and a minimum amount for buying and selling an investment. Limit orders can be good until (till) canceled (GTC), which means that the order stays in place until you cancel it or the security hits your maximum or minimum price requirements. Limit orders can also be day orders. That is, your limit order expires at the end of the day.

✔ **Market orders:** With a market order, you buy or sell a security at the then current market rate. A market order doesn't expire at the end of the trading day. For example, if you place an order after the market closes, it's usually filled immediately after trading opens the next day.

✔ **Stop orders:** After a security reaches the price set by the investor, the order becomes active. When the order is activated, the order is executed; however, the investor isn't guaranteed the execution price.

✔ **Stop-limit orders:** After a security reaches the investor's predetermined price, the order is activated. The order can only be executed at the set price or better, so the order may not be completed.

When placing your trade, you need to know a few things in advance. You need to know how many shares you're buying or selling, the ticker symbol for the security you want to trade, your target price for buying or selling the security, the type of order you're going to place, and when you want your order to expire. After you've placed your order, you receive confirmation on your screen. If you don't receive a confirmation message, telephone your brokerage immediately.

Many brokerages have online trading demos that allow you to practice trading. Even if you don't have a brokerage account, you still can try your hand at online trading by using the interactive simulation at Investing Online (`www.investingonline.org/isc/index.html`).

Sometimes you may experience the ever-so-common operator error when placing a trade, and your trade isn't completed. At other times, the servers at your brokerage may be offline or down because of a high volume of trades. Contacting your brokerage always is the best way to get to the bottom of problems. Whatever you do, don't enter your order again without first talking to your broker. If both orders are executed, you get double your order — and you may not want so much or be able to afford it!

A few caveats before you trade

Online investing has revolutionized the securities industry in several important ways. Not only can individuals readily use the Internet to access sophisticated research materials and financial data that previously were available only to financial institutions, but you also can use this newfound information to independently evaluate a security's performance. Online investors now can place trades without the assistance of a registered securities representative by entering an order with an online brokerage so that it's executed using traditional methods. Undeniably, online investing is an excellent opportunity and tool, but it has these limitations:

✔ Clicking a mouse is easy, but making a sound investment decision requires using a repeatable investment strategy. After all, if you find a great investment method, you want to implement it again and again. However, an easy investment isn't necessarily a sound investment. "Investigate before you invest" should be the slogan of all online investors.

✔ Making a trade with a click isn't the same as executing a trade. The technology is not instantaneous. Your order must travel through several market layers and may encounter delays before it's actually executed.

✔ Frequent trading doesn't necessarily equal successful trading. Trading again and again may work for some people, but for most traders, long-term investing in sound securities is the best way to realize profits.

> ✔ Trading fees may be more complicated and expensive than you expect. Read the fine print so you know the exact cost of the trades you expect to make. Additionally, you may want to find out, among other things, whether the online brokerage charges a fee for maintaining or closing your account.

Knowing When to Hold and When to Fold

Keeping your portfolio in balance may require you to replace or swap some of your investments for others. You can use online portfolio trackers to determine which investments need to be pruned. Most online brokerages include portfolio tracking; however, what your brokerage offers may not meet your specific needs. Here are a few examples of what you can find online:

✔ **GainsKeeper** (www.gainskeeper.com) provides accurate cost basis, capital gains tax lot data, and trade decision tools that can maximize your after-tax returns. With GainsKeeper you can import your portfolio information from your broker, *MS Money, Quicken,* or *Excel* files. You also can export results to *Excel* files, *Turbo Tax, Tax Cut,* and other tax software programs. Expect to pay $49 to track 100 stocks and $140 to track 1,000 stocks.

✔ **Morningstar.com** (www.morningstar.com) premium membership includes analyzers that can help you understand the tax and cost consequences of replacing a security within your portfolio. Additionally, you'll discover a plethora of online asset allocation tools that can help balance your holdings, determine your optimum asset allocation, and uncover the risk in your portfolio. The 14-day trial is free. Subscriptions are $12.95 per month, $115 per year, or $199 for two years.

✔ **Reuters** (www.reuters.com/finance.jhtml) requires your free registration to take advantage of its portfolio tracker. The Reuters portfolio tracker (formerly MarketGuide) is easy to use, allows you to set up multiple portfolios with on-demand research for domestic and international stocks, U.S. funds, and cash. You can edit your portfolios by adding or deleting companies, and changing investment amounts or shares. You can view your portfolios by performance (how the portfolio is doing), fundamentals (how investments compare with others), valuation (whether any gains or losses have occurred), and daily action (whether a trade is needed). Help icons provide additional information about portfolio functionality.

- ✔ **Risk Grades** (www.riskgrades.com) is based on a complicated scientific formula for calculating the risk of your investments. With your free registration, you receive five portfolios, graphing features, risk-versus-return analysis, risk alerts, "what-if" analysis, and historical event simulations. Using these tools, you can determine which investments are beyond your risk-tolerance level.

You can discover much more about the world of trading stocks, securities, and other financial instruments by getting ahold of a copy of *Investing Online For Dummies* by Kathleen Sindell (Wiley).

Chapter 9

Smart Bucks: Planning for College Online

A college education is expensive and getting more and more so every year. For that reason, it's good to know that you can use the Internet to calculate how much that college education will cost you or a favorite student you know today or in the future. For that matter, you can partner with the Internet to shop for the right school and visit many college campuses without ever leaving your desktop computer. And if that isn't enough, you can get a rough estimate of what Uncle Sam says your expected family contribution (EFC) will be and how it impacts your financial-aid situation.

Yes, how families pay for their students' educations is one of the easier methods of managing your money online. So in this chapter I show you how to do just that with a combination of financial aid, grants, scholarships, loans, and savings. You'll find out how special circumstances need to be brought to the attention of financial-aid administrators and how you can start the financial-aid process online, discover online sources for two types of *gift aid*, or free money.

You'll also uncover free search engines that comb online databases in an attempt to match your student's achievements and attributes with more than 3,500 scholarships. Top grades or test scores often play major roles in receiving financial aid, so I show you ways you can increase your student's test scores, and thus upgrade your financial-aid package, using online sources for improving test-taking skills. Likewise, you can find out how to navigate through the many types of loans that are available to help fund your student's education.

For parents who want to start a college savings plan, I show you how the Internet can help you get the biggest bang for your buck and pay fewer taxes to boot. You'll find out not only which colleges are giving discounts on college tuition but also how you can calculate your tuition discount online. Be sure to check out the online worksheets at the end of this chapter so you can compare financial-aid award packages to determine which is best.

For more offline information about funding your student's college education, see *Free $ For College For Dummies* by David Rosen (Wiley) or search on "Education Funding" at Dummies.com (www.dummies.com).

Higher (Priced) Education: The Cost of Going to College Today and Tomorrow

According to the Bureau of Labor Statistics (www.bls.gov), in its 2000–2001 study, a postsecondary education pays. The average weekly earnings of a college graduate are $896, compared with a community college graduate who makes only $598 and a high school graduate with no college who makes $506 every week. The average weekly earnings of an individual with less than a high school education are $360.

Visiting colleges without leaving your desktop

If you're like most people, you can't take several weeks out of your hectic life to tour the nation's campuses. CampusTours (www.campustours.com) is one example of a Web-based company that gives students and families an opportunity to observe a college and determine if it's worth a campus visit. You can visit the selected college without leaving your desktop computer by taking a virtual tour. If you like what you see, you may even be able to apply to the college of your choice online. In some cases, CampusTours is used to review a one-on-one campus visit. In other situations, CampusTours is used to introduce students to schools with which they may not be familiar but which they may decide to visit after they complete the virtual tour. For many institutions, CampusTours is a large part of their recruitment effort. Bear in mind, however, that you don't want to make your final decision about enrolling at a school until you and your family have seen the school up close and personal.

No wonder Americans see an education as the ticket to a better life. The CollegeBoard (www.collegeboard.com), a research company that tracks college trends, states that the average difference between the lifetime earning potential of someone who spends two years in college and a high school graduate is $250,000. The choice is yours.

Unfortunately, the costs of a postsecondary education are increasing at a rate that's higher than inflation. During the last ten years, for example, the cost of attending a four-year college has increased by 40 percent, while inflation has increased by 28 percent (according to the U.S. Department of Labor, Bureau of Labor Statistics, located at www.bls.gov/bls/inflation.htm). The CollegeBoard states that during the last few years, tuition at private colleges increased almost 6 percent annually, and at four-year public colleges, the increase was about 10 percent annually. During the same time frame, the cost of room and board also increased between 5 percent and 6 percent. If these annual increases continue through the next five years or so, you can expect a four-year education at a private college with room and board to cost around $175,000.

The bottom line is this: If you want your student to go to college, you need to begin planning now. Start looking for inventive and innovative ways to finance your student's education. A good starting point is the Internet. Many Internet users refer to online college planning sites in an effort to unravel the mysteries of financial aid, scholarships, and tax-free savings plans. Here are a few mega Web sites for college planning to get you started:

- **Fidelity** (www.fidelity.com) offers good advice for college planning. On Fidelity's home page, pull down the "Retirement & Guidance" menu and then click on "College Planning" to discover how Section 529 savings plans (named for Internal Revenue Code Section 529) can help you finance your student's education

- **MSN Money** (moneycentral.msn.com) offers insightful articles and online tools. Uncover different strategies that you can use for students at different ages. The Q and A (question and answer) section is quite useful, and the tuition savings calculator and portfolio tracker can help with your college planning.

- **SmartMoney's College Planning** (www.smartmoney.com/college) includes articles, worksheets, and calculators that cover various ways to invest your college dollars and to receive tax breaks. You can also discover the requirements of Section 529 savings plans.

Shopping for the right school

The decision to attend a four-year college, two-year program, or vocational school needs to be carefully evaluated. Any educational program takes time, effort, and money, so don't jump in without doing your homework. In making your decision, you need to consider the following factors:

- **Quality of education:** Verify whether the school is accredited, whether it has a good reputation, and what local employers say about the school. For example, the Wall Street Journal (`www.careerjournal.com/special reports/bschoolguide/overall.html`) and BusinessWeek.com (`www.businessweek.com/bschools/03/geographic.htm`) rank colleges and offer critiques of different schools.

- **Completion rate:** Find out how many students are enrolled at the school, how many actually graduate, and how many students transfer to other schools.

- **Job placements:** Check out whether the school has a career placement office and how many graduates are placed in jobs that are related to their chosen fields.

- **Availability of financial aid:** Dig up the dirt on what financial-aid programs the school offers and whether financial-aid counseling is available. You may also want to become acquainted with how the school's refund policy works.

- **Student complaints:** Check with the Better Business Bureau at `www.bbb.org` to see whether any serious complaints have been lodged against the school.

- **School crime rate:** Crime can be a problem on some campuses, so you need to check up on the campus crime rate. If it's high, you need to find out what the school does to protect students. You may also want to compare the school's campus crime statistics with the same from similar schools. The Department of Education Web site at `www.ope.ed.gov/security` is a good place to check on these factors.

Regardless of which type of educational program you select, you need to realize that continuing your education is often expensive, time-consuming, and requires maximum effort. So finding a school that matches your academic abilities, educational goals, and personality is important. The Internet offers several online college matching services, including

- **CollegeBoard** (`apps.collegeboard.com/search/index.jsp`): The CollegeBoard offers a free online service that matches your preferences to a database of more than 3,500 schools. All you have to do is answer an online questionnaire about the type of school, location, campus life, costs, and financial aid you desire.

✔ **Princeton Review** (www.princetonreview.com/college/research/advsearch/match.asp): The Princeton Review combines your academic and extracurricular histories and preferences to assist you in finding the right college.

✔ **USNews.com** (www.usnews.com/usnews/edu/eduhome.htm): *USNews & World Report* provides an annual best-colleges index that ranks schools. The magazine's online advanced college search tool can assist you in discovering a school that meets your requirements.

Calculating the future costs of college

Before you panic about the cost of sending your student off to college, getting a grip on just how much you're expected to pay is important. Bear in mind that most college expenses are paid with a combination of savings, financial aid, and student loans. If you think you may need a little financial assistance, you're definitely not alone. Millions of students go to college every year, and their parents are trying to figure out how to pay the price of admission. Statistics indicate that only one in three parents actually is prepared to fully fund his or her student's college education. Later in this section I provide a list of several online calculators that employ often-used federal formulas for calculating your financial need. They can give you a sense of how much you'll be expected to contribute to your student's education.

Finding financial aid when you have a special situation

Many families have special circumstances that don't fit on the standardized financial-aid form. Your unique situation may not fall into a neat package. Examples of several factors that illustrate what can make calculating your financial need difficult include

✔ **Divorce.** Divorced couples can expect the incomes of stepparents to be included in the family's contribution, which may not seem fair because stepparents have no obligation (and possibly no intention) of supporting the students of their spouses.

✔ **Siblings with special needs.** Many families have siblings with chronic illnesses or particularly high costs of living.

✔ **Special family living circumstances.** Some living situations affect a family's ability to pay for college. For example, say you're supposed to receive court-ordered child support but haven't received a dime.

If you have a special situation that doesn't fit on the financial-aid form, don't despair. Don't let your special circumstances prevent you from contacting the school of your choice and explaining what's actually happening with your family. These special circumstances need to be brought to the attention of the financial-aid administrator. However, before contacting the school, make sure that you can clearly state your case.

Financial need is defined as the difference between the *cost of attendance* (COA) and your *expected family contribution* (EFC). Your EFC is defined as the amount of money you're expected to be able to contribute toward your student's education as determined by the Federal Methodology (FM) needs analysis formula. The FM formula includes parent and student contributions and the student's dependency status. Other factors in the formula include family size, number of family members in school, taxable and nontaxable incomes, and assets.

Remember, no hard and fast rules exist about who does and who doesn't receive financial aid. How different institutions calculate financial aid can be subjective, varying from school to school. Many online college-aid calculators are available online. They can help you determine your EFC and estimate how much a certain student can receive in financial aid.

The following are a few examples of facts you need to know before using the online college-aid calculators:

✔ **The parental income:** In some situations, as much as 47 percent of a family's income can be applied toward a student's education. Parents with variable incomes need to pay heed to which years they report their incomes, because doing so can have an impact on financial aid. For example, if you're a business owner, you may have some discretion about when you can take tax write-offs or bonuses or report income.

✔ **The student income:** Financial-aid administrators usually assess the income of students at a higher rate than parental income, a factor that's important to keep in mind when you're setting up a college fund for your student or deciding when or how much to pay your student for working in your business. Bartering within a family-owned business can be a good approach to lowering the amount of your student's income without causing a rift. For example, if you're paying your student a minimum wage for one or two years before he or she starts college, you may want to barter with your student and pay less wages and more educational expenses later. The benefit of this is that it lowers your student's income by paying a lower wage now in exchange for paying room and board later on when your student is enrolled in college.

✔ **How and where money is held:** Savings accounts held in the student's name or in special accounts can negatively impact your financial-aid application. For example, any college fund for a student needs to be in the parent's name or in an account that's designated for the benefit of the student.

✔ **Assets:** Not all assets are counted by financial-aid administrators. For example, the cash value of insurance policies, deferred annuities, and collections aren't included in financial-aid applications for you or your student. Additionally, if your student's grandparents (as part of their estate planning) want to take advantage of a tax deduction and make a tax-deductible gift to your student, you may want to suggest precious metals or an insurance policy. For details about the Federal Methodology Needs Analysis formulas used by financial-aid administrators when tallying up parental assets, see FAFSA.com at `www.fafsa.com/fmtables.htm`.

The Internet provides many financial-aid calculators that can assist you in gaining an understanding of the amount of money your family is expected to contribute to funding your student's college education. The following are a few of the best and easiest online EFC financial-aid wizards:

✔ **College Cost Forecaster v10.1** (`www.mhec.state.md.us/financialaid/calculator/cacmarystart.html`) provides a college-aid calculator for Maryland students and their families. This online calculator estimates your family's EFC for public and for private colleges. The online calculator also

  • Forecasts an inflation-adjusted EFC any number of years into the future.

  • Calculates financial aid for what-if scenarios.

  • Computes education loan payments for Stafford, PLUS, Perkins, or other loans.

✔ **Mapping Your Future** (`www.mapping-your-future.org`), shown in Figure 9-1, provides useful calculators for estimating your expected family contribution. Additionally, students can discover the minimum salaries they'll need to cover their student loan payments after they graduate.

✔ **SmartMoney** (`www.smartmoney.com/college/finaid/index.cfm?story=need`) provides an easy-to-use worksheet for calculating your family's EFC contribution to your student's college education.

✔ **Xap.com** (`www.xap.com`) offers an online financial-aid calculator that breaks down the process into seven steps. You enter your personal information to find the cost of attending the college of your choice and your eligibility for a Pell Grant, Stafford loan, or other financial aid (additional scholarships, grants, or loans). You'll also discover the deadlines for filing for requests for financial aid at the colleges you select.

Figure 9-1:
Mapping
Your Future
calculates
your
Expected
Family
Contribution.

Brother, Can You Spare a Little Financial Aid?

Financial aid can make attending a private four-year school possible. For example, if your EFC is only $6,000, you may qualify for $24,000 in financial aid at a school that costs $30,000 per year to attend. Comparing that to a public four-year school with annual costs of $8,000, the EFC may leverage only $2,000 in financial aid.

Financial aid is determined by a combination of factors that are unique for each school and each student. According to the CollegeBoard (www.college board.com), a record $90 billion in financial aid was disbursed in 2003. About 75 percent of all students at private colleges and 60 percent of students at public colleges received some type of aid during that year.

Many people believe that financial-aid funds are available only for families that are hard-pressed to finance their students' educations. Currently, financial aid is not only for the very poor; families with incomes that are less than $70,000 per year also can qualify for financial aid. If your student is athletically or academically gifted, additional financial aid may be available.

Families with incomes of more than $100,000 per year with only one student in school will find it difficult to receive financial aid. On the other hand, whenever you earn more than $150,000 per year and have two or three students in school simultaneously, it's good to know that you may still qualify for financial aid.

Starting the financial-aid process online

You need to complete two forms to start the federal and financial-aid processes: the College Scholarship Service Profile (CSSP), which you can find at www.collegeboard.com is used by more than 600 colleges, universities, graduate and professional schools, and scholarship programs to determine the eligibility of students for nonfederal student aid. The Free Application for Federal Student Aid (FAFSA) is used to apply for student financial aid from the federal government, including the Pell Grant, Perkins Loan, Stafford Loan and work-study. You should complete the FAFSA form each year, even if you think you don't qualify for financial aid. After all, your financial situation may change. For example, a sibling may begin college, the financial situation of your family may change or other factors that affect your eligibility may come into play. You can complete the FAFSA form online at www.fafsa.org. To cover all your bases, both forms should be completed every year in which you apply for aid.

The FAFSA is used by public and private schools for their financial-aid decision-making. Public schools, however, adhere to the guidelines of the FAFSA more than private schools do. The FAFSA is frequently used to calculate financial-aid eligibility by subtracting the EFC from the cost of attending school.

If you use the online calculators listed in "Calculating the future costs of college," earlier in this chapter, you'll probably notice that your EFC is largely based on your income, assets, the number of years until your retirement, and the number of students in your family who are attending school at the same time.

Yet every story has at least two sides, and financial aid has many sides. For one thing, your personal situation can affect the number of dollars your student receives. For another, the college you choose may have hidden factors that influence the amount of financial aid it offers. The following are a few examples:

- ✔ If you're too slow in applying for financial aid from the school of your choice, the financial aid you're seeking may already have been given to other students. When the school's money is gone, you can do nothing about it but apply earlier next year.

- ✔ Student desirability sometimes plays a role in the amount of financial aid you can expect. Schools frequently offer attractive financial-aid packages to exceptional athletes and scholars. If your student is gifted in these areas, don't be shy about telling the financial-aid officer.

- ✔ The number of students needing financial aid varies every year. In some years, the number of students in need of financial aid is higher than in others.

You may be surprised to find out that many schools offer creative payment plans tailored to fit your individual needs. For example, you may be able to prepay four years of tuition or pay tuition on a monthly or quarterly basis.

A couple of the better online sources for information about financial aid are

- ✔ **FinAid** (www.finaid.com), a free service that's for individuals looking for ways to finance their education. This comprehensive Web site is a great starting point for your financial-aid search.

- ✔ **Princeton Review** (www.princetonreview.com/finance), which provides online help for completing financial-aid forms, tips on how to get the financial aid you want, and online tools to make your life easier.

Many college students believe that the award letters they receive are a sign that their troubles are over. Although that may be true (in some cases), you nevertheless need to complete the FAFSA. This annual application has a predetermined deadline. What's more, your school won't let you ignore it either. You may need additional funds for hidden expenses, and completing the FAFSA can help. If you don't need extra money, you don't need to activate the application, but if you do need the extra money, be glad you completed and submitted your FAFSA.

Getting free money for college: Grants

Everyone agrees that *gift aid* or grants are the best way to pay for college. The reason grants are best is simple: Grants don't have to be repaid. The first step in applying for a grant is completing the application form. No limits are imposed on the number of grants for which you can apply. Your time and effort and a postage stamp are the only costs of applying. Grants are awarded for two reasons:

- ✔ **As gift aid.** Gift aid can be a grant based on a student's athletic abilities, academic abilities, or other personal attributes. Many grants are based on need or other conditions. Some grants are based on who you are (American Indian, daughter of a firefighter, and so on) or where you live (many states offer grants for residents). Grants that are based on merit can be for a student's outstanding talent. The personal wealth of the parents doesn't enter into the equation, so the amount of the award is the same for all students.

- ✔ **On the basis of need.** Need-based aid usually is in the form of grants that require a qualifying grade (sometimes 70 percent) and the inherent financial needs of the student's family. Don't, however, think that your student shouldn't apply for grants because he or she isn't earning top grades.

Remember the saying: "It's difficult to be a hero in your hometown." When it comes to finding grants, this statement is patently false. Students frequently find more success in their search for grants in their hometowns. Good sources of educational funding are community groups, regional branches of professional associations, and churches that award academic scholarships. Your student's high school guidance counselor should have a list of these resources. Additionally, check with the alumni association of the school you plan to attend. You may qualify for one or more of the alumni grants that are available. Here are several online sources for grants:

- ✔ **Washington Higher Education Coordinating Board** (`www.hecb.wa.gov/index.asp`) is an example of how states sponsor financial-aid programs for college students. This Web site includes links to state grants offered in the state of Washington for undergraduates with significant financial need, state work-study programs, Washington Promise Scholarships, and educational opportunity grants targeted for undergraduate students who can't complete their educations because of family or work commitments, health concerns, financial need, or other factors.

- ✔ **Maryland Higher Education Commission** (`www.mhec.state.md.us/financialAid/descriptions.asp`) divides its financial assistance programs into need-based grants, legislative scholarships, loan assistance repayment programs, merit- and career-based scholarships, and grants for unique populations.

- ✔ **The Student Guide** (`studentaid.ed.gov/students/publications/student_guide/2004_2005/english/index.htm`) illustrates the types of student aid that are available. For example, you find the eligibility requirements for Federal Pell Grants (with an annual maximum limit of $4,050 for 2004–2005), which almost exclusively are for undergraduates and don't have to be repaid. Federal Supplemental Educational Opportunity Grants (FSEOG — with an annual maximum of $4,000) don't have to be repaid, either. They're geared for undergraduates with exceptional financial needs. Visit the Web site to see whether your student is eligible.

- ✔ **USNews.com** (`12.47.197.196/usnews/state.cfm`) offers an extensive listing of links to states that offer specific funding for college. You also can find information about state-based loans and scholarships. You need to check your state of residence for college grants. Each state offers different grants, but you still have to complete a FAFSA (nope, you can't get around it) and submit your application by the deadlines posted on the Web site.

Grants and scholarships often require special tests, oral and written essays, or high scores on the American College Testing Assessment Test (ACT). You can find out how you may stack up against the competition by taking any of the sample tests at `www.act.org`. Additionally, this Web site enables you to register online for the ACT test and to search for test dates and locations.

More free money: Scholarships

The difference between grants (free money) and scholarships is a huge one. Scholarships usually are awards for something you've already accomplished or something you can do, such as maintain a predetermined grade level, be a sports star, or be someone a college can be proud of in some other way.

Types of scholarships

Schools often categorize students into scholarship categories. A student needs to be familiar with these classifications to increase his or her chances of receiving scholarships from colleges, institutions, and foundations by highlighting personal achievements within those categories. A few of the attributes to emphasize so you can appear more attractive to the financial-aid administrators evaluating your applications are

- ✔ **Academics:** As the recipient of top grades, you've received a near-perfect grade or at least high scores on your SAT or ACT tests and you're ranked at the top of your class. Flaunt it; you're academically gifted and that's a plus.

- ✔ **Athletics:** You're the star of your school's football or basketball team, or you were named All-State as a field hockey player. You were a member of the track team, swim team, tennis team, or golf team. Athletic talents can spell financial aid.

- ✔ **Character and achievement:** Your science fair project was featured in a national magazine. You wrote a book. You're the winner of the national creative writing award. You traveled to a country as head of the school's debate team. You've demonstrated leadership in your community. Your business acumen is recognized. Tell financial-aid administrators about these attributes because they can be helpful in securing a better financial-aid package.

In some cases, scholarships can actually reduce the amount of financial aid your student receives. That's because colleges have rules against over-awarding, or giving students too many scholarships. The good news is that some scholarships can be used to reduce the amount of student loans (and yet not reduce the amount of grants).

Finding scholarships online

The Internet is a great source for finding scholarships that match your unique attributes. To avoid scholarship scams, bear in mind that the best online sources for scholarship searches are usually *free*. Here are some of them:

✔ **College Planning Network** (www.collegeplan.org) is a nonprofit organization geared for middle-school and high-school students who are seeking information about scholarships in the Pacific Northwest in the United States.

✔ **CollegeBoard** (apps.collegeboard.com/cbsearch_ss/welcome.jsp) provides an online tool to assist you in locating scholarships, internships, grants, and loans that match your educational level, attributes, and background. Complete the questionnaire, and the "Scholarship Search" tool locates potential opportunities from a database of more than 2,300 sources of available aid.

✔ **FastWEB** (www.fastweb.com) is divided into two sections. The first is the free scholarship search, where scholarships are sorted by due dates and award amounts. The second is the free search for colleges. Just plug in criteria like your student's grade-point average (GPA), hobbies, school activities, and so on.

✔ **FinAid** (www.finaid.com) is the granddaddy of all online college planning Web sites. On it, you'll discover in-depth information about scholarships, savings plans, and student loans.

✔ **Scholarship Experts** (www.scholarshipexperts.com) is by far the best scholarship search engine on the Web. If you think quality content (meaning no inappropriate ads) is worth $30 a year, then this is the Web site for you. If you subscribe, get ready to complete an extensive questionnaire.

Upgrading your chances of winning a scholarship

One way to increase your student's chances of winning a scholarship is to make certain that he or she gets top marks on tests and essays or is ranked at the top of the class. Several of the Web sites that follow offer full practice tests and suggests ways to improve test scores:

✔ **American College Testing Assessment Test** (www.act.org), called the ACT, is the counterpart of the Scholastic Aptitude Test (SAT). The Web site includes sample tests, test-taking tips, and online results.

✔ **GoCollege** (www.gocollege.com) provides full practice SAT and ACT tests. Student-submitted FAQs also offer unique insights about student life.

✔ **Kaplan** (www.kaptest.com) offers free membership to its Web site, sample questions, and analyses of past SAT tests.

The student loan labyrinth

Award-package shortfalls usually are filled in with work-study programs or student loans. Some student loans are subsidized, and others are unsubsidized. Student loans based on financial need are subsidized. When a student loan is subsidized, you usually don't have to pay yearly interest while the student for whom the loan was granted is still in college.

Checking out need-based student loans

Perkins student loans are subsidized, low-interest loans geared for students who demonstrate a high need. The financial-aid officer at the school you've selected will tell you whether you qualify. Schools decide who receives Perkins loans because they come from each school's federally funded loan pool and the graduates who are repaying their own Perkins loans. The maximum loan amount for undergraduates is $4,000, with interest rates (currently) of about 5 percent. Students must repay the loans beginning about nine months after graduation.

Repayment of Perkins loans can be spread across a ten-year period (or about $53 a month for the maximum loan). Perkins loans can be canceled (or forgiven) whenever a graduate is employed as a full-time teacher in a low-income area, becomes a special education teacher, or teaches math, science, or other specific subjects where a shortage of teachers exists. Others who qualify for forgiveness of Perkins loans are full-time nurses or medical technicians, law enforcement or corrections officers, employees of student or family service agencies in low-income communities, or Peace Corps volunteers.

Exploring other sources of college funding

Student-employment (or work-study) programs are administered by the financial-aid office of the college of your choice. The school's financial-aid officer helps students find jobs that pay an expected amount. Students enrolled in and qualifying for work-study aid programs earn money to help pay for educational costs, such as books, supplies, and personal expenses. To sum it up, work-study plans are federally sponsored programs that offer students part-time employment to meet their financial needs. Additionally, work-study programs can give students valuable on-the-job experience related to their career goals. For more information about the federal work-study program, see the College Zone at www.collegezone.com/student zone/416_876.htm.

Looking into unsubsidized student loans

Unsubsidized loans, which sometimes are called supplemental loans, can have payments that are deferred until after graduation. The advantage of unsubsidized loans is that they're not need-based, meaning anyone, including the richest person you know, is eligible.

Remember not to include unsubsidized loans whenever your student calculates and evaluates awarded aid. The names of some of the unsubsidized loans include:

- **Stafford loans:** They include reasonably low interest rates that are capped at 8.25 percent. Stafford loans have maximum amounts of $2,625 the first year, $3,500 the second year, and $5,500 the third and fourth years. Borrowers can have part or all of their loans subsidized (meaning the government pays the interest while the student is in school). Repayment begins six months after graduation. Graduate/professional students can borrow $18,500 per academic year.

- **Federal PLUS Loans:** These loans enable parents who don't have adverse credit histories to borrow the full cost of an education (less any financial aid) for dependent undergraduate students. Education costs include tuition, room and board, books, transportation, and additional expenses. Variable interest rates on PLUS Loans range between 2 percent and 9 percent. Repayment of interest and principal begins 90 days after the loan is fully disbursed to the school. PLUS loans aren't income-sensitive, so your family's income isn't a factor when determining eligibility. You also may be able to deduct some of your interest payments from your taxes.

- **Private-education loans for parents:** These loans are for parents and are available at banks. They aren't government backed. If considering this type of loan, you may want to start by checking out Nellie Mae (www.nelliemae.com). Nellie Mae offers EXCEL private loans with variable rates that are calculated monthly or annually. Annual rates generally amount to the prime rate plus 2 percent, calculated August 1, and the monthly rate is prime plus .75 percent, adjusted at the beginning of every month when needed. You can borrow the full amount of college expenses minus any financial aid the student receives. Recipients must be creditworthy, which usually means no delinquencies for at least two years, and your debt payments (for other loans, such as mortgages and EXCEL loans) can't exceed 40 percent of your gross monthly income. Expect to pay an upfront guarantee fee of 6 percent (2 percent with a co-borrower), which goes into a default insurance fund.

✔ **Home-equity loans:** Home-equity loans enable parents who are home-owners to borrow against the equity they've accrued in their homes. *Home equity* is defined as the difference between your mortgage loan and the fair market value of your home. The interest you pay for your home-equity loan often is tax-deductible. One limitation of this approach is the likelihood you'll have to pay an additional fee for the loan.

✔ **Borrowing against a whole-life insurance policy:** Late starters have a difficult time catching up with early college-fund savers. Check with your insurer; you may be able to borrow against your whole-life insurance policy at rates lower than those offered by PLUS lenders. If you don't mind depleting your death benefit, you may not have to repay the loan.

Many resources and tools are available online for explaining the details of student and parent loans. Here are a few examples of what you'll find:

✔ **CNNMoney** (money.cnn.com) provides a student-loan calculator that enables you to determine how quickly you can pay off your student loans. You can experiment with what-if scenarios of making higher monthly payments to shorten the length of your loan term or seeing how a change in the interest rate affects the payoff date.

✔ **CollegeBoard.com** (www.collegeboard.com) supplies an in-depth look at how you can fund your student's education. In fact, the information is so extensive that you sometimes forget your original question. At the home page, click on "For Parents." On the next page, click on "Pay for College" and then on "Aid & How to Pay."

✔ **SmartMoney.com** (www.smartmoney.com/college/finaid) offers a section about college planning. In the section on College Planning you'll discover an article titled "Student Loans Demystified." This article answers the most frequently asked questions about what the different types of student loans are, how much you need to borrow, and how you repay the loan.

Maximizing Your Savings for College

Most parents pay for their student's college education with a combination of financial aid, grants or scholarships, loans, and savings. However, many parents *incorrectly* believe they won't qualify for financial aid if they save for their student's college education. However, if your family earns more than $70,000 per year you may not qualify for financial aid anyway. Moreover, if you earn less than $70,000 per year or if you qualify for financial aid for some other reason, the cost of going to school is likely to be greater than the amount of financial aid you'll receive. And that means you probably will have to borrow the money to pay for your student's college education. Bottom line — if you aren't affluent, the more you save for college, the less you'll have to borrow to pay for it.

One way to avoid having to borrow a large amount of money is to start saving now. For example, say you and your wife have just had a baby, and you decide to stop buying your lunch and start taking your lunch to work. The resulting $6-per-day savings, or $120 per month, earning 4 percent annually for 18 years, yields almost $38,000 for your student's college education.

The five ways you can save for your student's education are

- ✔ **Section 529 savings programs:** These savings plans may be offered by a state, by an agency of the state, or by an educational institution. Some Section 529 college savings plans enable taxpayers to receive a tax deduction for contributions.

- ✔ **Coverdell ESA:** Savings in this plan go into a tax-deferred account created by the U.S. government to assist families in paying educational expenses.

- ✔ **Uniform Gifts to Minors Act (UGMA) and Uniform Transfers to Minors Act (UTMA):** UGMA enables a donor to contribute to a minor's custodial account without having to appoint a legal guardian or create a trust account. UTMA enables items other than cash or securities to be considered as gifts. Each year you can contribute $11,000 to each individual without incurring federal gift tax. Married couples can contribute $22,000 annually without incurring any federal gift tax. (For more information about the Uniform Gifts to Minors Acts and taxes, see Chapter 11.)

- ✔ **Qualified U.S. Savings Bonds:** U.S. Savings Bonds are debt obligations of the U.S. government that are backed by the Treasury Department and monitored by the Bureau of Public Debt. In 1990, the Bureau of Public debt began the Education Bond Program. Under this program the interest earned on savings bonds may be free from federal taxes when the principal and interest from the sale of the bonds are used to pay for the education of the bondholder or his or her spouse, significant other, or student. For details about the Education Bond Program, see the Bureau of Public Debt at `www.publicdebt.treas.gov/sav/saveduca.htm`.

- ✔ **Taxable accounts:** Taxable savings accounts, which often are managed by professional brokerages and have higher returns than state-managed programs, carry investment risks in return for the promise of higher returns. These accounts have no contribution limits.

It's important to remember that it's never too late to start saving for your student's education. The sooner you start saving the better because of the wonder of compounding interest. If you're uncertain about the amount of money you need to be saving every month, use FinAid's "Savings Growth Projector" at www.finaid.org/calculators/savingsgrowth.phtml. This online calculator can assist you in targeting the exact amount of money you need to set aside each month for your student's education.

Selec ing from two types of Section 529 college savings plans

Section 529 savings plans are prepaid tuition programs that pay future tuition costs at today's prices. Prepaid tuition plans enable families (or individuals) to establish an account in the name of the student and lock in a specific number of academic units or periods of instruction time at the current tuition rate. Prepaid tuition plans often are used for public four-year colleges. The account can be funded by periodic payments or in a lump sum. Prepaid tuition plans come in two flavors:

✔ **Prepaid units:** The buyer purchases units that represent a fixed percentage of the total tuition. Although the cost of a unit may increase each year, after a unit is purchased, its value remains the same percentage of tuition as when it was originally purchased regardless of any future increases in tuition costs.

✔ **Prepaid contracts:** The buyer purchases contracts that represent a specified number of years of tuition and mandatory fees, room, and board. The purchase price depends on the age of the student, type of payment (whether lump sum or installment), and the number of years of units purchased. For the most part, contract prices are lower for younger students because the proceeds can be invested for longer periods.

Today all 50 states sponsor Section 529 college savings plans. These college savings plans enable individuals to contribute to an account to pay for a student's qualified higher-education expenses at any eligible educational institution. Section 529 college savings plans are required by federal law to prevent contributions that are more than the amount required to fund the student's education, but the law doesn't otherwise specify any other limit on contributions. This means that each state can set its own limit. Most states estimate the amount of money required for seven years of postsecondary qualified higher education (undergraduate and graduate school). Because states can set their own cumulative contribution limits, the range is between $146,000 and $305,000. The average contribution limit is $235,000. (For more information, see Table 9-1 for a comparison of Section 529 college savings plans to Coverdell ESAs.)

For more information about Section 529 college savings plans, be sure to check out *529 and Other College Savings Plans For Dummies* by Margaret A. Munro (Wiley).

Rolling over with Coverdell ESAs

Once known as Educational IRAs (Individual Retirement Accounts), Coverdell Education Savings Accounts (ESAs) are tax-free when used to pay for qualified education expenses. They also enable investors to change beneficiaries. Control of account withdrawals transfers to the student beneficiary when he or she becomes of legal age (usually 18 years old in most states). The maximum annual contribution is $2,000.

Investing in a Coverdell ESA has many advantages over placing your savings in a taxable investment. An investment of $2,000 per year with an annual return of 8 percent beginning when your child is a baby can yield as much as $89,524 for college when your student reaches age 18. Invest those same amounts with similar returns in a taxable investment (and assuming that combined federal and state taxes are 28 percent), puts the yield at only $70,318.

Not only is knowing about the different ways you can save for college important, but you also need to know how *much* to save. FinAid features a calculator that is just the ticket at `www.finaid.org/calculators/savingsplan.phtml`. Using this calculator, you can design a savings plan that ensures you have enough money to pay future college bills as it fits in with your ability to save today.

The UGMA/UTMA enables individuals to set up a minor's trust account, invest in a wide variety of securities, and maintain custodian control of the account until the student reaches legal age. One limitation of the UGMA/UTMA approach is that beneficiaries can't be changed. For students younger than 14, the first $750 of annual earned income is tax-free, but the next $750 of earned income is taxed at the student's income tax rate, and anything more than $1,500 is taxed at the parent's tax rate. After the student reaches the age of 14, all income earned is taxed at the student's rate. Control of the withdrawals transfers to the student when he or she reaches legal age. When calculating financial aid, financial-aid officers treat this type of account as a student asset.

The federal formula for calculating EFC (expected family contribution) according to FinAid (`www.finaid.org`) is as follows:

- ✔ Parental Income: 22 percent to 44 percent of adjusted gross income
- ✔ Parental Assets: 3.0 percent to 5.5 percent of nonretirement assets (such as 529 savings plans and brokerage/mutual fund accounts)
- ✔ Student Income: 50 percent over $3,000
- ✔ Student Assets: 35 percent of all assets (such as UGMA /UTMA accounts, Coverdell ESAs, and other savings)

Getting a college break

Good news! If you file your tax return as a single taxpayer and your income is less than $40,000 ($80,000 for married couples filing jointly), your student qualifies for a Hope Scholarship (Tax) Credit of up to $1,500 each year for the first two years of college, even when he or she uses funds from a Section 529 savings plan for college expenses. As your income level climbs to $50,000 ($100,000 for couples filing jointly), the amount of the credit is gradually reduced until it's completely phased out. In subsequent years, you can claim the Lifetime Learning Credit; however, this credit is subject to the same income restrictions as the Hope credit. The Lifetime Learning Credit amounts to 20 percent of up to $10,000 of your (or a family's) tuition expenses, or a maximum of $2,000. *Note:* These tax credits apply only to tuition expenses and not room, board, or books."

According to FinAid (www.finaid.org), the student's 529 College Savings plan is considered an asset of the parent, not the student, and will have less effect on federal financial-aid calculations than savings in the child's name. The EFC formula assumes that between 22 percent and 44 percent of the adjusted gross of parental income is available for their student's educational expenses, but the formula only includes 3 percent to 5.5 percent of the parent's savings (which include 529 Savings Plans). The EFC formula assumes that 50 percent of student income and 35 percent of the student's assets, which include Coverdell ESAs, UGMA / UTMAs and other savings, are available to pay for college. Table 9-1 details how a 529 savings plan and a Coverdell ESA account compare in other ways.

Table 9-1   Comparing a Section 529 Plan with a Coverdell ESA

Type of Plan Attribute	529 Savings Plan	Coverdell ESA
Maximum annual contributions	Depends on the plan and can vary from $100,000 to $305,000	Limited to $2,000 per year (regardless of how many people contribute)
Offered by	States (often with the assistance of financial institutions)	Brokerages, banks, and mutual fund companies
Contributor attributes	No limit on parental income	Parent's modified adjusted gross income is less than $220,000 for married taxpayers filing jointly and less than $110,000 for single taxpayers

Type of Plan Attribute	529 Savings Plan	Coverdell ESA
Treatment of asset for financial-aid purposes	Considered an asset of the account owner (the parent)	If set up in the name of the parent, considered an asset of the parent
Account earnings	Tax-free for qualified expenses	Tax-free for qualified expenses
Investment options	A variety of variable investment options	A wide variety of securities
Able to change beneficiaries	Yes	Yes
Control of withdrawals	Owner of account	Transfers to student at legal age
Penalties for non-qualified withdrawals	10% penalty withheld on earnings	10% penalty withheld on earnings
Qualified use of proceeds	Any accredited post-secondary school in the U.S.	Any accredited post-secondary or qualified K–12 school in the U.S.
Tax implications for contributions	Contributions can be deductible for state income tax purposes	Contributions are not tax-deductible

Using the Internet to find savings advice

The Internet offers many online sources to help you become skilled at saving dollars for college. Because all states have Section 529 savings plans to assist you making the most out of each dollar you save, many Web sites offer screening tools that compare different Section 529 college savings plans, assist you in starting a college fund, and analyze which method of saving for college is best for you. Here are some of them:

✔ **CollegeSavingsBank** (www.collegesavingsbank.com) offers the CollegeSure CD, which pays an annual percentage yield that's tied directly to annual increases in college costs (with a 2 percent minimum interest rate). You can select a fixed maturity date from 1 to 25 years. CollegeSavingsBank also offers Section 529 plans and Coverdell ESAs.

✔ **FinAid** (www.finaid.org) includes a Savings link that offers a number of articles about Section 529 plans, gifts, and estate planning strategies that can assist you in financing your student's college education. The Web site is an excellent source for parents seeking financial aid.

✔ **Savingforcollege** (www.savingforcollege.com) provides a detailed guide to Section 529 plans. Be sure to check out the informative FAQ section, content from major news organizations, and original articles that provide timely insight into what you can expect from your Section 529 account. Additionally, Section 529 plans are described and ranked by state. A separate table shows performance results for each state's Section 529 plan.

✔ **The College Savings Plans Network** (www.collegesavings.org) offers answers to FAQs, articles, contact information, and a link to each state's Section 529 plan.

✔ **The Education Plan** (www.theeducationplan.com) includes two savings plan choices. The first is The Age-Based Choice in which your money is invested in one of five diversified mutual fund portfolios based on the student's age. The second option is The Custom Choice in which you select from eight different portfolios. All of the portfolios are professionally managed. The Web site includes college-saver information and online tools.

✔ **TIAA-CREF Tuition Financing, Inc.** (www.tiaa-cref.org/tuition) is a nonprofit organization that works with several states to provide state-sponsored and independent Section 529 plans. A recent change in the tax laws makes independent Section 529 plans possible. Today about 290 private schools have come together to form their own prepaid independent Section 529 plan. If your student decides not to attend one of the participating schools, the plan refunds your money along with the modest interest you've earned. Earnings aren't taxed if the proceeds are spent on higher education.

✔ **U.S. Department of Education** (www.ed.gov/thinkingcollege/early) provides a basic overview of how to plan for college early. Content includes links to other useful college planning Web sites and a screening tool that helps you find information about specific schools.

On Sale Now: Getting a Discount on Tuition

The tuition discounts we hear the most about are offered to college employees and their offspring, college alumni and their dependents, senior citizens, and siblings or married couples who are simultaneously enrolled. If you're in one of these categories, you're eligible for a tuition discount regardless of your personal wealth.

Calculating your tuition discount online

The National Association of College and University Business Officers (www.nacubo.org) reports in a study titled *Tuition Discounts* that in 2002, independent colleges and universities collectively discounted more than 39 percent of gross tuition with institutional funds, and the largest increases in tuition discounts have occurred at small colleges. Small colleges have indicated that more than 75 percent of all first-year students at 331 private schools receive awards of $7,000. At small schools that charge tuitions of less than $20,000, tuition discounts usually are higher. Some schools offer to discount half the published cost of tuition.

DePauw University is a good example of a school that offers merit-based tuition discounts. You can even calculate the amount of your academic award online at www.go2.depauw.edu. At the home page click on "Find Your Merit Award," and next click on "Go to the Merit Award Calculator." At the Merit Award Calculator page you'll need to enter your student's SAT or ACT score, grade-point average, and class ranking. The online calculator immediately indicates the amount of award DePauw University will offer. For example, a student with an SAT score of 1,020 and a GPA of 3.25 receives a discount of $3,000. A student with an SAT score of 1,200 and a GPA of 3.75 receives a discount of $10,000.

The other type of discounting is for the poor. Many Ivy League schools offer tuition discounts to financially needy students. In the past, middle-class and upper-middle-class students often were expected to pay full price for tuition so discounts could be offered to students in need.

Today, a new trend bases tuition discounts on merit or character. In other words, some colleges offer a discount because the student is attractive to the school. A recent survey shows how the best students can receive the best tuition discounts. Schools don't usually publish this information. However, if you go to the college's Web site and look for "university-sponsored discounts" in a footnote to the college's financial statement, you're likely to discover how much the school is discounting tuition. (Don't forget to read the fine print. Some schools mix grants with discounts, so determining an exact number is difficult.)

Discover exactly which private colleges offer non-need-based aid by visiting Kiplinger.com (www.kiplinger.com/tools/privatecolleges). Click on the article titled "Best Values in Private Colleges" for more information about tuition discounts. This article lists 100 top private colleges and describes how colleges provide non-need-based aid, in general. Keep in mind that 12 of the top 20 schools admit less than one in four applicants.

Creating an Online College Worksheet

When your student starts receiving acceptance letters, you'll also begin receiving awards letters. Calculating the real value of each school's offer is important. The best award packages consist of grants. Grants can be need-based, merit-based, federal, state, or institutional in origin. Grants usually are tax-free and don't have to be repaid. You'll need to compare award packages from each school to make an educated decision about which award package is best from a purely financial perspective. You can do so by following these three steps:

1. **Establish the amount of free money.**

   First, add up the grants. Grants are usually handed out according to need. Examples of need-based grants are Pell Grants and Federal Supplemental Educational Opportunity (SEOP) Grants, which are non-negotiable. Pell Grants have a maximum of $4,000 per year and are targeted for low-income families. SEOP Grants vary from $100 to $4,000 per year, come directly from the school, and can be mixed with other need-based and merit-based grants. Scholarships also are free money that doesn't have to be repaid. Scholarships usually are awarded for athletics, good grades and test scores, or other indicators of your student's merit.

2. **Determine the total cost.**

   Tuition, room, and board are only the beginning costs for attending college. Other costs include transportation, clothing, and entertainment.

3. **Calculate the difference, and compare award packages.**

   As you begin stacking up your award packages, you'll probably see clear-cut differences between the packages. For example, you may be flattered that one award is based on merit, but another award based on need may go further in funding your student's college education.

The following are online calculators that can assist you with comparing financial-aid packages.

   ✔ **CollegeBoard** (www.collegeboard.com) helps you compare financial-aid offers. You may want to show a better offer that you received from another school to the school of your choice, just to see whether the school you want to attend is willing to upgrade your financial-aid package.

   ✔ **U.S. News.com** (www.usnews.com/usnews/edu/college/tools/brief/awards_brief.php) points out that financial-aid awards are often difficult to compare, but the worksheet it provides enables you to compare financial-aid packages *and* check your out-of-pocket costs for each school.

Chapter 10

Online Retirement Planning

Many people expect their retirement years to be the best years of their lives. That's what makes retirement planning more than just investing and saving for the future. It's about enjoying your life and not being constrained by economics and worry. It's important to give plenty of thought to how you're going to spend your time when you're not at work.

Saving for your retirement requires discipline. Retirement often is 40, 30, 20, or even only 10 years away, but it just doesn't seem like it's going to happen anytime soon. A study by Hewitt Associates, a benefits consulting firm, shows how difficult it is for individuals to visualize their retirement years. The study indicated that about 49 percent of workers surveyed said they didn't think they were saving enough and another 18 percent just weren't certain.

This chapter is about how you can use the Internet to help you get ready for retirement. In this chapter, you find out how to use online tools provided by the Social Security Administration for determining how much you can expect in Social Security benefits. And you discover a breakdown of average retiree expenses so you can start calculating how much money you need for retirement. This chapter shows how you can use the Internet to develop an online retirement plan. An example of how you can fill the gap between your retirement income and expenses is provided, and to maximize your retirement savings, you can identify a few places online where you can create "what-if?" scenarios. Best of all, this chapter helps you explore the Net for the optimum ways to save for your retirement.

Pop Quiz, Hotshot: How Ready Are You for Retirement?

Everyone needs a game plan, a strategy for retiring. Individuals who write down their retirement plans have a better chance of achieving their goals than folks who keep putting off the task of taking a good look at what they need to do to secure their retirement. Bear in mind that your retirement plan is similar to creating a business plan. To get started you need to know:

- ✔ **Your current needs:** If you haven't calculated how much you need to keep your head above water, you need to figure it out now. Knowing your current expenses helps you compute your future expenses.

- ✔ **How much you need to retire:** Many people want to move to another state or travel to all the places they were too busy to see when they were working.

- ✔ **Your retirement time frame:** When do you plan to retire? What activities do you plan to participate in? Will your mortgage be paid, or will you have children in college?

- ✔ **Your retirement expenses:** Determine your fixed expenses. How much income overall will you need? How much do you expect to receive from Social Security? What about your company pensions and your own retirement savings?

And here are a few tips for the road ahead:

- ✔ **Get the most out of your 401(k) plan.** Taking full advantage of your employer's 401(k) plan today may make a huge difference in your retirement lifestyle.

- ✔ **Take advantage of other savings plans.** Most folks have a gap between their expenses in retirement and the retirement benefits they'll receive. You can compensate for this deficit with IRAs, Roth IRAs, SEP-IRAs and other savings plans.

- ✔ **Don't ignore your retirement investments.** Monitor your savings and investments. Compare your financial status with your retirement plan. Are there any problems?

- ✔ **Plan your quitting-time strategy.** Set a reasonable withdrawal rate from your nest egg. Manage your money so you don't run out of money before you run out of time.

- ✔ **Periodically revise your long-term plans.** Update and rebalance your plan as necessary. If you decide you want to travel more in your retirement years, you may have to increase your savings.

✔ **Be passionate about your retirement planning.** Give some real thought to how you want to spend your retirement years. Apply this enthusiasm to your retirement planning. Remember, each person gets only one retirement.

The Internet provides many online tutorials to help you become skilled at planning for your retirement. A few examples include

✔ **About.com Retirement Planning Tutorials** (retireplan.about.com), which offers tutorials and links to online resources for information about investing in 401(k) and 403(b) plans.

✔ **GE Center for Financial Learning** (www.financiallearning.com), which offers articles, worksheets, and an extensive tutorial about retirement planning. The online retirement tutorial takes about 45 minutes to complete.

✔ **Prudential Financial** (www.prudential.com), which offers an online retirement planning tutorial. On the home page, click on "Financial Planning." Next click on "Retirement Planning," and then click on "Retirement Planning Learning Guides" and then on "Retirement Planning Tutorial." Scroll down the page to the outline of the tutorial.

Developing a Retirement Plan

If you don't have a retirement plan, create one. If you have a retirement plan, review it, and put more into it. Most Americans know they're not saving enough for their retirement. Many individuals aren't saving because they've been shaken by recent stock market losses, and others just let life get in the way of saving.

Whether you have a traditional pension plan, 401(k) plan, or no retirement plan at all, the Internet can help you develop a do-it-yourself plan. The Net provides many sources, tools, and resources to help you build your retirement plan. In many cases, the Internet even does the math for you. The following are a few examples of Web sites that can assist you with building your retirement plan online:

✔ **Investopedia** (www.investopedia.com) offers an online introduction to retirement planning. Discover how much you need, the different types of retirement plans, and how taxes affect you and your retirement.

✔ **Morningstar.com** (www.morningstar.com) provides an online retirement planner to help you plan for your golden years. It requires your Premium membership, which costs $12.95 per month.

- ✔ **SmartMoney.com** (www.smartmoney.com) supplies one the Internet's best retirement planning tools. Get worksheets, information about how long your money will last, and more, without having to register or pay a dime. On the home page, click on "Personal Finance" and then on "Retirement."

- ✔ **The Motley Fool** (www.fool.com/retirement/retirementplanning/retirementplanning01.htm) offers an online retirement primer to get you started with planning your retirement.

- ✔ **The Wall Street Journal** (www.wsj.com) provides Personal Finance News and Tools to assist you with your retirement planning. It's powered by the SmartMoney's Retirement Worksheet Calculator. Subscriptions are $3.95 per month or $39 per year.

The foundations of the retirement plans of many people are their pensions and Social Security benefits. Both are discussed in the sections that follow.

Pensions

Pension plans are defined as a promise by a sponsor, usually a company or a union, to pay a pension to the plan member. A variety of pension plans are in place. Here are two examples of traditional pension plans:

- ✔ **Defined benefit plan:** In a defined benefit plan, the promised pension is based on a clearly defined formula, such as years of service or hours worked.

- ✔ **Defined contribution plan:** In a defined contribution plan, the sponsor or company makes contributions to an investment fund in the plan member's account. The plan member's account grows with the contributions and with the investment earnings from the fund. At retirement, accumulated funds are used to purchase an annuity or similar financial product that pays the retirement income.

For more about different types of pensions, see the U.S. Department of Labor Web site at www.dol.gov/dol/topic/retirement/typesofplans.htm. You'll discover descriptions of various pension plans and find out what you need to know about pension plans and your rights.

Cashing in your Social Security benefits

In 1935, Social Security was enacted to provide a safety net for America's destitute older citizens. As of September 2000, the program was issuing benefits to some 32 million retired workers and their dependents, and nearly 7 million survivors of deceased workers. Social Security taxes cover five categories: retirement, disability, family, survivors, and Medicare. At this time, workers with earnings of less than $87,000 per year pay 7.6 percent of their income to Social

Security. (Employers match workers by paying in the same amount.) The self-employed pay a total rate of 15.3 percent of income less than $87,000 per year.

As you work, you earn credits toward your retirement. People born in 1929 or later need at least 40 credits to receive retirement benefits. Your actual earnings determine the amount of Social Security benefits you receive. Full retirement age gradually is increasing, depending on the year of your birth. You can receive benefits at age 62, but they're reduced. The average age of retirement is 65. If you hold off until age 70, you get a larger benefit check.

Your Social Security statement details all three scenarios. Since 1999, the law requires the Social Security Administration (SSA) to send a Social Security Statement every year to all workers who are ages 25 and older who aren't receiving Social Security benefits. If you don't automatically receive your statement, you can request one online at `www.ssa.gov/online/ssa-7004.html` or call toll-free 800-722-1213 and request that form SSA-7004 be mailed to you. You'll receive your statement in the mail in about two to four weeks after your online request.

If you're uncertain about when to cash in your Social Security benefits, refer to the Social Security benefits calculators located at `www.ssa.gov/planners/calculators.htm`. You'll find three styles of calculators:

✔ **Quick calculator:** This quick-estimate calculator makes use of your date of birth and years' earnings. To use this calculator, you must be older than 21 years old and younger than 65 years old.

✔ **Online calculator:** This online calculator requires your date of birth and complete earnings history, and it projects your future earnings. This calculator is similar to what's shown on your Social Security statement — the one you receive on a regular basis from the SSA.

✔ **Downloadable detailed calculator:** The third calculator is a free downloadable program that provides the most precise and detailed estimates. Keep in mind that your Social Security records are private.

For more information about your Social Security benefits, check online at one of these sites:

✔ **AARP** (`www.aarp.org/socialsecurity`) maintains a Social Security Center on its Web site. You can find answers to some commonly asked questions about Social Security.

✔ **ElderWeb** (`www.elderweb.com`) provides the latest Social Security news and links to other sites that offer information about Social Security. On the home page click on "Finance & Law." Scroll down the page and click on "Social Security."

✔ **FinanCenter.com** (`partners.financenter.com/consumer/calculate/us-eng/retire02n.fcs`) offers a calculator to help you determine the amount of your benefits.

Using the Internet to Determine How Much You Need to Live On

What expenses will you have in retirement? Table 10-1 shows how the average percentage of income is allocated for most retired people. Table 10-1 indicates that you still can expect to pay taxes and will be required to save well into your retirement years.

Table 10-1	Retirement Expenses
Expense	*Average Percentage*
Housing	20%
Groceries	11%
Personal care	5%
Automobile	9%
Un-reimbursed medical expenses	4%
Insurance	4%
Recreation	5%
Gifts to charity and others	2%
Interest on consumer loans and credit cards	4%
Other items	8%
Taxes and savings	28%
Total	**100%**

Knowing how much your expenses will be in retirement is important. Many financial planners suggest that retirees will require the use of 80 percent of their current income. Many retirees require more income in their retirement years than when they're working. Some retirees cruise around the world. Other retirees take up expensive hobbies. Many retirees just travel to visit their children and grandchildren. Regardless of how you envision your retirement years, you need to know the costs in advance. Here are a few Web sites that can help you focus on retirement expenses:

✔ **Argone Credit Union** (`hffo.cuna.org/story.html?doc_id=491&sub_id=14953`) supplies an easy-to-understand article about how you can quickly and easily calculate your retirement needs.

✔ **Financenter.com** (`www.financenter.com`) offers an online calculator titled "What will my income be after I retire?" This extensive calculator includes future one-time investments, your monthly taxable income, and your monthly savings for tax-advantaged accounts, such as: 401(k)s, SEPs, Keoghs, traditional IRAs, and Roth IRAs.

✔ **Living to 100** (`www.livingto100.com`) offers an online calculator to assist you with planning for your retirement. Fill out the Web site's questionnaire, and you'll even discover your life expectancy. The longer you live, the more savings you require.

✔ **Today's Seniors** (`www.a-guide-for-seniors.com/pages/retirement_calculator_b.html`) offers a retirement calculator to help determine how long your money will last. Simply select the age at which you plan to retire, or your current age, if you're already retired.

Figuring out how much to save: A real-world example

When you subtract your projected retirement expense from your expected retirement income, to your dismay you may discover a shortfall (a negative cash flow). When you know the amount of the deficit, you can determine how much you need to save.

What follows is an example for a hypothetical Mr. Jones. Here's how things shape up for him:

✔ **The outflows:** Mr. Jones used Table 10-1 to calculate his after-retirement expenses. He believes he has a good handle on the types of expenses he'll have when he retires at age 65.

✔ **The inflows:** The foundation for all retirement plans is Social Security. Mr. Jones worked for the last 35 years and contributed the maximum to the Social Security system. He estimates that he will receive $1,807 per month, a total of $21,684 per year. The amount he actually receives at retirement is adjusted for inflation.

✔ **The difference:** Mr. Jones has determined that there's a gap between what he will receive in his Social Security benefits and what he'll need to live on. Mr. Jones estimates that he will live for 20 years after he retires. The shortfall is about $40,000 per year.

Estimating what Mr. Jones will need to save by the time he turns 65 years old and determining whether he's going to live in his usual style are good starting points. The following formula and amounts from Table 10-2 show how much Mr. Jones needs to accumulate to cover his $40,000 shortfall, if he's going to live in the style to which he's accustomed. Things are a little complicated here, but try to follow along (the message is important). During the twenty years of Mr. Jones's retirement, he will deduct $40,000 per year from his savings (which he hopes will be earning a return of 10 percent). He needs to know exactly how much he must having in his savings by the time he retires at age 65 to meet this requirement. Using the formula below, the total amount he'll need to acquire before he retires is $373,832. The formula looks like this:

Required Savings = Annuity ÷ Table 10-2 Factor × $1,000

$373,832 = $40,000 ÷ 107 × $1,000

Table 10-2	Present Value of an Annuity Due Factor Table			
	Assumed Annual Percent Earnings Rate (per $1,000 of Savings)			
Years of Annuity	*8%*	*9%*	*10%*	*12%*
5	232	236	240	248
10	138	143	148	158
15	108	114	120	130
20	94	101	107	120

Mr. Jones should have about $375,000 in savings when he retires to compensate for the gap between his Social Security benefits and his living expenses. To reach that goal, he needs to set aside an equal amount for each of the next 20 years. Mr. Jones expects an 8 percent return on his savings. Using the Deposit Calculator at Nolo.com (www.tcalc.com/tvwww.dll?Save), Mr. Jones can determine exactly how much he needs to save to reach his goal. At the home page, click on "Law Centers," and next click on "Calculators." Using the Deposit Calculator, enter the appropriate data and click "Compute" to calculate the results. Mr. Jones needs to save $7,600 per year to meet his retirement goal. This means that Mr. Jones needs to save about $637.00 per month.

If Mr. Jones started earlier and could set aside an equal amount for each of the next 30 years, with an expected return of 8 percent, he would only have to save $252.00 per month (about $3,024 per year). Bottom line, this example illustrates the importance of starting early to save for retirement. For more information on this topic see the following Web sites:

✔ **FundAdvice.com** (www.tcalc.com/tvwww.dll?Save) offers a calculator that can be used in two ways. To calculate how much you can save, enter your dates and amounts and leave the Savings amount field empty. To calculate how much you will need to save to reach a particular goal, leave the deposit amount empty and complete the remaining fields. Click "Compute" to calculate the results.

✔ **Harris Direct** (www.harrisdirect.com/pre/edu_ret_worksheet.htm) offers an online calculator that indicates exactly how much you need to save this year to meet your long-term retirement goals.

✔ **The National Endowment for Financial Education** (www.nefe.org/pages/multimedia.html) provides resources on saving, budgeting, and retirement planning. Don't forget to read "Guidebook: Help Late Savers Prepare for Retirement."

Luckily, you don't have to calculate the math to determine how much you'll need to save if you have a shortfall; the Internet can do the work for you with online calculators that take the guesswork out of retirement planning. Here are a few of the best Web sites to help you get started:

✔ **FinanCenter** (partners.financenter.com/consumer/calculate/us-eng/retire02a.fcs) provides "Am I saving enough" online retirement calculator. Expect a lengthy questionnaire and calculator to assist you in determining how much you need to save for retirement.

✔ **Investopedia** (www.investopedia.com/calculator/PVAnnuityDue.aspx) offers an easy-to-use online calculator that shows, for instance, if you want to retire with a steady stream of income per year, exactly how much money you need to have today.

✔ **The Ballpark Estimate** (www.asec.org/ballpark) is an easy-to-use, one-page worksheet that helps you quickly identify approximately how much you need to save to fund a comfortable retirement. The Ballpark Estimate takes complicated issues like projected Social Security benefits and earnings assumptions on savings, and turns them into language and mathematics that are easy to understand.

Using "what if?" scenarios

You can prepare for your retirement in many different ways. Some industry experts say that your retirement nest egg needs to be limited to 5 percent withdrawals per year. Therefore, if you expect to live for 20 years after you retire and plan to deduct $30,000 per year from your nest egg to supplement your pension, Social Security, and other sources of income, your nest egg needs to be $600,000.

Although that's one way to make certain your money lasts, you can try other scenarios. The Internet is a no fuss, no muss way to help you try a wide variety of "what if?" scenarios. This experience can help you gain a better understanding of the possible outcomes of what you do today so you can maximize your retired tomorrows. Here are a few examples:

- ✔ **American Savings Education Council** (www.asec.org/ballpark/ballpark.htm) offers a thorough online calculator titled "How do I plan for my retirement?" To plan for a different scenario, don't use the back button. Just re-enter your data on the worksheet.

- ✔ **About.com** (retireplan.about.com/cs/calculators/a/calculators.hrm) offers an online retirement calculator and retirement workshop for online retirement planning.

- ✔ **Financial Engines** (www.financialengines.com) is often considered the Cadillac of online planners. Developed by 1990 Nobel Prize–winning Stanford University Professor William Sharpe, Financial Engines is costly ($39.95 per quarter), but it's worth every penny. Easy-to-understand graphics make retirement planning a pleasure.

Saving for Retirement

The number of traditional retirement plans has continued to decline, and many employers are replacing them with more-conventional retirement options like 401(k) plans. Doing so takes much of the burden off the employer and enables employees to have greater control over their accounts. However, according to the American Association of Retired Persons (AARP — www.aarp.com) about 55 percent of participants forget the purpose of the 401(k) plan and cash out when they change jobs. In other words, they unnecessarily incur taxes and a 10 percent penalty (if the participant is younger than 59½ years old).

If you accumulate $10,000 in a 401(k) plan, for example, and you cash out at age 25, you pay a big chunk of the money you receive in income taxes to Uncle Sam and you pay an early withdrawal penalty that amounts to $1,000. If, on the other had, you didn't touch the funds until you turned 65 years old, and that $10,000 was earning an average 8 percent annual return, you'd have $200,000 for your retirement. Granted, you couldn't buy a yacht, but you could get a pretty decent sailboat.

The joys of 401 (k) plans

The Revenue Act of 1978 created new retirement options for employee retirement plans. Instead of traditional pension plans, employers can offer workers 401(k) plans. Eligibility for most plans is set for employees of a certain age

(21 years old, for example) and for a predetermined number of hours of annual service (more than 1,000 work hours per year, for example).

Workers can make contributions to the plans in four ways:

- After-tax dollars (the "thrift plan").

- Worker contributions that are matched by the employer. For example, a worker contributes 10 percent of his or her paycheck, and the employer provides a 5 percent matching contribution, so the employee ends up with 15 percent.

- Nonelective contributions, which are automatically deducted and placed in plan.

- Worker-elective pretax contributions, where you can sock away part of your salary each year for your retirement.

The best part of a 401(k) plan is that employers and employees can contribute to the plan without being taxed. As a general rule, total contributions by employer and worker are limited to less than 25 percent of the employee's compensation or a maximum amount of $30,000, whichever is smaller. Employer contributions aren't required, and employers have flexibility in matching their employee's contributions.

The distribution of funds from 401(k) plans can occur whenever you terminate your employment, retire (at age 59½ for many plans), or suffer a hardship, such as medical expenses, college tuition, disability, and in the worst case — death. Of course, you must pay taxes when you withdraw the money. When you begin making regular withdrawals, your tax bracket at that time, it's hoped, will be lower than it was when you were making contributions so that the IRS isn't taking such a large chunk of your 401(k) savings.

For more information about 401(k) plans check out

- **About.com** (`retire.about.com/cs/401k/a/401k.htm`), which offers more information about 401(k) plans.

- **SmartMoney.com** (`www.smartmoney.com`), which provides a 401(k) planner. Discover how increasing or decreasing your 401(k) contribution affects your take-home pay and the amount of money you'll have for retirement.

- **The-Adviser.com** (`www.the-adviser.com/Questions/401kplans.htm`), which offers all the information you want about withdrawals, changing jobs, retirement, and minimum required distributions.

- **The Wall Street Journal** (`www.wsj.com`), which offers the Money Toolbox. Financial/Retirement planning tools include an online retirement planning worksheet, 401(k) planner, and 401(k) contributions calculator. Subscriptions are $3.95 per month or $39 per year.

Employees of nonprofit organizations can have 403(b) plans, which are similar to 401(k) plans.

Individual Retirement Accounts (IRAs)

When you open an Individual Retirement Account (IRA), you have to decide whether you want a traditional IRA, a Roth IRA, or an education IRA (for more information about education IRAs, which are now called Coverdell ESAs, see Chapter 9). Each type of IRA has its own advantages and limitations.

Traditional IRAs

Congress created traditional IRAs in 1974 as a means of saving for retirement without having to pay taxes on the money you earn in your account until you start withdrawing the funds during retirement. You may also be able to deduct your annual contribution to a traditional IRA from your yearly income taxes. Being able to do so depends on how much you earn.

Several rules affect withdrawals from traditional IRAs. For instance, you can't begin withdrawing funds without penalties until you reach 59½ years of age. If you withdraw funds before that time, you pay a tax penalty. In addition, you must withdraw funds when you turn 70½ years old, which is when you no longer can contribute any more money to the IRA. Expect to pay taxes on any funds that you withdraw. As such, spreading your withdrawals across as many years as possible is a wise choice, so you won't be hit with a large tax bill when you're older than 70.

Roth IRAs

Roth IRAs were created in 1997. Table 10-3 shows the annual contribution limits for traditional and Roth IRAs.

Table 10-3	Annual Contribution Limits for Traditional and Roth IRAs	
Year	*Under Age 50*	*Age 50 and Older*
2004	$3,000	$3,500
2005	$4,000	$4,500
2006–2007	$4,000	$5,000
2008	$5,000	$6,000

Roth IRA withdrawals are tax-free if the account is held five or more years and you're 59½ or older. Withdrawals also are tax-free if you become disabled, if you're purchasing a home for the first time, or if the account holder dies. Roth IRA eligibility is based on adjusted gross income (AGI) and phases out for individuals with AGIs of more than $95,000 and for couples who file a joint tax return with combined AGIs of more than $150,000 in 2004.

Keep in mind that as long as you have earned income, you can contribute to a Traditional IRA until you turn 70½. Investors older than 70½ can't contribute to a Traditional IRA but can contribute to a Roth IRA. If you don't have earned income but are married and file a joint return, you still can contribute to an IRA based on your working spouse's income.

For more information about this topic, see these Web sites:

- **Employee Benefit Research Institute** (www.ebri.org) is a nonprofit, nonpartisan organization that provides information and education about employee benefits. Find the latest information about IRAs.

- **Kiplinger.com** (www.kiplinger.com/basics/managing/retirement/roth1.htm) provides a large online retirement center that includes articles, resources, and online calculators.

- **Roth IRA Web Site home page** (www.rothira.com) offers technical and planning information about Roth IRAs to practitioners and consumers.

- **The Motley Fool** (www.motleyfool.com) provides "The 60-second guide to opening an IRA account." This online guide offers step-by-step guidance for opening an IRA and a calculator to determine what type of IRA account is best for you. You'll also find suggestions about where to invest your cash and brokerage comparisons.

Online calculators for determining the best IRA account

Several kinds of IRA accounts are available. The Vanguard Group (http://flagship3.vanguard.com/web/planret/PTRetireCenterOV.html) has a Retirement Center that offers an online calculator that can help you determine what kind of IRA is best for you. At the Retirement Center, click on "I'm starting to save for retirement," and then click on "What kind of IRA is best for me?" You'll discover whether you can contribute to a traditional or Roth IRA, find out whether you're eligible to deduct your traditional IRA contribution, calculate your maximum allowable contribution, project the long-term returns of each type of IRA, and then compare your options.

The Internet provides other online IRA comparison calculators at these Web sites:

- ✔ **Morningstar.com** (`screen.morningstar.com/ira/iracalculator.html?tsection=toolsiracal`) provides an IRA calculator to help you make better IRA decisions. Discover your eligibility, determine your contributing limits for Roth or Traditional IRAs, compare various scenarios to uncover which IRA is best for you, and discover whether you need to convert your traditional IRA to a Roth IRA.

- ✔ **Calcbuilder** (`http://www.calcbuilder.com/cgi-bin/calcs/IRA1.cgi/themotleyfool?Question=Income`) offers an online calculator to help you determine which type of IRA account provides you with the most retirement income.

Retirement plans for small businesses and the self-employed

Simplified Employee Pensions (SEPs) frequently are best for business owners who have high incomes. These individuals want to maximize their contributions, keep their plans simple, and pay low fees. You can contribute up to 20 percent of your compensation if you're unincorporated, and if you're incorporated, you can contribute up to 25 percent of your compensation up to $41,000 per year. In other words, if your business is unincorporated, your income must be at least $200,000 to reach the $40,000 contribution level. Keep in mind that if you have employees, you must contribute the same percentage of compensation for your employees that you do for yourself. The following Web sites offer a few examples of more online information:

- ✔ **Internal Revenue Service** (`www.irs.gov/retirement/content/0,,id=97203,00.html`) offers a full menu of high-quality articles about retirement plans for small businesses and the self-employed.

- ✔ **Retirement Planner** (`www.retirementplanner.org/index.html`) offers a full menu of retirement advice. Discover how to safeguard your 401(k) plan, IRAs, and annuities.

- ✔ **Workindex.com** (`www.workindex.com`) offers links to retirement benefits and services sites on the Internet. Enter "Retirement Benefits" in the search box on the home page.

Other retirement options

If you're shut out of a 401(k) plan for some reason and can't qualify for an IRA account, you may want to consider investing in a variable annuity. You can purchase a variable annuity that guarantees a 6 percent return. That is, you're guaranteed to earn at least 6 percent annually and may make a higher return. Say you invest $200,000 with a 6 percent guarantee. In ten short years, your investment grows to be worth a minimum of $360,000. During this time the stock market hits a high, and your investment is worth $500,000. The stock market also hits a low, and your investment is worth $300,000. When you begin to make monthly or annual withdrawals from your guaranteed annuity, your payments will be based on the high of $500,000. For more information about annuities see these Web sites:

- ✔ **Annuity.com** (www.annuity.com) offers a broad spectrum of information about annuities, including definitions, rates, quotes, and online calculators.

- ✔ **Federal Consumer Information Center: About Annuities** (www.pueblo. gsa.gov/cic_text/money/annuity/annuities.htm) covers the different types of annuities, including fixed, variable, deferred, and immediate annuities. You'll also find information about the advantages and limitations of investing in annuities.

Chapter 11

Pass It Along: Simple Online Estate Planning

In This Chapter

▶ Gaining an understanding of estate planning over the Internet

▶ Comparing wills and trusts and determining which is best for you

▶ Partnering with the Internet to start on your estate plan

▶ Using online resources to design an estate plan that fits the different stages in your life

▶ Selecting and meeting an estate planner with help from the Web

▶ Calculating the value of your estate online to determine your tax liability

*E*state is a legal term, but its meaning is more personal than that. An estate, regardless of how large or small, planned or not, is simply how folks refer to or describe what you've accumulated throughout your life. People always have plenty of excuses to put off planning their estates, including "I'm too young and much too busy," or "It's depressing to think about what will happen when the inevitable happens," or "All my relatives are insincere ingrates and don't deserve my time and consideration."

Adding fuel to these burning embers, estate tax rules are changing each and every year (at least through 2010), creating even more reasons to avoid estate planning. However, in spite of all the Congressional wrangling with this tax, flexible estate planning is becoming more important than ever.

This chapter focuses on estate planning, which can include life insurance policies, financial planning, and retirement planning. However, those topics are covered in Chapters 10 and 18. The parts of estate planning that this chapter deals with are what's important to include in your estate plan and how the Internet can solve the mysteries and ease the dread of taking care of who gets what from your estate.

I start out this chapter with a definition of estate planning so you can see just how easily you can create a will without leaving your computer, get tips on how to avoid probate, set up trusts, and use other estate-planning techniques. This chapter explores simple and complex trusts and wills, and you'll see comparisons of both so you can determine which is best for your personal situation.

This chapter also points you toward several online estate-planning courses that are informative but not time-consuming, shows you how to get started with your estate planning, and points out the top estate-planning issues you can expect to encounter at different stages of your life. And, of course, I provide suggestions about how to use the Internet to help you calculate the value of your estate online, select an estate planner, and decide what to bring to your first meeting.

Using the Internet can help you find out about your estate-planning options, discover online tools to get organized, and in general, point you in the right direction. Even so, having a professional review your goals and help you implement your plans is a good idea and can help you avoid any unpleasant surprises. After all, you don't want dear old Uncle Sam to enter the family picture at the last moment, claiming a major part of your estate.

Estate Planning: What It Is and Why You Need It

Estate planning isn't exclusively for the affluent; moreover, the principles of estate planning are simple. What you accumulate throughout your lifetime is yours, and you want to protect it and transfer it to your heirs according to *your* wishes. Doing a little estate planning ahead of time (while you're still alive, of course) can help your beneficiaries avoid many headaches and heartaches.

The results of planning your estate need to assure you that the beneficiaries you select will enjoy the fruits of your labors. Consequently, a good way of approaching estate planning is by thinking of it as *family wealth planning*. Your family wealth plan needs to address your values, mission, philosophy, and long-term goals. Many people believe that estate planning means dealing with disability, death, and taxes — all the things we usually struggle to avoid. Although for the most part they're right, the fact is, estate planning assists you in providing for your loved ones — after disability, after death, and after taxes.

To get estate planning correctly in focus (and to help you see just how important estate planning is) begin by looking at estate planning as another part of financial planning. Answer the questions that follow, and when you look at your responses, you'll probably want to start your estate plan right away:

✔ **What will happen to my property?** Do I know exactly what I own?

✔ **Who will care for my minor children or aging parents?** Who will they turn to if I'm not around?

✔ **Will my spouse and children be provided for?** How will they pay the bills?

✔ **Will the family business continue?** Have I allowed for any type of succession?

✔ **Will the estate settlement be conducted by someone with the family's interests at heart?** Do I have a family or an estate-planning attorney, or at least someone in mind as an executor?

✔ **Will estate and death taxes, probate fees, and other administrative and legal costs be held to a minimum?** How will my survivors pay for the costs?

Overall, estate planning helps make life less stressful for your heirs at a time that's usually full of grief and anxiety. Unnecessary expenses can be reduced or eliminated, and administrative hassles and taxes can be dealt with in the best way possible. You can leave a lasting legacy that everyone in your family can enjoy.

TECHNICAL STUFF

How your estate-tax liability grows

A table that can be found at Banksite (www. banksite.com/calc/estate) shows you how much you may have to pay in estate taxes if you happen to die from now through 2050. This table (go to the Banksite Web site listed in the first sentence and click on the "Watch the Estate Grow" button at the bottom of the page) assumes that your IRA or 401(k) plan will be $59,500 in 2001 and will increase with inflation because such plans are tied to your salary. According to the table, in 2001, your other investments, life insurance, home equity, and cash will total $179,725, and the total value of your estate will be $243,225. Life insurance, cash, and personal property also are expected to increase with inflation. The value of your car remains the same because automobiles depreciate and are bought and sold frequently. The calculations used in this table also assume that Congress won't change current tax rules. Using these and other assumptions about interest rates and annual yields, if you die in 2021, you can expect the value of your estate to increase to $1,468,151 and your estate-tax liability to be $196,305. Die ten years after that (in 2031 — as if you have the choice) and your estate climbs to $3,395,826, but your estate-tax liability keeps pace, growing to $1,162,704. These amounts show how important it is to work online and with professionals to adjust your will, trust agreements, and financial plans so you can explore estate-tax reduction and other tax-saving moves in advance. You may also want to build some flexibility into your strategy. For example, instead of stating that a certain amount flows into your trust, specify that the maximum amount of the federal exclusion for the applicable years needs to flow into the trust.

Dying without an estate plan is a bad idea

Everyone needs an estate plan. If you don't have a will, trust, or some sort of estate plan, your state of residency decides how to dispose of your assets according to a preset formula. And that can cause big problems for your family if your estate doesn't fit a standardized model. Your spouse, significant other, or children won't have any say in the decision-making; moreover, the state doesn't care one iota about your dreams, fears, and values. But caring is exactly what estate planning is all about — protecting and controlling your assets to provide for your loved ones, minimize estate taxes, and protect your business (if you own one).

Taxing estate-planning issues

The primary goals of estate planning are avoiding estate taxes, transferring your assets to the right people, and easing the burdens your demise places on your survivors. In June 2001, new federal estate-tax rules went into effect in the United States. The law replaced a $675,000 unified estate-tax credit with a $1 million unified credit exemption for 2003. That's the amount each individual can freely pass on to beneficiaries; it's the amount of an estate that can be *excluded* from having to pay any federal estate taxes. The amount of the exclusion (the unified credit exemption) increases incrementally to $3.5 million from now until 2009. The federal estate tax is repealed in 2010, so exclusion isn't needed that year because no one will be paying estate taxes that year. Table 11-1 illustrates how federal estate-tax exclusion will affect you through the year 2010.

Note how the amount each person can pass along to his or her heirs free of federal estate taxes increases through 2009 before the tax is repealed in 2010, when entire estates can be passed along to a relative free of federal taxes. Although the tax is repealed, the repeal may last for only a year. Therefore, if your estate is valued at more than $1 million, you'll probably have to spend some planning time so that you can maximize what you pass on to your inheritors.

Some beneficiaries have to pay state estate taxes even when they owe nothing to the Internal Revenue Service. For example, states such as New Jersey, Wisconsin, and Rhode Island have exemption rates that are as little as $675,000 (at this time the federal exemption rate is $1.5 million and gradually increases to $3.5 million in 2009). However, states can add independent state death taxes at any time. At the moment, a few havens may be safe. States such as Florida, California, and Nevada appear to be protected because they have constitutional rules against independent state death taxes.

Table 11-1	How Estate Taxes Vary by Year	
Calendar Year	*Exemption*	*Highest Rate*
2004	$1.5 million	48%
2005	$1.5 million	47%
2006	$2 million	46%
2007	$2 million	45%
2008	$2 million	45%
2009	$3.5 million	45%
2010	Everything you own	0%

Calculating the Value of Your Estate Online

Knowing the value of your estate can help you determine how to plan to distribute your estate. A wide variety of online calculators can assist you in determining its value. A few that you may find useful are

- ✔ **Charles Schwab** (www.schwab.com) offers an online estate tax and probate calculator. You can use this Internet calculator in one of two ways: One is for detailed calculations about your asset values, and the other is a quick calculation. To find the online estate-planning calculator, go to Schwab's home page and click on "Planning," then click on "Tools," and then click on "Estate Tax and Probate Calculator."

- ✔ **Smart Money** (www.smartmoney.com/estate/index.cfm?story=estatetax#worksheet) uses what it calls an "Estate Tax Exposure Meter" to show you how to take advantage of higher exclusion amounts. Higher exclusion amounts and good estate planning can help you reduce or even avoid estate taxes. The calculator assesses how much you'd owe today.

- ✔ **Fidelity** (http://web.fidelity.com/EstatePlanning/tools/tax/taxM1.jhtml?_requestid=421673) provides an online federal estate-tax calculator. Enter your personal data to project your estate, and allow the calculator to estimate your potential federal estate-tax burden based on current tax laws. Additionally, you can consider your potential future estate-tax estimates. At the home page click on "Retirement and Guidance" in the top header and then "Estate Planning." Next, click on "Estate Tax Calculator."

The More Popular Tools: Wills and Trusts

The most accepted way of transferring assets to survivors and beneficiaries is through a will or a trust. A *will* is defined as a legal document that describes how you want your resources to be distributed after your death. The distribution is controlled by a legal process called probate. Probate is Latin for "prove the will." If one or more of your heirs contests your will (or if there's a lack of agreement among your heirs), a supervised probate will be required. Supervised probates need formal reports from appraisers, accountants, and attorneys. These documents will be reviewed by the court at each stage of the proceedings. All court actions, including the presentation of the facts and figures from the formal reports that relate to your estate, are conducted in open court. This means that nothing is private. After the probate process begins, your family no longer controls your estate; the court, probate attorneys, and named executors are in control of all your assets. For individuals who are incapacitated due to illness or injury, this is a good thing. For widows with children, this can cause a delay in the payment of living expenses.

A *trust* is a document that enables you, the *grantor,* a fancy word for the owner of the estate, to establish a separate entity (much like a corporation) to hold, manage, and eventually distribute your assets in the manner you desire to your beneficiaries. A chief benefit of establishing a trust is that it's not a public document that goes through probate. A trust offers your heirs an element of privacy. However, establishing a trust (or trusts) frequently is more costly than creating a will. Trusts can be established in a variety of ways to meet your individual needs and requirements. I describe the different types of trusts later in this section.

For now, though, here are some more Web sites where you can find more information about estate planning:

- **I Hate Financial Planning** (www.ihatefinancialplanning.com/topics/topic_page.jsp?tid=3) recognizes that "you can't take it with you," so it provides a good overview of the elements of estate planning. On the home page, in the section that states "Why Am I Here?", scroll through the topic box until you reach "To Plan My Estate," and then click on your selected topic.

- **Prudential Financial** (www.prudential.com) provides an easy-to-understand overview of estate planning. On its home page, click on "Financial Planning," and then click on "Estate Planning Overview."

- **Kiplinger.com** (www.kiplinger.com) offers suggestions for starting your estate planning and articles about the top estate-planning issues and tools. On the home page, click on "Planning" and then on "Estate Planning."

Hunting good will

All your estate planning goes to waste if your survivors don't know where you kept your will or trust documents. Sometimes these documents aren't stored in obvious places, like a desk drawer, file cabinet, or home safe. For example, some folks actually wrap these documents in foil and store them in their freezers.

When you can't find the documents at home, check the person's safety deposit box. Also, don't forget to check desk drawers and file cabinets at his or her place of business or look for the lawyer's name and contact information. *Note:* You'll need a key to the safety deposit box and an official death certificate.

Where there's an online will, there's a way

Creating a will is one of the easiest estate-planning tools you can use to help your family. Unfortunately, as many as 70 percent of all Americans don't have a current and valid will. Wills describe to members of your family how you want your estate to be distributed. Dying *intestate,* or without a will, can cause additional work and expense for your survivors. A qualified estate-planning attorney, although recommended, isn't required. Many courts accept handwritten wills, drawn up without legal counsel. You can even put together a will online. A proper will usually includes

- ✔ How you want your property to be distributed among your heirs. Remember to avoid vague instructions that can lead to costly legal bills and squabbles between your beneficiaries.
- ✔ The name of the executor (or personal representative) of your estate.
- ✔ How the costs incurred in settling your estate will be paid.
- ✔ Who you're designating as guardian for your minor children and the name of a trustee to protect any money they inherit.

Some of the factors that can cause a will to be considered invalid are

- ✔ **Improper execution:** The individual who wrote the will must be at least 18 years old. Three witnesses must attest that the will is real, and the document itself has to conform to the formalities of the state in which it was drawn.
- ✔ **The grantor was not mentally competent:** The individual who is establishing the last will and testament must be of sound mind, know the nature and extent of his or her property, and be able to identify the people who ordinarily would share in the estate.
- ✔ **The will was made under duress:** A will must represent the free and willful act of the individual for whom it was drafted.

If the will is proven to be invalid, then the estate is considered intestate (without a will). At that point, the probate court uses all the preset formulas for distributing assets. If no living relatives are found, the estate then reverts to the state.

Where there's a will, there's a way to avoid probate

Probate is a legal process that identifies and catalogs all of your property, appraises the property, pays all debts and taxes, and distributes the remaining property to your heirs according to your instructions.

Probate often takes several months to complete, is frequently cumbersome, and can be expensive. All probate records are open to the public. These records are exposed to con artists who view grief-stricken family members as easy targets and can use the information they gain from public records to prey on survivors.

Probate records aren't private; relatives, friends, and associates can view these public records and petition the court for a share of your estate. For that reason, avoiding probate can prove valuable to many people. In most cases, all you need to do is sign a form to help your family avoid additional grief. However, you can immediately implement several easy-to-use techniques in an attempt to get around having your will probated. You need to

- ✔ **Take advantage of special procedures for small estates.** Some states enable you to cruise beneath the radar and avoid probate whenever your estate is less than $100,000. These rules vary by state, so make finding out the minimum part of your estate-planning homework.

- ✔ **Set up payable-upon-death bank accounts.** Doing so enables your representative to draw money from your bank account so your wife and children can have something to live on while the estate travels through the probate system.

- ✔ **Register vehicles and investments with transfer-upon-death forms.** When you do, the transfer of ownership doesn't have to pass through probate.

- ✔ **Hold property in joint ownership.** Doing so enables survivors to immediately take possession and ownership of the property. A word of caution: Joint ownership can cause problems if one of the owners is incapacitated.

✔ **Create a living trust.** For some individuals, creating a living trust is the best approach to estate planning. Frequently, a living trust is called a "probate avoidance trust." A living trust enables the grantor to avoid probate completely because the trust does all the work and the state has nothing to administer.

✔ **Take advantage of the gift-giving tax exemption now.** Current law allows you to give $11,000 a year to each child, grandchild, niece, nephew, and so on. (A couple can give $22,000 per year to each relative.)

If you're executing any of the fiduciary duties associated with someone's will, it's a good idea to get more than one copy of the official death certificate. Many of the agencies that you run into will ask for an official copy of the death certificate. Therefore, obtaining a half dozen or more is often a good idea and a timesaver in the long run.

The Internet provides much of what you need to know about wills. Here are a few of the best will Web sites available:

✔ **Legalzoom** (www.legalzoom.com) helps you create a will that's valid in any of the 50 states without ever leaving your computer. In just three steps, you can complete your will and have it reviewed for the most common mistakes. Answer a few simple questions, and you're ready for delivery within 48 hours. The price is $59 for a standard last will and testament. Same-day processing is an additional $20.

✔ **Probate FAQ** (www.nolo.com) provides you with the basics of what probate is, who is responsible for handling probate, and how you should avoid probate. On the home page under "Browse the Law Centers," click on "Wills & Estate Planning," and then click on "Living Trusts and Avoiding Probate."

✔ **SaveWealth** (www.savewealth.com/planning/estate/probate) provides useful guides to how the probate process works in California, Colorado, Florida, Georgia, Hawaii, Illinois, Indiana, Maine, Massachusetts, Mississippi, Ohio, Pennsylvania, Texas, and Virginia.

✔ **The Funeral Directory** (www.thefuneraldirectory.com/planityour way/samplewill.asp) offers a fill-in-the-blank sample will that serves as an easy-to-understand outline of what needs to be included in a will.

✔ **Wills FAQ** (www.nolo.com), at NOLO Law for All, shown in Figure 11-1, illustrates what happens if you die without a will, the validity of hand-written wills, and what makes a will legal. On the NOLO home page, go to "Browse the Law Centers" and click on "Wills & Estate Planning," and then click on "Encyclopedia." Scroll down that page to "Wills FAQ," and click on it.

Figure 11-1:
The NOLO
Law Center
provides
easy-to-
understand
information
about wills.

Getting the Basics of Trusts

Trusts (excluding a living trust that replaces a will) can be flexible and valuable tools for the allocation of your assets. Trusts come in several flavors and
can be created and funded during the grantor's lifetime or by the terms of a
will. The terms of the trust may allow for changes to be made by the grantor
or even for it to be revoked in its entirety. By contrast, the terms of the trust
may also be fixed or irrevocable on the date it's conceived. Although several
types of trusts can be administered, each involves the following three factors:

- ✔ **Grantors transfer (or arrange for transfer of) ownership of their assets
  to a trustee during their lifetimes.** Trusts often aren't expensive to
  maintain. Therefore, grantors don't have to be wealthy to have a trust.

- ✔ **A trustee holds the resources defined by the trust for the benefit of
  the inheritors.** A trustee can be an attorney, banker, financial planner,
  family member, or trusted friend.

- ✔ **The beneficiaries or inheritors receive the assets as intended by the
  grantor.** Trusts provide flexibility and need not alienate inheritors from
  the decision-making process.

You can have a simple trust or a complex trust. *Simple trusts* may require the trustee to distribute all ordinary income annually. A *complex trust* may rely on the trustee's discretion to retain or distribute income. You're free to select whichever type of trust meets your needs. Several benefits of establishing a trust are

- **Asset management:** The responsibility of making decisions and maintaining adequate records is transferred to another person or entity. For individuals with young children, having someone else managing your youngster's assets may be the most important aspect of having a trust.

- **Asset protection:** A trust can protect assets from the creditors of your beneficiary; moreover, a trust can protect assets from a former spouse in the event of the divorce of the beneficiary.

- **Provisions for multiple beneficiaries:** A trust is an efficient way to disburse the assets of a grantor. When you have a number of beneficiaries, using a trust enables you to use the discretion of a trustee for disbursing assets.

- **Provisions for special needs:** In some cases, one of several beneficiaries may have special needs, such as tuition for college, healthcare, or other finance-related issues. A trust can address these special requirements.

- **Tax planning:** A trust can assist you in taking full advantage of the unified credit exemption (see "Taxing estate-planning issues," earlier in the chapter) and make certain that all necessary assets are available to the surviving spouse.

Table 11-2 compares wills to trusts in terms of their respective benefits and limitations. A will or a trust can be the best way for you to protect your assets, but bear in mind that estate planning often includes more than just one of these approaches. It's a plan that needs to cover all unforeseen events that you may encounter.

Table 11-2	A Comparison of Wills and Trusts
Wills	*Trusts*
Wills are used to implement your estate plan.	Trusts provide continuity to the management of your assets upon your death or disability.
With a supervised probate action, several weeks may pass before the court appoints an executor who is authorized to deal with income and expenses of your estate.	Upon the grantor's death, trustees can distribute assets more quickly. A more rapid distribution of assets may be important for a surviving spouse or beneficiaries.

(continued)

Table 11-2 *(continued)*		
Wills		***Trusts***
If you suffer any physical or mental incapacity, a court proceeding may be required to determine conservatorship of your assets. (Conservatorship is a process in which the court appoints a person to make certain legal decisions to protect them from neglect, financial abuse, and isolation.)		A trust protects the grantor against mismanagement or nonmanagement of his or her assets during physical or mental incapacity.
Probate is often expensive. For their fees, probate attorneys receive 2% of the first $1 million and 1% of the next $9 million of assets passing through probate.		To reduce costs, a family member or close friend may be appointed as trustee or executor.
Open court probate records are available to the public.		Trusts, for the most part, are not open to the public.
Death tax returns and the payment of death taxes must be completed.		Death tax returns and payment of death taxes must be completed.

ADAPTED: "Estate Planning Basics" by the National Association of Financial and Estate Planning (1999 and 2001). Available online at www.nafep.com on April 8, 2004.

Alternatives to probate are frequently used for small estates with assets of less than $100,000 and for property passing outright to the surviving spouse. These alternatives generally are inexpensive but effective. When planning your estate, you need to keep these alternatives in mind.

Trusting in Your Living Trust to Avoid Probate

There are several types of trusts. A *living trust* is the creation of a fictitious entity for the purpose of holding ownership of an individual's assets during that person's lifetime and for distributing those assets after his or her death. The individual who creates a living trust is called the grantor and names a trustee. The trustee follows the instructions of the grantor after he or she dies. While the grantor is living, the trustee may administer the living trust and control the assets even though they belong to the living trust.

Living trusts are active during an individual's lifetime. A will does not spring into effect until after death. During your lifetime, you transfer ownership of your assets to the living trust. This is called *funding the trust*. Keep in mind that merely executing the living trust doesn't automatically cause the living trust to be funded. For example, the grantor has to transfer title of any bank accounts, stock certificates, or real estate into the living trust.

A word about your privacy and your living trust: As part of the funding process, if you're transferring mortgaged real property to your living trust, the consent of the mortgage company is required. The mortgage company usually requires the recordation of the living trust, with the deed, at the office of the county clerk. At this point, the living trust can become part of the publicly accessible records.

Often, a living trust enables you to bypass probate if you fund your trust while you're alive, meaning all your assets are owned by the trust, and no assets are held separately outside the trust for the probate court to administer. Upon your death, ownership of your assets passes to the successor trustee of your living trust, who then distributes your resources according to your instructions.

Remember, other estate-planning devices can also assist you in avoiding probate. For example, you can use joint tenancy, life insurance policies, and IRA and Keogh accounts.

A *pour-over* will is necessary for any personal property that wasn't included in the living trust or is acquired after the grantor established the living trust. The pour-over will and the living trust make certain all your assets are distributed to your heirs in accordance with your instructions and no laws of intestacy (that is, state laws for people without wills) apply. Unfortunately, a pour-over will must go through probate if the decedent dies owning assets that must go through the will.

Here's an example of how the state of New York handles pour-over wills and living trusts. A will becomes a matter of public record during the probate process. Anyone can request the Surrogate's Court to send a copy of a will. A living trust is a private document that isn't open to public scrutiny. However, a pour-over will becomes a matter of public record when it's submitted for probate, and the pour-over will often includes the living trust by reference.

The living trust can be revocable or irrevocable:

- ✔ **Revocable trusts** enable the grantor to keep the right to change how he or she manages their assets and allows the grantor to change the trustee at any time.

- ✔ **Irrevocable trusts** cause the grantor to give up control and ownership of the property that's placed in the trust but offer tax advantages for grantors with estates that exceed the federal estate-tax exclusion and gift-tax credit.

Keep in mind that a will doesn't spring into effect until you pass away. A living trust can assist you during a lifetime of planning. That is, a living trust can preserve and increase your estate while you're alive and yet still offer you protection if you become incapacitated or mentally disabled.

For more information about trusts, check out

- ✔ **CNN Money 101** (`money.cnn.com/pf/101/lessons/21`), which illustrates how trusts aren't just for the super wealthy. You'll discover whether creating a trust is the right type of estate planning for you or if it's something you don't need to worry about.

- ✔ **Forbes** (`www.forbes.com/2003/0609/106sidebar1_print.html`), which offers tips about how your age, where you live, and what you own are deciding factors for creating a trust.

- ✔ **NOLO** (`www.nolo.com`), which introduces you to living trusts and shows why they're a popular way of avoiding probate. At the NOLO home page, go to the "Browse the Law Center" menu, click on "Wills & Estate Planning," and then click on "Living Trusts and Avoiding Probate."

- ✔ **The Assets Protection Law Center** (`www.rjmintz.com/funding-living-trust.html`) provides an online asset-protection law library. Discover how to fund your trust and more at this Web site.

The Joy of Joint Tenancy and Beneficiary Arrangements

Not everyone's family fits into a standardized model. Today, many families are blended, meaning they include first and second spouses and children from a new spouse's former marriage. Additionally, because people live longer, seeing widowed senior citizens getting married isn't uncommon. These situations require some more complex thinking and considerations when it comes to estate planning.

Joint tenancy is a concept that enables two or more people to be listed as owners of a property. The result of this joint ownership is that upon the death of one of the owners, the property immediately is transferred to the other owner without the property having to pass through probate court. Using rights of survivorship, individuals A and B jointly own the property and agree to pass title to the property one to the other when one of the joint owners dies. However, whenever one of the joint tenants becomes incapacitated, the property can be held in limbo for years.

Beneficiary arrangements are situations in which assets are transferred to heirs without the benefit of legal instruments like a will or trust. For example, a beneficiary may be specified in a pension plan, insurance policy, annuity, or investment account. When the original owner dies, the assets remaining from these financial arrangements can be transferred to the specified heirs without having to go through probate. Several drawbacks to this type of transfer exist. For example, beneficiary distribution can be subject to lawsuits, bankruptcies, and divorce problems experienced by the inheritor.

The Internet provides many online courses about estate planning. These online courses are comprehensive but not time-consuming. Here are a few of the best:

- ✔ **AARP** (www.aarp.org) provides sound advice for estate planning. On the home page, click on "Money and Work," and next click on "Financial Planning." In the left margin, click on "Estate Planning." Click on the "Estate Planning Guide" to gain an understanding of everything you need to know about estate planning.

- ✔ **GE Center for Financial Learning** (www.financialearning.com) provides an online estate-planning course in Spanish and English. Find out how to value your estate, plan for the unexpected, create a will, choose an executor and guardian, and avoid probate and estate taxes. Discover planning strategies with trusts, and find out when to review your estate plan. The online course concludes with an estate-planning checklist. On the home page, just click on "Estate Planning" in the left margin and then on "Courses" to get started.

- ✔ **SaveWealth** (www.savewealth.com) provides estate-planning insights that can help you get a better grip on the ins and outs of estate planning. On the home page, just click on "Estate Planning."

Picking Up Lose Ends and Anticipating Problems

Filling out a few forms sometimes can eliminate extra costs, arguments between family members, and plenty of pain and suffering. Signing a *durable power of attorney form* (which isn't the same as giving someone the power of attorney) designates someone as your agent in case you're incapacitated and thus enables that agent to make financial decisions on your behalf. Having a durable power of attorney does the following:

- ✔ Avoids the appointment of a guardian or conservator if you happen to become debilitated or disabled

- ✔ Provides for the management of your personal finances: paying bills, collecting Social Security benefits, and depositing and cashing checks

- ✔ Creates valid legal debts: buying and selling real estate, continuing the operation of your business, beginning or continuing your estate planning

Signing a *health-care proxy* also can eliminate much of your family's pain and suffering if you become terminally ill or are injured in an accident and don't want to live by use of artificial means. A health-care proxy enables your agent to make health-care decisions for you when you're unable to make them for yourself. For example, your health-care proxy

- ✔ Provides specific medical guidelines for your health-care representative.

- ✔ Permits your agent to take your religious and moral beliefs into consideration when making a decision about your care.

- ✔ Permits you to name an alternative representative if your first-choice representative is unavailable or refuses to serve as your agent.

Whenever you hire an attorney to draw up your will or trust, he or she probably will include documentation for a durable power of attorney and health-care proxy either for free or for a minimum charge.

You can pick up the forms for designating durable power of attorney and initiating a health-care proxy from most stationery stores. These days, with the Internet, you can even save yourself that trip to the mall by going online and downloading those same forms for free. Here are several sites where they're available:

- ✔ **CCH Financial Planning** (`www.finance.cch.com/tools/poaforms_m.asp`) offers free online state health-care proxy forms. Just click on the link for the state you desire. Keep in mind that some forms are guidelines and may enable you to make modifications that suit your individual needs. Other forms may have to be completed as is.

- ✔ **Family Care Givers Online** (`www.familycaregiversonline.com/legal-medical.html#Power%20of%20Attorney%20Forms`) offers easy-to-use online education and information resources for anyone helping older adults and provides free, downloadable durable power of attorney forms.

- ✔ **The Funeral Directory** (`www.thefuneraldirectory.com/planityourway/livingwill.asp`) provides a free downloadable medical-directive form that's an invaluable form for getting things organized in a hurry.

Not all heirs are created equal

If you don't have any heirs and your personal situation fits into the formula for settling an estate in your state, you may not need a will, trust, beneficiary arrangement, or joint tenancy. However, most people live in a complicated world of blended families and ties that go beyond the narrow limits of probate court. Therefore, if you want to have some say in how your assets are allocated among your heirs, you need to do a little planning.

If you write a will and own property in your name, your estate probably will have to go through probate court. All court proceedings are open to the public. This situation exposes your estate to public scrutiny. A living trust is a good way to avoid the rigors of probate and the prying eyes of potential swindlers. The trustee of your living trust can quickly and easily transfer your assets to your heirs. Beneficiary arrangements can be used to transfer assets in particular pension plans, retirement accounts, insurance policies, annuities, bank accounts, and brokerage accounts. Some married couples (or unmarried couples) use joint tenancy with rights of survivorship as their way of holding a title together. Table 11-3 shows which of these approaches are best for certain situations. As for the abbreviations: *W* stands for will, *T* stands for trust, *B* stands for beneficiary arrangements, and *JT* stands for joint tenancy arrangements.

Table 11-3 Which Is the Best Way to Transfer Assets?				
Transfer Planning Issue	*W*	*T*	*B*	*JT*
Controlling gifts to specific heirs	X	X	X	X
Beneficiary dying before the owner of the estate	X	X	X	X
Ensuring that funds will be used for the heir's education		X		
Dealing with a mentally or physically disabled heir		X		
Managing an heir who has bad spending habits or drug- or alcohol-related problems		X		
Dealing with a couple's children from previous marriages (when one spouse has more children than the other)		X		
Managing to disinherit or omit an heir or heirs	X	X		
Specifying property, such as a house or car, to go to a particular heir or heirs	X	X	X	X
Controlling at what age heirs receive their shares of the estate or detailing different ages as payment milestones		X		
Ensuring that inheritors receive equal or unequal shares (based on several factors) that the estate owners specify	X	X	X	

ADAPTED: "Estate Planning Basics" by the National Association of Financial and Estate Planning (1999 and 2001). Available online at www.nafep.com on April 8, 2004.

These examples are for illustrative purposes only and may not be appropriate for your exact situation.

Don't keep your estate plans hush-hush

Many of the items you own have sentimental value to your children. Sometimes more angst besets the question of who gets the gravy bowl than just about anything else. And surprising your beneficiaries isn't a good idea either. Make certain that everyone knows who gets what and why. That way no one feels left out or mistreated.

Divorce causes a blending of many families and tends to complicate estate planning. Teen or adult children from first marriages and young children from second marriages need to be provided for in different ways. Sometimes using the benefits of a life insurance policy can ensure that your children actually receives what you want them to have, thus keeping the money out of the hands of an estranged former spouse. However, you must decide whether you want your children to have a large lump sum (that can be swallowed up if the child divorces) or graduated payments so any bad money-management habits can be minimized.

Frequently, the family doesn't know what type of funeral and burial plan a relative wants, so writing down funeral instructions for survivors is important so they can carry out your last wishes.

Estate Planning for All Ages

As you progress through the cycle of life, you need different types of estate plans to cover different situations. I have divided estate planning into three distinct categories based on age. Each age-based estate plan may not meet your exact needs, but it provides you with the basics for getting the right plan for the right time. Several estate planners that can help you get started are available online. A few of the better ones include the following:

- ✔ **Charles Schwab** (www.schwab.com) determines an estimated value of your estate and the amount of taxes you may incur. At the home page, click on "Planning," then "Planning Your Estate," and then "Estate Planning Steps." Return to the Estate Planning home page and click on "Alternatives" to see which estate-planning approach is best for you.

- ✔ **CNNMoney** (money.cnn.com/pf/101/lessons/24) offers a full course on estate planning starting with the top ten things you need to know, followed by how to assess your assets and the differences between wills and trusts. The online course includes a glossary and quiz.

> ✔ **Fidelity** (personal.fidelity.com/planning/estate/) has an online Estate Planner that's designed to help you illustrate potential planning strategies. It provides descriptions of various estate-planning techniques based on your inputs and various assumptions. Your particular circumstances are unique and affect actual planning done by an estate-planning professional; however, you can use the online Estate Planner to help point you in the right direction. *Note:* All examples are hypothetical and are intended only for illustrative purposes.

Your estate-planning priorities will probably change as you grow older. College-age students don't have the assets or responsibilities of older individuals. Older individuals may want to donate to charities or give gifts to fund the college educations of their grandchildren. Overall, estate planning is a family issue. It can be simple or complex, depending on your personal situation.

I've divided estate planning into these three life stages:

✔ Young singles and adults with children

✔ Middle-aged adults who have accumulated a few assets

✔ Seniors or retirees who are conserving their personal wealth for their retirement or off-loading assets so their heirs can pay a minimum of estate taxes

Keep in mind that these suggestions cover the top issues and may not fully address your unique needs.

Under 30 and loving it

When you're younger than 30, the likelihood of your dying is remote. Your estate plans can be short and sweet unless, of course, you have a dangerous job that places you in hazard's way on a regular basis. If you're just starting out, the value of your estate probably comes in under the radar of your state's requirement for going to probate court. If you're a wealthy young person, you can write a will and leave your possessions to your favorite cause or relative. If you don't write a will, the state gives all your assets to your surviving parents.

If you have a significant other but aren't married (there are some exceptions), then your closest relatives inherit everything. One alternative to this scenario is owning big-ticket items, such as your house, car, boat, and so on, in joint tenancy so the surviving joint owner automatically owns the property. Joint tenancy, however, has its own perils, so don't forget to read the fine print. For example, if you or your spouse becomes incapacitated, the ownership of jointly held assets gets really messy and usually ends up in court.

If you're married with young children, you have plenty to think about. You need to identify your future goals and concerns for you, your spouse, and your children. You may want to consider

✔ Writing a will that leaves your property to your spouse (or a designated person) and names a guardian for your children. Remember, if you don't have a will, probate court may give half of your assets to your spouse and the other half to your children. If your spouse needs money for the children, he or she has to go to court.

✔ Determining the future cost of tuition and finding the best way to reach your goal of providing for your children's educations. For more information about the tax advantages of savings plans, Section 529 plans, and using home equity to finance education, see Chapter 9.

✔ Completing health-care proxies and durable powers of attorney so that a family member can direct the health-care and financial decisions of the family if you and your spouse are out of action at the same time.

A durable power of attorney enables the person you select to represent you in case you become incapacitated and cannot represent yourself. For more information about a durable power of attorney, go to the ExpertLaw Web site at `expertlaw.com/library/pubarticles/Estate_Planning/durable_power_of_attorney.html`, which offers a free durable power of attorney form. This sample form covers the general provisions of establishing a durable power of attorney. Keep in mind that your durable power of attorney form needs to be reviewed by an attorney to make certain that it meets your legal needs and is valid in the jurisdiction where you live.

✔ Creating an estate plan that minimizes estate taxes and maximizes the accumulation of wealth. It's never too early to purchase life insurance (see Chapter 18) and consider retirement planning (see Chapter 10) to round out your estate planning.

Grooving in your midlife

If you're middle-aged and just hitting your stride, you've probably accumulated a few assets. Wanting to keep court and legal costs to a minimum, you may want to consider a revocable living trust as a way to distribute your assets to your heirs.

Living trusts don't affect your current lifestyle and generally are easy to set up, and they enable your assets to be quickly transferred to your beneficiaries upon your death. The trust can be revoked at any time while you're alive.

Some families get caught in what I call the "boomer sandwich" — when they're shelling out money for their children's college education, paying for assisted living for their parents, and trying to save enough for their own retirement. As a result, their estate plans must maximize each and every dollar. Here are a few ideas:

If the going mortgage interest rate is at least 1 percent less than what you're paying now, refinance. The cost savings can help you pay tuition. Additionally, taking out a home equity loan to pay for college can create some tax advantages.

Your life insurance needs to provide coverage in an amount that provides income in case one of the parents dies. For more details on how life insurance can assist you in conserving assets and providing liquidity for your estate planning, see Chapter 17.

Your health-care proxies, durable powers of attorney, and trusts need to be reviewed on a regular basis. Other items to consider are

- ✔ Making your bank account into a payable-on-death account by signing a form that your bank supplies. Name your executor or trustee or anyone in the family to inherit whatever funds are in the account upon your death.

- ✔ Setting up an annual gift-giving plan to reduce the size of your estate, especially if the property you own is greater than the estate-tax exemption amount.

- ✔ Reducing estate and income taxes by forming a charitable trust, which can include making a gift to charity and getting some payments back.

- ✔ Investing in disability and long-care insurance, which are wise investments at this point in your life. These types of insurance can protect your family against the expense of a long-term disability.

For more information on gift taxes and charitable trusts, see

- ✔ **NOLO** (www.nolo.com), which provides an easy-to-understand "Estate and Gift Tax FAQ" section for estate planning. According to the NOLO Law Center, most estates don't owe taxes. However, it pays to be informed. Answers to FAQs about estate taxes and gift giving to reduce taxes are written in a way that clears up any misunderstandings you may have about complex estate planning. On the home page, go to "Browse the Law Centers" and click on "Wills & Estate Planning" and then on "Estate Taxes."

- ✔ **MSN MoneyCentral** (www. moneycentral.msn.com/articles/retire/taxes/1242.asp) shows the basics of charitable trusts. See how charitable trusts offer income tax breaks and income.

- ✔ **Prudential** (www.prudential.com/simpleArticle/0,1470,intPage ID%253D1724%2526blnPrinterFriendly%253D0,00.html) explains the ins and outs of charitable trusts and taxes. At the home page, click on "Financial Planning." Next, click on "Estate Planning" and "Estate Planning Learning Guide." Click on the first item in the table of contents. At the Estate Planning page, scroll the "Skip to" dialog box to "Charitable Trusts and Taxes."

Retired and enjoying the good life

Retirement often is a wake-up call for getting your estate plan in order. Some folks play golf or bridge for years, and other retirees may suddenly become ill. Either way, now is the time to get going and make your estate plans. One of the most important decisions you need to make involves healthcare. You may want to consider assigning someone in your family the task of making your health-care decisions for you if or when you become incapacitated. After all, a doctor or the court doesn't know you the way members of your family do. A family member needs to have your durable power of attorney (they don't have to pass a bar exam to do it) to act as your agent. You can stipulate that the durable power of attorney won't go into effect unless you're incapacitated. Don't forget to have the form signed and notarized so that it's legally valid.

Folks near retirement and retirees need to consider the best way to provide growth potential for their assets and preserve capital. One protective strategy is a charitable remainder trust. A *charitable remainder trust* offers an immediate tax reduction and can help reduce capital gains.

Estate planning dictates that you must understand that you can't take it with you. So you may want to consider

✔ **Contributing to the grandkids:** If you can afford it, you can give the maximum amount of money allowed each year to your grandchildren's Uniform Gifts to Minors (UMG) accounts or set up a Section 529 plan to supplement their education funding while using the accompanying tax advantages.

✔ **Disbursing money to your favorite charities:** Doing so reduces estate taxes. Don't forget, charities also can also be named as beneficiaries of a trust.

✔ **Transferring the benefits of your existing life insurance policy to a trust to protect your heirs:** If you're a business owner or are self-employed, transferring the benefits of your insurance policy (or policies) to your trust may be valuable to your heirs. This estate-planning technique can protect the inheritance of your heirs in case of bankruptcy, divorce, or some other unforeseen event

According to U.S. government statistics, more than 50 percent of women and 33 percent of men age 65 and older either require assistance with day-to-day activities or enter a nursing home. Long-term-care insurance can help protect you from the high cost of this type of care.

Selecting an Estate Planner

Although the Internet can point you in the right direction and provide the basic education you need to understand different approaches to estate planning, an estate-planning attorney is necessary to make certain your beneficiaries don't run into any unpleasant surprises.

Finding a qualified attorney can be difficult. You may want to start by asking friends and family for recommendations. Your broker or accountant may be able to recommend a good estate-planning attorney. The estate-planning attorney you employ needs to meet certain criteria. He or she must

✔ **Have at least five years of experience practicing estate-planning law.** Check out your state's bar association records to determine whether the attorney has ever been party to an ethical complaint or inquiry.

✔ **Have at least 75 percent of his or her practice focused on estate planning.** Hiring an experienced estate-planning attorney helps you make certain that you're presented with all your estate-planning options.

✔ **Not actively solicit your business.** If an attorney tries to solicit your business, I suggest you run (don't walk) in the opposite direction. An attorney who contacts you directly or has someone contact you on his or her behalf may be breaking the Legal Rules of Professional Conduct.

✔ **Be covered by professional liability insurance.** This type of insurance covers you in case the attorney makes an error.

✔ **Offer a free initial consultation to discuss your needs and desires.** *Note:* Make certain you know how to fire your attorney before you hire him or her.

✔ **Bill on a fee-for-service schedule (not hourly).** Make sure that you know what you're paying for.

✔ **Make you comfortable when working together.** After all, estate-planning relationships can last many years.

Keep in mind that financial planners also can provide advice for investments, insurance, taxes, wills and trusts, and mortgages. The following Web sites can help you locate someone who is an expert in estate planning, elder law, post-mortem services, and financial services:

✔ **American Academy of Estate Planning Attorneys** (www.aaepa.com) is a professional association that educates estate-planning attorneys and provides consumers with valuable information. Search on "Estate Planning" and click on "Other Academy Links." The Center can assist you in finding a trusted attorney and protecting your personal wealth.

✔ **Estate Planning Law** (www.estate-planninglaw.com/#lawyers) offers a listing of estate-planning attorneys by name. All the attorneys listed have Web sites, so you can view their major practice areas, estate-planning approaches, and attorney profiles.

✔ **National Directory of Estate Planning, Probate & Elder Law Attorneys** (www.search-attorneys.com) can assist you in finding an attorney in your area who focuses on estate planning. You can search the national directory by location, firm name, or attorney.

✔ **LegalMatch** (www.legalmatch.com) enables you to anonymously describe your estate-planning concerns online to qualified, prescreened local lawyers for free. Lawyers respond to your case with an offer. You can access detailed information about each attorney and then choose the one with the experience, consumer ratings, and fees that you like best. Try using the online demo to find out how it works.

Preparing to Meet Your Estate Planner

Your first meeting with your estate-planning attorney needs to be a working meeting, which means you need to bring a file that includes copies of bank and brokerage statements and your existing will or trust (if you have one). If you're prepared, such a meeting can be a time to review your personal information and discuss fees. The following quick checklist gives you an idea of what you need to prepare before the meeting with your estate-planning attorney. Remember to use the Internet to help you gather, organize, and collect the documents you'll need:

✔ An inventory of your assets. You can use the online estate-planning calculators I mention below to help you get started.

✔ Copies of automobile titles, home deeds, and other assets you've listed in your inventory.

✔ A printed copy of your most recent online brokerage account statement. (For details on using an online brokerage and trading online, see Chapter 8.)

✔ Copies of your insurance policies. If they're locked up in your safety deposit box, bring copies of your paid insurance policy invoices.

✔ Copies of your pension plans. You may want to contact the Social Security Administration (SSA) for your latest statement. For information about contacting the SSA, see Chapter 10.

✔ Copies of paperwork for large debts. For example, go online and print a copy of your most recent mortgage and credit-card statements. (For information about viewing your statements online, see Chapters 3 and 13.)

✔ Copies of any existing wills or trusts and previously filed gift tax returns that you may have. The status of these documents may mean your estate plan will either stay the same or you'll have to start all over again.

✔ Copies of any powers of attorney or letters of intent or last instructions you may have completed and signed.

✔ A list of your Social Security number and the Social Security numbers of members of your family.

✔ Copies of your and your family members' medical insurance cards. This information may be used to clear up any misunderstandings that may occur.

For more online information about preparing to meet with your estate planner, check out the online sources in the list that follows. Although these Web sites promote the services of different organizations, they also include valuable estate-planning information and data sheets.

✔ **GE Center for Financial Learning** (www.financialearning.com) provides a detailed data sheet that can assist you in preparing to answer the common questions that arise during the estate-planning process. On the home page, click on "Estate Planning," click on "All Our Articles," and then click on "Preparing for a Meeting with Your Estate Planner."

✔ **Deloitte** (www.deloitte.com) provides timely articles, tools, and advisors to ensure that your plans address your family's values and long-term goals. On the Deloitte home page, pull down the "Global Site Selector" menu and select "United States." Next, pull down the "Services" menu, click on "Tax Services," scroll down to and click on "Private Client Advisors," and then click on "Family Wealth Planning."

✔ **The National Financial Planners Association** sponsors a National Financial Planning Support Center (www.fpanet.org/public/tools/estate_planning_checklist.cfm), which provides a printable checklist that's useful for getting the documents you need for a meeting with your estate-planning attorney. On the center's home page under the "Learning Tools" menu, click on "Checklists & Quizzes," and then click on "Is your estate in order?"

Part IV
Purchasing Online

The 5th Wave   By Rich Tennant

"Can you explain your loan program again, this time without using the phrase, `yada, yada, yada`?"

In this part . . .

In this part of the book, I offer some timely advice about how you can tell a good deal from a scam, some guidelines about determining the time to sell, and how to spot the green flags for buying.

Chapter 12

Click Locally, Shop Globally

*O*nline shopping has improved through the years. Now you can create a virtual model to try on the clothes you select at Lands' End (www.landsend.com), zoom in on different product features at Nordstrom (www.nordstroms.com), and change the color of the products that interest you at Eddie Bauer (www.eddiebauer.com). When a dress is available in three colors, you now can see how each color looks on the catalog model (or on a virtual model that looks just like you). Online retailers also are offering shorter shipping times, free shipping, and liberal return polices that often include free return shipping.

The Nielsen//NetRatings service, an Internet ratings company, reports that online sales (excluding travel) in November and December of 2003 were $18.5 billion, reflecting a 35 percent increase in sales during the same two months of 2002. Some of the growth of online shopping is fueled by the rising number of high-speed broadband links that now connect more than 50 million American homes to the Internet and make online shopping more convenient and faster than in the past.

In this chapter, I show you who's shopping online and how to shop safely. You also find out how to check out online merchants, save time by using handy shopbots to quickly find the best deals, and discover how to save money and benefit from cash-back shopping, money-saving coupons, free samples, and giveaways. Additionally, this chapter shows you how to locate the best online sales and get free shipping for your purchases.

How to Be a Savvy Online Shopper

Smart offline shoppers use a few precautions to make certain they don't become victims of credit-card theft. Savvy online shoppers also need to follow these guidelines to ensure that shopping online is as safe as going to the local mall:

- **Using a secure Web site:** Make certain the *checkout page* (the page where you pay for the items in your online shopping cart) is *encrypted* (a methodology that scrambles the information you send and receive over the Internet). For example, the checkout page may use Secure Socket Layer (SSL) or Secure Electronic Transaction (SET) methodologies to make certain your personal customer information is indecipherable. You don't have to do anything but look for the padlock icon at the bottom of your screen to verify that the checkout page is encrypted.

- **Checking out the vendor:** Anyone can set up a catalog on the Internet. Check out the vendor before making any purchases. (Find out how to check out vendors in "Trust but verify: Checking online vendors before buying," later in this chapter.)

- **Reading the privacy policy:** Vendors with privacy policies are obliged to protect your personal information, and that means they can't sell your e-mail address to third-party vendors who bombard you with spam.

- **Using a credit card:** Remember you're protected by the Fair Credit Billing Act, which gives you the right to dispute any charges under certain conditions (for example, whenever you receive defective or damaged merchandise).

- **Keeping a paper record:** Print a copy of your purchase confirmation number and order for reference. You may want to start an offline file of all your purchase orders from online purchases.

Make certain that you use a credit card when shopping online. Credit cards offer you more safety than cash, cashier's checks, or money orders because you're insured by the Fair Credit Billing Act. Don't forget about the differences between debit cards and credit cards. Whenever you use a debit card, you forfeit any leverage that a credit card gives you.

Trust but verify: Checking online vendors before buying

If you're unfamiliar with the seller, checking him or her out online is a good idea. Most Web sites include a section titled "About Us" that usually includes information about when the company was started, its management team, company goals, and contact information. Although a logo from the Better Business Bureau (www.bbb.org) on a company's Web site indicates its reliability, it isn't an absolute guarantee.

Shopping bots are fundamentally like search engines except that instead of finding information they're intended to help shoppers find the products or services they're looking for on the Internet. Many of the comparison shopping bots (such as Shopping.com at www.shopping.com) feature customer reviews and feedback. Small merchants can gain an edge on large merchants by providing outstanding customer service, especially when customers write favorable reviews. That's how small merchants gain prominent listings without having to purchase them. Shopping.com is one comparison Web site that's driven by 25,000 users who have given small companies the thumbs up for providing on-time delivery and customer support and meeting expectations during the past four years.

Following are a few consumer-rated comparison Web sites that can assist you in checking out a merchant:

- ✔ **4Consumers.com** (www.4consumers.com) offers product reviews from leading consumer Web sites all on one page. You also can find customer reviews, opinions, and complaints for thousands of Internet stores and vendors. Enter the name of the product you're researching in the search window and click on "Search for Reviews."

- ✔ **Bizrate.com** (www.bizrate.com) rates more merchants than any other comparison-shopping Web site online. One drawback: Items and merchants for which fewer or less frequent searches are conducted don't receive as much attention as the ones that receive more such hits, even though Shopping.com requires stores to be reviewed by more than 20 customers before they're given a rating. Some popular stores have thousands or even tens of thousands of customer reviews.

- ✔ **ConsumerNow** (www.consumernow.com) is an annotated listing of top-ranked consumer Web sites. At ConsumerNow, you find tips about how to make online shopping easy, inexpensive, and safe.

- ✔ **Shopping.com** (www.shopping.com) includes detailed and objective store data and extensive user reviews of products and stores. Keep in mind that customer reviews can be anecdotal. Shopping.com helps refine your search for the item you desire. ***Note:*** Shopping.com is a combination of the Dealtime shopping search engine and Epinions, a consumer review and ratings platform.

Web hazards and warranty policies

You need to make sure that you read the merchant's warranty, privacy, refund, and cancellation policies. After all, you're paying in advance for an item that you may have never seen. After checking a vendor at one of the Web sites mentioned earlier in this chapter, you may, for example, want to send them an e-mail message. Say you're interested in cookware. You may want to ask the merchant what the difference is between a stockpot and a Dutch oven. (The stock pot is tall and uses a burner on top of a stove; a Dutch oven is covered and can be placed in an oven.) Use the response you receive from the merchant to help determine whether you want to place an order.

When visiting the merchant's Web site, see whether it posts the Better Business Bureau (BBB) Online Reliability Seal. Although doing so isn't the same as a warranty, it does indicate that the online merchant lives up to the BBB's standards of service.

Don't forget to read the return policy

Returning unwanted online purchases requires online merchants to invest in reverse logistics. By that, I mean a way for customers to easily return or exchange merchandise. For many individuals, the absence of a good way to complete returns has stopped them from shopping online. Most online merchants include a return-shipping label with your purchase.

According to Forrester Research, about one of every ten products sold online in 2003 was returned. Some companies outsource their returns to other companies that are known as return management services (RMSs). Three good examples of RMS providers are the U.S. Postal Service (USPS), United Parcel Service (UPS), and Federal Express (FedEx). You can print a label and then call one of these companies for an immediate pickup of the product that you want to return. A variation of this service is returning your product directly to the RMS. You can go to a USPS office, for example, get instant credit for the return, and ship it back to the merchant at the same time.

Following are the descriptions of four RMSs that can assist you in returning your online purchases:

- ✔ **United States Postal Service (USPS)** (www.usps.com/send/waystosend mail/extraservices/merchandisereturnservice.htm) provides information about how you can return unwanted purchases. For example, after downloading a postage-paid label directly from the merchant's Web site, you can slap it on the package and then either drop the package into a collection box or give it to your letter carrier.

✔ **FedEx NetReturn** (`www.fedex.com/us/solutions/netreturn.html?link=4`) offers FedEx Return Manager, an automated Internet-based solution that enables your merchant to do one of the following:

- Transmit a return FedEx shipping label to you via e-mail

- Electronically dispatch a driver for shipment pickup at your location on the same or next business day

- Preauthorize a future pickup

✔ **UPS OnLine WorldShip** (`www.ups.com/content/us/en/bussol/offering/worldship/offering.html`) offers returns for U.S. and international customers who can be traced using the UPS tracking service. UPS gives you two options for using the return service. The first option is OnLine Call Tab, where drivers bring the label to your location on the date you specify and pick up the package. The second option is Print Return Label Service, where the merchant sends you a pickup label with instructions to drop the package off at a UPS customer counter or authorized shipping site.

Getting Online Advice for Exactly What You Want

Trying to research the latest technogadget or big-ticket item online can be frustrating because Web sites include tons of data that make it tough for you to know whether the information is up-to-date. Likewise, anonymous reviews are easy to find, but they may not be reliable. So you may want to get started by reading a wide range of manufacturer reviews to gain an understanding of what features you want and how much you'll have to pay.

Online professional reviewers write about new products every day. Their reviews are often easy to find and frequently include comparisons of similar products. As product buyers, many customers write online reviews about the same products, and they're also liberally sprinkled throughout the Internet. A customer's hands-on knowledge can differ greatly from the experience of an editorial reviewer. Looking at both types of reviews can assist you in gaining the best understanding of the product. An expert reviewer has a wide perspective, while the user has an operational approach about the best and worst features of the product. The following are several examples of where you can find product reviews online:

✔ **Amazon.com** (`amazon.com`) offers thousands of customer and editorial reviews of a wide range of products. In the search box, enter the name of the product you're researching and click "Go!" On the next page, in the left margin, click on "Editorial Reviews" or "Customer Reviews."

✔ **ConsumerREVIEW** (www.consumerreview.com), with your free registration, offers customer reviews and buying advice for outdoor sporting goods and consumer electronics. Find out how to buy or sell the products showcased within its network of web communities, including sites like AudioREVIEW.com. Discover the products you're interested in, read and write reviews, participate in discussions, compare prices, and shop online.

✔ **Consumersearch** (www.consumersearch.com) offers links to professional reviews. All reviews are evaluated by the Web site's editors and are rated for quality and credibility.

Comparison Shopping with Shopbots

Online shoppers primarily use shopping bot Web sites to save time and money. In fact, according to Nielsen//NetRatings, more than 21 million customers visited shopping-comparison Web sites in 2003. According to Forrester Research, Inc., about 18 percent of American online consumers use online price-comparison Web sites. Individuals who use comparison shopping spend about 24 percent more than the average online shopper.

For the most part, shopbots are easy to use. All you have to do is tell the bot (robot) what you want, and it searches online retailers for the best deal for the item you've selected. Unfortunately, using shopbots isn't always that simple; they aren't always perfect. The following is a short list of some shopbot limitations:

✔ They may provide you with a selection of merchandise only from the bigger retailers with higher prices. In other words, some categories are not well represented. One reason is that small retailers don't list their products online.

✔ Some merchants block shopbots from their Web sites. These merchants may have lower or higher prices, but either way, they don't want to be compared.

✔ Some shopbots offer preferred placement. In other words, merchants have paid for placement before a lower-priced product.

The first screens of a comparison Web site probably show merchants that have paid for preferential placement. Click again to sort either by price or quality to get more-objective advice. Don't stop your comparison shopping with just one search. You need to use several shopbots to find the best price. After you find the best price, search for a coupon or free shipping to knock off a few more bucks before you buy.

Most comparison Web sites differ in the way they determine placement, but all use some type of algorithm that considers elements such as price and availability to list products. Many Web sites add the amounts vendors pay for placements into their mix. The list that follows includes a few examples of online comparison-shopping Web sites. Some of them include merchant ratings, customer product reviews, and information about taxes and shipping so you can calculate your final bill.

- ✔ **Bizrate.com Inc**. (www.bizrate.com) accepts payments from merchants for preferential placement. It searches more than 34,000,000 products in around 47,000 stores but enables you to sort them by price and store name.

- ✔ **CNet Shopper** (shopper.cnet.com) offers price comparisons of electronic gear from desktop computers to digital cameras. Discover popular, new products and price drops. You can search CNet Shopper by part number, product, keyword, manufacturer, or category. If you like to read the specs for electronic equipment, this Web site is for you. Sign up for free newsletters and alerts about special offers.

- ✔ **Froogle** (froogle.google.com) is unique because it doesn't sell preferential placements to merchants. Merchants are listed according to Google's proprietary search algorithm, which in layman's terms means that small merchants don't get lost in the shuffle.

- ✔ **MySimon** (www.mysimon.com) offers price comparisons and shopping guides with advice on how to purchase items such as laptop computers. With your free registration, receive weekly newsletters and special offers.

- ✔ **PriceGrabber.com** (www.pricegrabber.com) is a highly rated price comparison Web site where products are presented well and total costs (shipping and tax) are included. Merchants that pay for preferential placement are clearly labeled. By the way, PriceGrabber.com doesn't charge merchants to list their products in its storefront section; however, it charges them $1 for a product that costs less than $15.75 and a fee of 7.75 percent for merchandise that costs more than $15.75. Pricegrabber.com includes a paid Featured Merchant section.

- ✔ **PriceSCAN** (www.pricescan.com) is an unbiased guide to finding the lowest prices on books, computers, digital photography, electronics, prescription drugs, home and garden items, movies, music, office equipment, sporting goods, video games, watches, and more. The database consists of publicly available product and pricing information. The company gathers data from magazine ads, vendor catalogs, Web sites, and so on, and then presents this information in a searchable form.

- ✔ **Shopping.com** (www.shopping.com) is the renamed and redesigned Web site for Dealtime, Ltd. Find what you want from thousands of products, compare the latest prices, read millions of reviews, and buy the right product through trusted stores. With your free registration, you can receive exclusive offers for the Web's top-rated stores, write reviews about products and stores, and receive e-mail alerts about Web site enhancements and features. Shopping.com accepts bids as low as a nickel for perennial merchant placement. The higher the merchant's bid amount, the greater the merchant's prominence in the consumer's results.

Helping others through online shopping

Hundreds of online-shopping Web sites partner with charities. That means if you shop at a certain merchant's Web site, a percentage of the amount you spend is directed toward a charity. Here's how it works: Merchants give referral fees to online entities for directing online shoppers to their respective Web sites. When you start with certain sites, the referral fee goes to the charity work of the referring Web site without additional cost to online shoppers.

Some merchants sponsor specific charities, while others are open to all charities. Online shoppers can point their donation to a selected charity. Keep in mind, however, that charity shopping sites are for-profit enterprises that earn their revenue from advertising, the profit remaining from a sale, and/or by taking a small percentage of the donation transaction. The following are a few examples:

✔ **Igive.com** (www.igive.com) requires your free registration. You can select which charity receives your donation. You download a tracking bug that pops up to notify you when you're shopping at one of the 540 Igive.com merchants. The pop-up window states how much of your purchase will be donated to charity.

✔ **SchoolMall** (www.schoolmall.com) requires your free registration. You select which school receives your donation. Vendors that sell products on this Web site agree to pay a commission. SchoolMall takes a percentage of the commission to cover costs of technology and expanding services. The remainder goes to the school of your choice.

✔ **Shop for Change** (www.shopforchange.com) tries to help consumers save time by shopping online, and it creates a better world. Every time you purchase merchandise from one of its merchants, Shop for Change donates up to 5 percent of the price to nonprofit groups working for peace, equality, human rights, education, and a cleaner environment. Shop and raise money for groups such as Planned Parenthood, Rainforest Action Network, and the ACLU.

Black-Belt Online Bargain Shopping

Everybody loves a bargain. I define *black-belt online bargain shopping* as taking your knowledge of online shopping and getting the best deal you can. This section of the chapter is filled with insider tips, expert shopping tools, hands-on advice for new and experienced Internet users, and lists of the best shopping Web sites you can find in cyberspace. This section covers

✔ **Making a purchase online and picking it up at the store:** This section shows how many online shoppers live in Internet time but like the convenience of local bricks-and-mortar stores.

✔ **Checking daily, weekly, and special sales:** This information works espe-cially well for folks who want big discounts on brand names. Some people are looking for the right product at the right price and don't care if they have to wait.

✔ **Stretching the purse strings to the limit through rebates:** Rebates target online shoppers who want to stretch their dollar a little more. Rebates can result in a check in the mail that can be used for the holi-days or in a donation to your favorite charity.

✔ **Finding online coupons:** Regardless of whether you get them offline or online, coupons are an American favorite. This section shows how the rules have changed about printing your own coupons.

✔ **Using discount coupons codes:** Everyone loves promotional codes. Free shipping is nice, but getting a few more bucks off your purchase is great.

Buying it online, picking it up at the store

Although this proposition may seem a little backward, it's popular. Many people don't want to interact with a salesperson and know that they can return their purchase if it isn't what they want or expected. Some people don't want to wait for the company van that promises delivery within a four-hour time window that stretches into six hours or more. Many stores offer this option, including

✔ **Circuit City** (www.circuitcity.com), where you can order the product you want online and immediately pick up your purchase after you've received your online order confirmation. You can pay for your purchase using a credit card or PayPal and avoid any shipping charges by using Circuit City's Express In-store Pickup option.

✔ **Sears** (www.sears.com), which responded to customer preferences by enabling them to order clothes dryers, dishwashers, and other items online and then pick them up at a local store.

✔ **Recreational Equipment, Inc.**, (www.rei.com), which enables shoppers to order items online and have them shipped to their local store at no extra charge.

Companies like Orvis (www.orvis.com) and the Gap (www.gap.com) have access to the full database of all their respective company products and sizes (for example, plus and petite sizes and maternity wear). While at a store, whenever a customer wants a certain item but can't find it in the store, a store clerk can order the item for the customer and have it delivered to the customer's home, free of charge.

Daily, weekly, and special sales

The Internet can let the sale come to you by offering Web sites that are updated hourly about sales at your favorite stores and sending you e-mail alerts about what's on sale. The list that follows shows a variety of sale Web sites that offer black-belt online shoppers the opportunity to shop for that Prada handbag at a bargain price:

- ✔ **Best Web Buys Deal of the Day** (www.bestwebbuys.com/hotdeals) is a tidy little Web site that divides products into five categories: electronics, books, music, videos, and bikes. Each day Best Web Buys tracks down Web sites that offer special promotions and coupons.

- ✔ **Dealoftheday** (www.dealoftheday.com) is a general interest site that posts the Deal of the Day and has a popular freebie-finder feature. You also find coupons and comparison shopping.

- ✔ **DealOne.com** (www.dealone.com/deals/156460.asp) offers links to one-day deals and weekly specials from online merchants across the Internet.

- ✔ **Fatwallet** (www.fatwallet.com) includes a Latest Deals section that provides you with up-to-the-minute news about online sales. If you're interested in a certain product, sign up for Fatwallet's alert service so you'll be notified immediately when an item you're seeking goes on sale.

- ✔ **Techbargains** (www.techbargains.com) searches the Internet and local stores for the best deals on products. You find hot deals on the latest tech products and great prices for just about anything you're looking for. The Web site includes Bargain News Headlines that cover all the latest sales, bargains, and deals. The home page includes the latest listings of what's on sale so you can save the most money. The Web site offers discount coupons, rebates, and vendor information. Techbargains also recommends which products you should purchase, and there's even a free newsletter.

Getting something back: Rebates

All rebate Web sites require you to register for their services. Some rebate Web sites require only your zip code and e-mail address, and others want you to complete a lengthy questionnaire so that online marketers have more insight into your buying preferences. There appears to be no correlation between how much information you're asked to provide and the size of your rebate.

Merchants offer rebates in differing amounts for your entire purchase. Each rebate Web site offers hundreds of small and large *e-tailers* (electronic retailer) to select from. Rebates vary from one online merchant to another. Buy.com (www.buy.com) and the Gap (www.gap.com), for example, offer low rebates of only a percentage point or two. Online merchants with large rebates include 1-800-Flowers (www.1800flowers.com) and Drugstore.com (www.drugstore.com), which offer at least a 6 percent rebate on your purchase. By contrast, Amazon.com doesn't offer any rebates.

If you're cost-conscious, you want to comparison shop for rebates at different rebate Web sites. Bookseller Barnes & Noble, for example, offers a 4 percent rebate on EBates.com yet offers only a 2.5 percent rebate at Rebateshare.com; however, you can use a coupon code to receive $5 off a purchase of $50 or more.

In most situations, you have to start at a rebate Web site to receive a rebate. Click on the name of the merchant's linked site. (If you go directly to the merchant's Web site, you won't receive your rebate.) Some rebate Web sites automatically deduct your rebate from the purchase price, and others apply a credit to your account, but remember that one rebate Web site is different from the next.

Keep in mind that every online rebater has different and ever-changing discounts. You can check out several online rebate Web sites in the list that follows:

- **Bondsonline.com** (www.bondsonline.com) enables online shoppers to recoup a small percentage of their purchase price in the form of a U.S. Savings Bond. Register at the Web site, and each time you complete a purchase at one of its 150 listed retailers, between 2 percent and 10 percent of your purchase price is placed into your account (depending on the merchant you're dealing with). Savings bonds start at $50. Keep in mind that Series EE Savings Bonds pay about 2.84 percent in interest. If the interest rate on the credit card you're using to make your purchase is greater than 2.84 percent, you don't save any money.

- **Butterflymall.com** (www.butterflymall.com) pays consumers to shop online. Sign up, shop at more than 600 e-tailers, and pay the listed prices. In return, the Web site then pays you 40 percent of your purchase price in Butterfly dollars. (Does anyone remember S&H Green Stamps?) When the Butterfly dollars appear in your account, you can redeem them for their cash equivalents. You must acquire at least $15 worth of Butterfly dollars before they can be redeemed or sent to you in a check.

- **BonusTree** (www.bonustree.com) is the place to go whenever you're interested in a sale at your favorite online merchant. The rebate program kicks back 50 percent of the merchant's commission fee to customers. Refer a new member to BonusTree and you receive up to $2. You can have your referral fee added to your account or donated to a charity. BonusTree also includes other freebies.

✔ **EBates** (www.ebates.com) offers its online members up to 25 percent cash discounts on purchases at more than 700 online stores. As you shop, you see a pop-up window that indicates when you're visiting an EBates-sponsored, Web-based merchant. Although the pop-up can be annoying, the check you receive in the mail makes up for it.

✔ **FatWallet** (www.fatwallet.com) offers cash-back shopping at its FatWallet's Cash Back Mall. Register, log on, and go to the Cash Back Mall. Click on the name of the merchant, and earn your Cash Back rebate. You can usually use coupons or discount codes and still receive your rebate.

✔ **Rebateshare.com** (www.rebateshare.com) offers coupons and rebates. Using specific codes provided by the site, you can save a predetermined percentage of your total purchase in addition to the rebate you earned. You need to accumulate $25 in credits before you can get a check in the mail.

Clipping online coupons

Something about saving a few extra bucks on your online purchases makes shopping online feel like a really good deal. According to *BusinessWeek*, about 80 percent of Americans clip coupons every year. In 2001, the number of Web surfers who clipped virtual coupons increased nearly 30 percent, compared with a 23 percent hike during the previous year. E-coupons help merchants retain current customers and entice new ones. Consumers regularly use e-coupons for groceries, books, health, music, beauty, fast food, apparel, and toys.

Savile Row by mouse click

If you have a hard time finding shirts or pants that fit, you may want to try purchasing customized clothes at Lands' End (www.landsend.com). At the Web site, click on "Lands' End Custom Clothing" in the right margin. Select either men's or women's, depending on your gender, and then select what type of custom clothes you want. Women can get custom blouses, jeans, and chinos. Garments for men include custom dress shirts and pants, custom jeans, and chinos. When completing the questionnaire about your body size, you don't have to take any complicated measurements. However, some of the questions are a little unusual, such as "What is your shoe size?" Answer all the questions because your answers help determine your general body type. Lands' End develops a mathematical model of your body by comparing your responses with a database of 5 million data points. Your garment is then individually cut and sewn to a pattern based on your unique fit profile. If the fit isn't just right the first time around, you can nip and tuck your profile accordingly. Lands' End Custom Clothing is cost-free, with a 100 percent customer satisfaction guarantee. Make sure you allow four to five weeks for delivery.

Unfortunately, the process for obtaining coupons online isn't quite as straight-forward as clipping coupons from your Sunday newspaper. Although many sites offer coupons, most don't allow users to print coupons directly from the Web site because of concerns about potential tampering. Instead, shoppers select the coupons they want, and they're mailed.

Sites that do allow you to print out coupons also require you to download software that's used to print the coupons. Other sites require you to enter information about your shopping habits to qualify for and receive coupons. Like rebate sites described in the preceding section, the suitability of using these sites depends on how comfortable you are with providing this type of information to online marketers. The following are a few examples of Web sites that provide online coupons:

- **Eversave.com** (www.eversave.com) is a free service that sends you coupons via e-mail that you can print out and redeem at local businesses, grocery stores, and famous national retailers for top brand-name products. It also offers online coupons for Internet purchases, searches for online sales, and compares prices to let you know where to go for the best deals. You can even get free samples offered by the Web site's advertisers.

- **SmartSource.com** (www.smartsource.com) is the same company that provides discount coupons in your Sunday newspaper. This free service enables you to print real, money-saving coupons on your own printer. Just download *Print Manager* (it uses about 40K of memory), and you're in business.

- **Valupage** (www.valupage.com) requires you to log on and enter your zip code and the name of your favorite supermarket. You'll see about $40 worth of national-brand coupons appear on your screen. You can print these coupons and redeem them at the supermarket. You receive a credit for the amount of your coupons that you can use for your next shopping trip to the supermarket.

Using coupon codes to save money

Unlike offline coupons that require you to bring an actual piece of paper to the store, online coupons work with codes and sometimes with special coupon links. Many e-tailers provide a discount on your next purchase as a thank-you gift. These discount coupons or dollars-off coupons can often be used online or offline via telephone or when visiting the local store.

How do you use an online discount coupon? Place the item(s) you want in your virtual shopping cart and then enter the coupon code (which also may be called a promotion code, discount code, promotional code, source code, or promo code) during the checkout process. A discount coupon code can dramatically reduce the amount of your purchase. For example, one researcher

I know purchases toner and boxes of paper from Staples.com. She also is a member of Staples' Business Rewards program and regularly earns discounts that can be applied to her purchases. Staples also offers discounts for certain office products. Additionally, if the order is more than $50, shipping is free. The researcher recently reduced a bill for $135 to only $75 by using her $35 Business Rewards discount coupon code and received a second discount by buying two large boxes of paper for the price of one (she entered a special code to get the second box of paper for free). Because the order was for more than $50 worth of merchandise, shipping was free.

Where can you find these discount codes? Go to Google at www.google.com, enter the merchant's name, and search for a promotion or discount code. Your search needs to look something like this: "Eddie Bauer Coupon." Your search results will include Web sites that specialize in discount codes for purchases from Eddie Bauer. Make sure you read the fine print about required minimum purchases and the expiration date of the discount code. If your discount doesn't show up prior to submitting your order, the coupon code or link may have expired.

Remember some of these Web sites are more efficient than others in updating their content. Some of them also have more-comprehensive lists of e-tailers. Consequently, you may have to check one or two Web sites before you find the right discount code for your purchase. Here are a few examples of Web sites that specialize in discount codes:

- ✔ **CouponMountain** (www.couponmountain.com), shown in Figure 12-1, offers discount codes for hundreds of e-tailers. If you haven't used a discount code before, try the Web site's five-step tour. CouponMountain is a clean, well-organized Web site that's been helping online shoppers save money since 2001.

- ✔ **Dealcatcher.com** (www.dealcatcher.com) lists popular coupons, new coupons, and expiring coupons for hundreds of stores. The Web site is updated throughout the day by its staff and forum members.

- ✔ **Dealcoupon.com** (www.dealcoupon.com) selects, compares, and verifies Web-based coupons so you don't have to. The Web site is arranged so that you can search by merchant name, product or service category, and discount coupon popularity. You can even set up e-mail alerts so you can automatically receive coupons from your favorite merchants.

- ✔ **FindSavings** (www.findsavings.com) provides a centralized and easy-to-use portal that aims to enhance your online shopping experience by offering users a single interface with access to products from more than 300 merchants and to promotional discounts and coupons that aren't normally accessible to users.

- ✔ **JumpOnDeals.com** (www.jumpondeals.com) offers online sales, coupons, and deals. The front page looks cluttered, but it has everything you need for finding a wide variety of stores, deals, and expiration dates.

Investigating used and refurbished products online

Discover deep discounts on the Internet for factory-reconditioned products. These items are cleaned, quality-checked, and returned to like-new condition by the manufacturers and are being sold at prices substantially lower than retail. Most manufacturers of refurbished or reconditioned products are well-known and offer manufacturer warranties. Here are some of them:

- **Amazon.com** (`amazon.com`) provides factory reconditioned or refurbished products that include manufacturer warranties. Amazon.com offers kitchen and home appliances, tools, hardware, DVDs, home theaters, cameras and photo equipment, computer add-ons, office electronics, and more.

- **Dealnews.com** (`www.dealnews.com`) searches the Web for the best deals available for the products you want. You find a variety of items, but Dealnews.com specializes in electronics. Visit the basement for links to refurbished Palm Pilots, computers, iPods, and more.

- **Dell Outlet** (`www.us.dell.com/content/products/compare.aspx/inspn?c=us&cs=&l=en&s=dfh&`) offers refurbished Dell equipment with a variety of configurations. Supplies are limited to stock on hand, which means no rain checks. Pricing, specifications, and availability are valid only in the U.S., and they're subject to change without notice. Taxes, fees, and shipping charges (other than a free shipping offer when applicable) are extra and vary. You may be able to combine your purchase with other offers or discounts.

Clearing the shelves: Online outlet shopping

The Internet is a terrific way for offline merchants to get rid of unsold goods. Online merchants can easily remove an item from their online catalog whenever it sells out. Many companies, such as Patagonia (www.patagonia.com) and Recreational Equipment, Inc. (www.rei.com), feature an online sales outlet. These merchants save money because they don't have to create a printed discount catalog.

Whenever merchandise remains unsold, the online merchant may resort to a liquidator or jobber. Jobbers typically pay 6¢ to 10¢ on the dollar for the merchandise they purchase. Liquidators often purchase merchandise by the pallet, which enables merchants to clear their shelves and requires minimum manpower.

Overstocks are a fact of life for online merchants. Web-based liquidators can operate with extremely low overhead by selling directly to consumers and thus saving shoppers from waiting in long lines at discount stores. Remember that the reasons leftovers haven't sold may be good ones. A pink-and-green-striped suit, for example, may not be to your liking, or if it is, it may only come in an unusual size.

Some coupons prove there's no free lunch

Coolsavings.com (www.coolsavings.com) is an example of an online discount coupon supplier. In 2004, coolsavings.com had a database of 11.5 million active households. Nielsen// NetRatings and Media Metrix (two Internet rating companies) consistently point out that coolsavings.com is one of the Internet's most popular Web sites for coupons, discounts, and rebates for packaged-goods manufacturers, national retailers, media publishers, and financial, travel, and personal service providers.

Coupons are printable or electronic (discount coupon codes). The only drawback is that cool-savings.com collects detailed, permission-based personal information from each individual consumer, including demographics and categories of interests. Coolsavings.com tracks each member's activity on its Web site to gather key behavioral and attitudinal data, such as shopping preferences. *Note:* Not all discount coupon Web sites include tracking software, but some like cool-savings.com can't help themselves.

The following are a few Web sites that offer outlet shopping online:

- **Bluefly.com** (www.bluefly.com) purchases directly from manufacturers so that it has a better range of sizes than many other online outlet stores. Bluefly.com accepts all returns for any reason within 90 days of purchase.

- **Overstock.com** (www.overstock.com) offers savings of up to 80 percent on your favorite name brands. Inventory includes thousands of DVDs, books, and more. Some online shoppers may have to pay at least a $2.95 restocking fee for returned items.

- **Smartbargains.com** (www.smartbargains.com) purchases directly from manufacturers so it can have a wider range of sizes than other Web-based outlet stores. It often charges at least a $6.96 restocking fee for returned items.

Shipping and Handling and Other Hidden Costs

What is shipping and handling? *Shipping* makes sense because your purchase has to be sent to you, but do you want someone handling your purchase? *Handling* usually refers to the person who gets the product from the shelf, puts it into the box (combining other items you've ordered), seals the box, and sticks the mailing label addressed to you onto the box. Some e-tailers don't let you know the real total cost of your purchase until you receive your order-confirmation e-mail.

Other, more enlightened Web sites include an upfront chart that itemizes fees for shipping, handling, and taxes so you won't order that extra item that puts you in a higher shipping-and-handling cost bracket.

A few more hidden costs that you may not have considered are

- **Customs and duties:** Discovering whether additional costs or regulations apply regarding customs and duty fees is important when you place international orders.

- **Membership fees:** Some Web sites promise to save you money if you join their organizations. However, completing a cost/benefit analysis for online shopping convenience versus traveling to the local mall is pretty difficult.

- **Shipping policy:** Understanding exactly how much you'll be charged for shipping and handling is important. A friend of mine recently won a *free* $500 online shopping spree. Shipping and handling costs were $179. That's not much of a bargain.

✔ **Taxes:** Find out whether a state retail tax will be added to your purchase — from either your state or the state in which the Web site does business.

✔ **Time:** Remember that time is money. More and more online merchants request your free registration to personalize your online experience and to speed up your checkout. Additionally, you may have to spend several hours searching online for a special item that just isn't available at a discount.

Amazon.com discovered that free shipping was key to the satisfaction of its customers. Following the leader, more e-tailers than ever before are offering free shipping. The following list includes several directories that show which online merchants offer free shipping. Don't forget to read the fine print. Some online merchants require a minimum purchase amount or grant free shipping only for seven- to ten-day ground transportation.

✔ **Bizrate.com** (`www.bizrate.com`) lists online merchants that don't charge for shipping on orders of $100 or more. Bizrate also offers reviews of merchants and products.

✔ **CouponMountain** (`www.couponmountain.com/freeshipping_coupon.html`), an online savings portal, aims to help online shoppers save up to 25 percent instantly when shopping at hundreds of Internet retail sites at no cost and without registration. CouponMountain offers a listing of free-shipping offers available only through its Web site. Some of these free-shipping offers have minimum-purchase requirements or require a coupon code.

✔ **FreeShipping.com** (`www.freeshipping.com`) offers access to one of the Web's largest directories of merchants that provide free shipping. FreeShipping.com requires your membership. Membership includes a 30-day free trial and then a subscription of $4.99 per month. All you do is

- Select a merchant that offers exclusive free shipping from the directory.

- Follow the links from Freeshipping.com.

- Shop and order as usual.

- Complete the free shipping rebate form.

Shipping rebates are for $10 per order with a maximum of $500 per year.

Chapter 13

Home Sweet Home! House Hunting Online

*I*f you're looking to purchase a new home, the first place to start is at your computer. You can collect Internet-based information about which homes are the best in the neighborhood and run the numbers to see whether you need to rent or buy. You can find out exactly how much house you can afford and what type of real estate is consistent with your best interests. You can likewise determine what type of house you want and select the features that you must have, desire, or don't want at any cost. Find out how you can take virtual tours of homes in your city or state or across the nation. Get free (or fee) reports about neighborhood crime levels, rankings of nearby schools, and even the general background of your neighbors.

Making Important Preliminary Decisions

Before you go house hunting, it's extremely important to figure out if buying a home is your best option. You also need to come to grips with how much house you can afford. Additionally, you need to determine what your housing priorities are. Do you want to be next to the mall or a school, for example? You also need to list the features that you absolutely need or just sort of want in your dream home. Taking care of all these issues first makes your house hunting a little easier.

Should you rent or buy?

There are many reasons for purchasing a home, but the two main financial reasons that make buying a home more advantageous than renting are that you can deduct the interest from your income taxes and that over time real estate tends to appreciate in value. This rate of appreciation is often greater than other investments. And yet owning a home isn't all gravy.

Online calculators can help you make your rent-versus-buy decision, and keep in mind that you can revisit your decision as often as you like. Here are several of them:

- **Ginnie Mae** (www.ginniemae.gov/rent_vs_buy/rent_vs_buy.asp?subtitleypth) provides a rent-versus-buy comparison chart that indicates how buying a home can cost you money if you move within a five-year period and how staying put can add big dollars to your pockets.

- **Mortgage101.com** (www.mortgage101.com) offers a flexible, easy-to-use calculator that assists you in analyzing the benefits of homeownership.

- **Realtor.org** (www.realtor.org/libweb.nsf/pages/fg301) offers an online field guide to buying versus renting. Its contents include statistics and studies on buying versus renting, consumer information, tips, and resources.

Why homeownership may not be for you

Several reasons can explain why home buying may not be for you. Here are some of them:

- You can't stay in one place for long or your job requires you to move often. The cost of buying and selling several homes within a three- to five-year time frame can make homeownership costly.

- Renting is cost-effective because it can excuse you from having to pay big increases in property taxes and hefty increases in flood or environmental insurance premiums.

- Homeownership requires you to be responsible for landscaping and home maintenance and repair. These items can be the source of surprise bills that can total thousands of dollars. Surprise bills can include a new water heater or furnace or even a new septic system.

- Not all house prices increase in all areas of the nation. At any time, housing prices are decreasing somewhere in the United States. If you buy now, you may have to sell in a market with declining prices.

If you can't stay in one place for a long time, or if you'll have to relocate soon because of your job or other obligations, purchasing a home may not be in your best financial interest. Sure you won't get the interest deductions on your tax return, but the cost of buying and selling a home can mean that you'll lose money on the deal. Additionally, if the real estate market in your area is slow, you may even have to sell the house at a price that's lower than your purchase price. Ouch!

Why homeownership may be just right for you

When you purchase a home, you can do anything you like to it. That is, unless your home is part of a historic district or homeowner's association, or if it's in a similar situation. Even if there are restrictions on the exterior of your home, you can frequently paint the interior walls with polka dots or install a purple countertop in the kitchen, if that's what you want. Although homeownership has its drawbacks, it can increase your net worth in these three ways:

- The value of your home may increase with the rate of inflation. Additionally, in a hot real estate market, homes prices can increase at incredible rates.

- With every monthly payment, your home becomes a source of emergency cash in the form of equity. You don't have to sell your home to take advantage of this profit.

- The mortgage interest you pay is deductible from your income taxes, which can lead to substantial tax savings.

How much house can you afford?

Understanding how much house you can afford is important. One general rule is that you can afford a home that's 2.5 times the amount of your annual salary. For example, if you make $100,000 per year, you probably can afford a $250,000 home.

After figuring out how much you have for a down payment, you need to determine your ability to pay the mortgage. Your monthly mortgage payment *can* include all of the following. Bear in mind that even though your lender doesn't require you to pay each of these expenses on a monthly basis, they still need to be paid:

- **Principal:** Repaying the actual loan amount.

  In the early years of the mortgage, most of the mortgage payment is applied to interest. In later years, most of the mortgage payment is applied to the principal.

- **Interest:** What you pay the lender for borrowing the money to purchase your home.

   Note: Individuals who are credit risks often pay higher interest rates than people with perfect credit.

- **Real estate taxes:** Taxes based on the value of your home that are collected by the local governmental unit to pay for services, such as schools, road and street maintenance, and so on.

   Real estate taxes can change each year and can range from .4 percent to 1.7 percent of the assessed value of your home.

- **Homeowner's insurance:** The amount of lender-required insurance that you have on your home that covers the possible loss of your home and other buildings on your property.

   Homeowner's insurance covers losses caused by fire, lightning, explosion, smoke, theft, vandalism, or water damage due to defective appliances in the home.

- **Private mortgage insurance (if applicable):** Required by the lender whenever the buyer is unable to make a down payment of at least 20 percent of the home's sales price.

   In cases in which the borrower defaults, this kind of coverage insures the lender against the market value of the home being less than the amount owed by the defaulting borrower. The cost of private mortgage insurance (PMI) depends on the amount of the loan. Sometimes lenders charge higher interest rates to cover this additional risk.

Private mortgage insurance usually is required for loans that are greater than 80 percent of the property's value. A loan that's valued at 80 percent of the total value of the property has an 80 percent *loan-to-value ratio,* or LTV. In other words, the lower the LTV, the higher the equity in the house. Whenever you sell the house (for its appraised value), the equity is the amount of cash (20 percent in this case) that you'd have after you completely repaid the loan balance. Conventional wisdom on the part of the lender says that the more equity you have in a property, the less likely you are to default on the loan. As a result, when you have a loan with a high LTV, the lender will probably require you to maintain PMI coverage on the property.

When it comes to calculating mortgage payments that include most or all of these factors, I suggest using one of several home-affordability calculators that are available online to do the math for you. Here are some of them:

- **LoanApp.com** (www.loanapp.com/calculators) provides six calculators that help answer your home-financing questions. Check the mortgage qualification calculator to determine how much income you need to purchase a home.

✔ **CNNMoney Calculators** (http://cgi.money.cnn.com/tools/) offers an online calculator that follows the guidelines that most lenders use. You can factor in your gross annual income, down payment amount, monthly debt, mortgage rate, annual property taxes, and annual homeowner's insurance to determine (conservatively or aggressively) the price of the house you can afford, the loan amount, total monthly payment, and so on. At the online calculator's home page, click on "How Much House Can You Afford?"

What kind of home do you want?

Determining what type of house you want is important before you begin your online search. Many baby boomers (people born as part of the exploding population in the decade or so following World War II) are now looking for homes that are located in assisted-living communities, can be easily adapted for the handicapped, or have only one floor. Four-floor townhouses require plenty of stair climbing and don't work well for people with arthritis or other joint troubles. Knowing the type of home you want and the features you require can reduce the amount of time you spend in the back of your real estate agent's car.

Is the timing right, and does it matter?

The residential real estate market always experiences up cycles and down cycles that usually last about seven years. The most recent down cycle was from 1992 to 1998. During that time, in some areas of the country, real estate prices decreased as much as 30 percent. That decline represented the steepest decrease in real estate prices since the Great Depression. Only recently have prices in the areas hit hardest returned to their early 1990s values.

During the last ten years, as family incomes have increased and families have grown, mortgage rates reached historically low levels. Housing shortages likewise forced buyers into bidding wars for homes in a few locations. All of these elements combined caused home prices to increase. Even after you total all these factors, whether the current up-tick in the real estate cycle has reached the top still isn't known.

The housing market will take a downturn at some point. Trying to time the housing market is as difficult as trying to time the stock market. In general, the housing market is unpredictable because it relies on so many factors. The fluctuations (increases or decreases) in interest rates, the number of homes that are available, and the types of new or established homes are elements of the housing market that are constantly changing. The bottom line is this: The best time to buy a home is when it's best for you.

If you enter the market, you take your chances. What makes your home a good investment is whether prices go up more before they begin to decrease again.

Married couples can create questionnaires about the type of home and which features need to be included in their dream homes. Among the several types of homes that are available are

- **Single-family homes:** They're set apart from the house next door and have between one and four levels. The house may have its own yard and from a few inches to a few acres separating it from the house next door. A single-family dwelling usually is larger than other types of homes. If you don't like mowing lawns and landscaping, then a home with a large yard isn't for you.

- **Townhouses:** These dwellings are similar to single-family homes, but they usually share a wall or two with the next-door neighbor. In most cases, townhouses have two to four levels with small front yards and backyards. Townhouse communities often share common areas and charge homeowner association fees. Common areas can include such amenities as landscaping, pools, lifeguards, clubhouses, roads, gates, doormen, or security guards. The population is denser in townhouse developments, so parking may be at a premium.

- **Condominiums:** This type of home can look like a single-family dwelling, townhouse, or apartment. The difference is that ownership refers to a specific dwelling and an undivided interest in common areas such as hallways, parking, and recreation areas. Condominium owners are expected to pay condominium fees that cover the expenses of maintaining the common areas. In general, condominium living reduces the responsibility of exterior home maintenance. However, some condominium fees can be greater than the monthly fee for the individual dwelling.

- **Co-ops:** Popular in large cities like New York, Chicago, San Francisco, and so on, ownership in a co-op provides the owner with an interest in the corporation that owns the unit where his or her individual dwelling is located. In many situations, co-ops interview prospective owners and decide whether they can live by the rules of the co-op. As part of the interview process, individuals may have to provide financial statements to the interview committee. One reason for the close scrutiny of new owners is that co-ops usually are densely populated and require neighbors to be neighborly.

- **New home versus established home:** Another decision you must make is whether you want a new or established home. If you're someone who's handy with fixing things, then an established home may be the way to go. If you purchase an existing home, be prepared for repairs such as heaters or air conditioners that may fail. If you frequently travel or don't know one end of a hammer from the other, buying a new home may be the best decision. If you purchase a new home, however, be prepared to landscape the yard (or fill in what the builder has provided) and buy window treatments, extra shelving in the garage, and so on.

Most homeowners sell their homes in five years, which means that when you select your housing type, you need to consider the resale value of your home. Realtor.com (`www.realtor.com`) provides these suggestions:

- The most popular single-family dwelling has three bedrooms and two baths.

- A one-bedroom condominium is harder to sell than a two-bedroom condominium.

- Two-bedroom, single-bath single-family dwellings are harder to sell than three-bedroom homes with two baths.

- Homes on busy streets or near commercial buildings often are harder to sell and may sell for less money than homes located in more-residential neighborhoods.

Remember that ocean view isn't the same as ocean front.

What features do you want in your home?

Before you spend hours searching for a home, having a good idea of the home features that you require, desire, and just don't want is important. Table 13-1, adapted from my book *Unofficial Guide to Buying a Home Online* (Wiley, 2000), shows one way you can sort your priorities.

Table 13-1   Features You May Want or Need in Your New Home

Gotta Have Features	Wanna Have Features	Not on Your Life Features
Close to the school you want your children to attend	A good view	High crime area at night
Located in a specific neighborhood	A deck	Located next to a highway or congested area
No city or county restrictions against a home-based business	A specific type of architecture	A specific type of architecture
Built on one level with no or few steps or the ability to adapt to the handicapped	Hardwood flooring throughout the house, entertainment center	Other features that are not acceptable

(continued)

Table 13-1 *(continued)*

Gotta Have Features	Wanna Have Features	Not on Your Life Features
Enough room for you, the family, furniture, your office, pets, and other things that make your life comfortable	Neutral colors or specific colors for carpeting, walls, the exterior, roof, and so on	Other features that are not acceptable
Enough bedrooms and bathrooms to accommodate the family and several guests	Whirlpool in the master bedroom (unless it is for medical reasons)	Other features that are not acceptable
Backyard or enough room on your lot so the children can play outside	Built-in bar, brass lighting fixtures, faucets, door handles, and skylights.	Other features that are not acceptable
Storage space, ample closets, and eat-in kitchen	Bay windows, special window treatments, and swimming pool	Other features that are not acceptable
Garage, central heating and air conditioning	Swimming pool and built-in bookshelves	Other features that are not acceptable

House Hunting without Leaving Your Computer

The convenience of the Internet enables home buyers and mortgage seekers to save time and money. For most people, purchasing a home is the largest and most important financial decision they ever make. Investing in a home is a long-term commitment. The money you've invested in your home won't be available for emergencies or to provide you with a quick source of cash. Although the current real estate market is heated, you can lose money even in a hot market. Sometimes homes are difficult to sell because nearby schools close, neighborhood crime increases, or more homes are built, increasing the population density to an uncomfortable level. Sometimes a home decreases in value simply because a beautiful view is blocked or destroyed in some way.

The following list of online home buyer megasites can help you get your online search started in the right direction:

- ✔ **iVillage** (www.ivillage.com) provides easy-to-understand articles about home buying. At the home page click on "Money," and then click on "Home" or "Mortgage."

- ✔ **MSN House & Home** (www.houseandhome.msn.com) offers information about buying a home, loans and financing, insurance, moving and relocation, and more.

- ✔ **Real Estate Article.com** (www.realestatearticle.com) includes articles about agents, appraisals, mortgages, foreclosures, insurance, moving, and more.

Hooking up with a real estate agent

The Internet assists home buyers in understanding the price ranges of homes in specific neighborhoods, the types of houses that are for sale, and who the top-rated agents are in your area of interest. In the early years of the Internet, it looked like the Web might put real estate agents out of business. The *opposite* is true. The Internet makes real estate agents more important then ever. Agents can advertise their access codes in newspaper ads, so potential customers can see the listings (and get 360-degree virtual tours of homes for sale) and contact the agents by e-mail, telephone, or pager. In other words, real estate agents help you leverage the information you receive online. They also offer market expertise, assist with buyer/seller negotiations, and help you find financing for your dream home.

Real estate agents come in several flavors. Selecting the wrong flavor can cost you more dollars when you purchase your home. The following list describes different types of real estate agents:

- ✔ **Brokers or brokerages** are state-licensed to conduct a real estate business. Some brokers also are agents and combine sales and management.

- ✔ **Real estate agents** are salespeople who help home buyers or home sellers. In some cases, a real estate agent may represent both buyer and seller in a transaction. If you're a home buyer and the real estate agent is also representing the home seller, make sure you know which party the real estate agent truly represents.

- ✔ **Realtors** are agents or brokers who belong to the local or state boards of realtors, which are affiliated with the National Association of Realtors (NAR). These agents and brokers follow a code of ethics that's stricter than state laws. They sponsor the Multiple Listing System (MLS), which they use to list several million homes for sale throughout the nation.

- ✔ **New home agents** represent builders or building representatives, which can be an insurance company, bank, or other entity. You can select the new home agent or your own agent to represent you. Either way you go, the builder needs to pay for the agent's commission.

Taking a close look at agents reveals that they can be broken into several categories. For example, you can select an agent who represents the seller, an agent who represents the buyer, or an agent who represents the buyer and the seller. Here's how those differing situations are described:

- ✔ **Listing agents:** These agents usually represent the seller. In other words, they must negotiate in favor of the seller and put the seller's interest first.

- ✔ **Subagents:** These people usually bring information and deals to buyers but nevertheless represent the seller.

- ✔ **Buyer agents:** These people represent home buyers. Only the buyer agent can legally negotiate for the buyer. The buyer agent puts the buyer's interests first. The buyer agent works for the buyer and provides information and client-level advocacy.

- ✔ **Exclusive buyer agents:** These agents work for firms that represent only buyers. These companies don't list properties but are bound by the National Association of Exclusive Buyer Agents (NAEBA) standards of practices and codes of ethics. They are 100 percent loyal to the home buyers they represent and can advise buyers when not to purchase a home and point out property flaws.

- ✔ **Dual agents:** These agents play the role of mediator. A dual agent represents the buyer and the seller. The only one who actually wins in this situation is the agent. Hiring a dual agent may not be in the best interest of the home buyer.

As a general rule, a buyer agent or an exclusive buyer agent is best for a home buyer. Buyer agents can show you any home that's for sale and negotiate on your behalf. Buyer agents provide unbiased facts about the true value of a home, the market, and obvious housing defects. Additionally, a buyer agent helps you find financing and often suggests that you seek preapproval for a home loan.

For more information about buyer agents, see the following companies' Web sites:

- ✔ **The Home Buyer's Center** (www.homebuyerscenter.com) offers information about the duties and responsibilities of exclusive buyer agents, links to homes for sale, and a useful comparison checklist of buyer agents versus seller agents.

- ✔ **Exclusive Buyers Agents.com** (www.exclusivebuyersagents.com), which provides geographical listings of exclusive buyer agents. You can find your local exclusive buyer agent with this listing.

- ✔ **National Association of Exclusive Buyer Agents** (www.naeba.org) provides information about types of buyer agents, suggested interview questions, and links to other relevant Web sites for home buyers. You also can find information about how you can search for an exclusive buyer agent in your area.

- ✔ **1agent** (`www.1agent.com`) is a free service designed to assist you in finding the best real estate agent in the area where you want to live. The company looks into the educational backgrounds of the agents who are recommended. Brokerages pay a fee to 1agent.com to be included in their recommendations.

Taking virtual home tours

The Internet is ideal for offering online tours of homes. At any given time, more than 2 million homes are listed for sale on the Internet. Most well-known real estate brokerages have Web sites that enable you to view the homes they represent. Overall, the Internet offers many online tours of homes. You can search a database of properties for locations, home types, and features you're seeking and then take a virtual tour of the homes that meet your requirements. The following are a few examples of what you'll find online:

- ✔ **Coldwell Banker** (`www.coldwellbanker.com`) includes photos and lengthy descriptions of homes that may interest you. Tools like Neighborhood Explorer rank schools, median income, and age of residents. Your Personal Retriever tool continues your search and sends the results to your e-mail box. You even get a personalized Web page called My Coldwell Banker that lets you save listings or other information.

- ✔ **Homegain.com** (`www.homegain.com`) assists you in finding and comparing real estate agents; viewing new, existing, and foreclosed homes for sale; finding a mortgage; and determining how much your home is worth.

- ✔ **Homeseekers.com** (`www.homeseekers.com`) is a nationwide database of all types of real estate listings for sale or lease.

- ✔ **NewHomeGuide.com** (`www.newhomeguide.com`) offers online publications about new homes and the new-homes market.

- ✔ **Realtor.com** (`www.realtor.com`), illustrated in Figure 13-1, is *the* starting place for anyone beginning his or her home-buying search. This Web site includes more than 2 million listings in the 50 states and Canada. The sophisticated search engine can refine your search requirements so you don't receive tons of useless results.

Home insurance companies look at your dream home's claims history. You can order a copy of the same report from the Comprehensive Loss Underwriting Exchange (CLUE) for $13 at `www.choicetrust.com`.

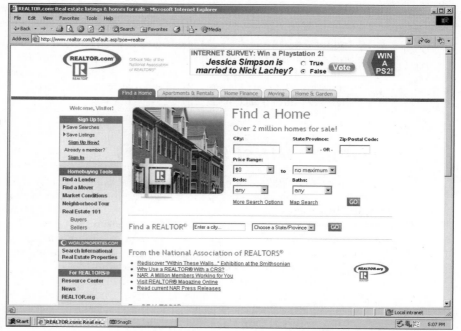

Figure 13-1:
Realtor.com
is the home
of the online
Multiple
Listing
System
(MLS) and
includes
more than
2 million
homes
for sale.

Getting online neighborhood reports

Homeseekers.com (www.homeseekers.com) can help you discover whether a
home is overpriced. You can search for homes here and in countries such as
England, Spain, France, and Korea. Homeseekers.com includes the ability to
check the sales prices in a certain neighborhood and find out about homes
in foreclosure. Property listings include many details. You can narrow your
search by selecting specific features, such as saunas, views, or swimming
pools.

✔ **Realtor.com** (www.realtor.com) offers neighborhood reports that
   include information about schools, the city, and crime. At the home
   page, click on "Moving." Next, click on the report in the left margin that
   you're seeking.

✔ **Crimecheck.com** (www.capindex.com/resframe.html) provides up-to-
   the-minute neighborhood crime reports. The price is $9.95 for the first
   CrimeCheck report and $7.95 for subsequent reports (at time of order).
   You receive the only address-specific crime-risk report available.

✔ **Homegain.com** (homegain.relodigest.com) offers detailed neighborhood profiles for any zip code within the U.S. Reports include weather, crime statistics, demographics, wealth breakdown, and more.

The Internet can assist you in spotting overpriced homes. You can determine the value of your dream home by using Internet-based automated-valuation models. Some automated-valuation reports are free and others are fee-based. For instance, HomeRadar.com (www.homeradar.com) is an excellent example of what you can find online. House Clicks, at www.houseclicks.com/selling/cma.html, provides good articles about the usefulness of competitive market analysis (CMA) and shows how you can prepare your own CMA analysis. Remember you may pay less than you expect by using CMA online tools.

Chapter 14

Financing a House Online

- -

In This Chapter

▶ Getting a grasp of the jargon used in mortgage lending

▶ Overcoming the down payment hurdle

▶ Qualifying for your dream home

▶ Making sure you can pay the closing costs

- -

This chapter covers quite a bit of ground. First I help you come to grips with the mortgage process and selecting a mortgage that's right for you. Then I show you how you can finance your dream home — that is, apply for a mortgage — online. You can use the Internet to calculate your maximum mortgage amount so that if you're caught in a bidding war for the home you desire, you know when to stop. And I help you locate the best Web sites for online mortgage shopping.

You gain a better understanding of different types of home loans and discover special programs that can help you overcome the down-payment hurdle. You likewise find out how creative financing, gift-assistance programs, and special first-time-buyer deals can make your dream home a reality and how you can use the Internet to prequalify or receive preapproval for a loan.

I discuss what lenders look for when they check out your credit report, how much you must pay in closing costs, and how you can lower your costs by providing a few tips to help you lower the expense.

Understanding the Mortgage Process

Most of us don't have the ready cash to pay for a home, so we need to apply for a mortgage. A *mortgage* is a loan that's secured by the value of the property that you're purchasing. In other words, your home is collateral for the mortgage. Homebuyers can obtain a mortgage from an online mortgage lender, an *online aggregator* (a company that screens loan applicants for lenders), traditional savings and loans, banks, or credit unions.

You can work directly with the lender or mortgage broker. Mortgage brokers work for a fee in a manner that's similar to independent insurance agents'. For a fee, brokers bring lenders and borrowers together for loan origination. More than 50 percent of all loans in the United States are originated by brokers. Employing a mortgage broker is advantageous whenever your finances don't fit a cookie-cutter mold. For example, a broker may find a loan program that fits your unique situation. In some situations, a broker can find funding for you whenever your credit history isn't flawless, when you're self-employed, or when you have variable income.

Brokers can speed up the closing time, oversee the processing, and get you a good interest rate, but all of these services aren't free. You pay a commission that may be included as a document-preparation or document-processing charge. Brokerage fees vary, so make sure to ask your broker exactly what the fee is and who pays it.

Mortgage banker is a term that refers to loan officers who work at banks. A mortgage bank usually sells underlying loans to investors but continues to service the loans. Because these loans frequently are bundled or sold together in the secondary mortgage market, the entire operation doesn't include much flexibility.

The mortgage process relies on the basic steps that I outline in my book *The Unofficial Guide to Buying a Home Online* (Wiley, 2000). You can expect some differences from lender to lender, but you can expect the following even if you apply for a mortgage online. The nine steps are

1. **Completing the application.**

   The application takes about 30 minutes to complete online and about 45 minutes to complete if you're working offline. The application is a standardized form used by all lenders. Be prepared to pay appraisal and application fees when submitting your application.

2. **Checking your credit rating and prequalifying.**

   With your approval and payment, the lender checks your credit report. Before you apply for a mortgage, it's wise to check your credit rating so you can determine the types of loans for which you qualify and don't qualify, if you don't already know.

3. **Hearing from the lender by telephone.**

   If you've applied online, a loan officer contacts you via e-mail or telephone to verify your loan application information.

4. **Locking in your interest rate and appraising the property.**

   After the loan type and amount are determined, you can lock in the interest rate and loan approval for about 45 days. The lender then orders an appraisal of the property.

5. **Putting together loan documentation, verification, and other paperwork.**

   At this point, you receive a copy of your application, disclosure forms, and a document checklist via fax or the U.S. mail, and the lender analyzes your loan for completeness, verifies the information you submitted, confirms the value of the property with the appraisal, and determines whether the property has any encumbrances, judgments, or liens.

6. **Submitting the loan to the lender.**

   When all the paperwork is collected, the package is submitted to the lender for underwriting.

7. **Underwriting the loan and final approval.**

   A loan underwriter reviews the loan package and faxes an approval and any conditions that need your approval to your mortgage banker or broker.

8. **Delivering loan documents by express mail.**

   The lender completes the loan package and forwards the package to the escrow agent. The escrow agent contacts you and coordinates a convenient time to sign all the documents. The loan closing is coordinated with the loan closer, the seller, the real estate agent(s), and the escrow agent.

9. **Attending the closing when the big day is finally here.**

   You go to the office of the settlement attorney and sign the documents. The lender reviews the documents, and the escrow agent requests a wire transfer of the loan funds and then records and closes the transaction. Although the exact closing procedure may vary from state to state, the results are the same. When you finish the closing, your dream home is yours.

 At the request of regulators, mortgage applicants receive an optional form from the lender that asks about the borrower's race or national origin and gender. Whether you complete this form doesn't play any role in whether your loan application is accepted or denied.

The Most Common Types of Mortgages

The most popular home loans can be divided into four categories:

✔ **Fixed loans:** Fifteen- or thirty-year fixed-rate loans have payments that are the same for the life of the loan. Borrowers tend to be conservative. If interest rates increase, you benefit because your interest rate remains the same for the life of the loan. These loans are best for borrowers who plan to stay put for at least seven years.

✔ **Adjustable-rate mortgage (ARM) loans:** The interest rate for an ARM is fixed for a specific period of time, but then it changes on a predetermined basis (either monthly, quarterly, or annually). An ARM is for borrowers who can accept the risk of moderate interest-rate fluctuations and are willing to take the chance of higher payments in the future for lower payments now. Borrowers who are likely to move or refinance their homes within five years of purchase benefit most from ARMs, and so do borrowers who can live with the possibility of higher interest rates in return for lower short-term monthly payments and interest rates.

✔ **Interest-only loans:** Only interest is paid for a predetermined period of time, and then interest and principal payments are paid. Borrowers who use this type of loan can accept high-interest-rate risk. They want to keep payments as low as possible in the short term (but expect much higher payments later). Borrowers benefit by making payments that are as much as 20 percent less than usual to start out. This type of loan usually is best for borrowers who believe their incomes will increase in the future.

✔ **Piggyback loans:** Piggyback loans are a type of two-for-one loan — two mortgages (or a mortgage and a line of credit or equity line) at the same time. This type of loan benefits borrowers who can't meet the down-payment hurdle and also want to avoid private mortgage insurance (PMI). Some borrowers use piggyback loans to avoid jumbo mortgage rates. This type of loan often is ideal for buyers whose cost for PMI is greater than the interest on the piggyback loan.

These four types of loans are only the beginning of what's available. Because of the broad range of loan offerings, a mortgage that's tailor-made for every applicant probably can be found. Using the Internet, prospective homebuyers often find loans that meet their unique needs and desires.

The Internet can help you with what may be the biggest financial decision of your life — purchasing a home. Sites on the World Wide Web like the ones in the list that follows provide vast amounts of information on selecting and financing your dream home:

✔ **Bankrate.com** (www.bankrate.com) offers many articles about selecting a conventional mortgage. At the top of the home page, click "Mortgages," and then scroll down the page, clicking on titles that are of interest to you.

✔ **HUD** (www.hud.gov/buying/insured.cfm) offers unbiased information about FHA guidelines and requirements.

✔ **SmartMoney.com** (www.smartmoney.com) offers information about what kind of conventional home loan you need to select, worksheets, and more. At the top of the home page, click on "Personal Finance" and then on "Real Estate."

✔ **VA Loans** (www.homeloans.va.gov/veteran.htm) offers online pamphlets about eligibility, education for first-time homebuyers, Veteran Administration–approved lenders, and more.

FHA and VA Loans

FHA loans are home loans that are insured by the Federal Housing Administration. FHA loans are open to qualified home purchasers. Just about anyone who qualifies for an FHA loan receives a loan. You don't have to be a U.S. citizen, but you must have a Social Security number and be eligible to work in the United States. The property you're purchasing must be your principal residence.

The FHA has maximum loan limits that are determined by the county in your state. The FHA Mortgage Limits page (`entp.hud.gov/idapp/html/hicostlook.cfm`) allows you to look up FHA mortgage limits for your area or several areas and then lists them by state and county of Metropolitan Statistical Area.

To qualify for an FHA loan, you're required to show that you have sufficient income to pay a mortgage. You're required to use at least 3 percent of your own funds for the purchase of your home. If you don't have the funds, you're allowed to receive a "gift" from a family member, your employer, a charitable organization, or government agency. The gift must not be expected or imply repayment. A letter from the gift giver is required. The letter should state that the gift giver doesn't expect to be paid back. FHA focuses on your overall credit paying history, not just isolated incidences of financial problems. For more online information about qualifying for an FHA loan, see the following Web sites:

- **HUD's Homes and Communities** (`www.hud.gov/buying/insured.cfm`) states that HUD doesn't give you the FHA loan directly. (You need to apply at your local HUD-approved lender.) However, this Web site offers information about how to qualify for an FHA loan.

- **MSN House and Home** (`houseandhome.msn.com/financing/guides/specialloans.aspx`) offers an online guide that can help you determine whether you qualify for a FHA, VA, or other special loan designed to bring homeownership to first-time and low- to moderate-income buyers. Don't hesitate to check out this Web site to find out more about these money-saving options.

A *VA loan* is defined as a loan guaranteed by the U.S. Department of Veterans Affairs (VA). VA loans are made to honorably discharged veterans or their unremarried widows or widowers. Such loans require a small or no down payment and offer lower interest rates. The advantages of a VA loan include

- No down payment in most cases

- Loan maximum up to 100 percent of the VA-established reasonable value of the property

- No private mortgage insurance (PMI) premiums

- Assumable mortgages, subject to VA approval of the assumer's credit
- 30-year fixed loan rates
- No prepayment penalty

To receive a VA loan, you must apply for a home loan with a VA approved lender. The VA guarantees the home loan with the lender. Lenders must also comply with VA income and credit standards. For more about how you can qualify for a VA loan, see these Web sites:

- **VA Loan Guaranty Homepage** (www.homeloans.va.gov) offers online guides, pamphlets, and videos to show how the main purpose of the VA home loan program is to help veterans finance the purchase of homes with favorable loan terms and at interest rates that are competitive with the rates charged on other type of mortgage loans.

- **VA Mortgage Center.com** (www.vamortgagecenter.com/prequalify.htm) offers information about the eligibility requirements for a VA loan. If you'd like to prequalify for a VA loan, fill out the form on the page. A VA loan specialist will help you determine how much you prequalify for and can also answer any questions you have. You'll be contacted within three business hours with your approval information.

Shopping for a Mortgage Online

You can shop online for a mortgage in one of two ways:

- Go directly to one online lender and apply for a mortgage.
- Go to an aggregator's Web site and complete the same home loan application forms. (An *aggregator* enables buyers within a market to select among various competitors by combining information about the market and suppliers and providing this information via the Web site.)

The aggregator screens your application before it's sent to multiple lenders. These mortgage lenders then render a decision on the application.

Top-rated online mortgage lenders

About one in ten mortgages originates online every year. This number is expected to increase in the future as the Internet matures and more people become experienced with managing their money using the Internet. The following are several of the nation's top online and offline mortgage lenders:

- ✔ **Chase Manhattan** (`mortgage02.chase.com/noframes/gateway.jsp`) offers a step-by-step guide to getting an online mortgage. Detailed information is included in "Upfront Planning," "Finding Your Home," "Getting a Mortgage," and "Summary of Key Steps."

- ✔ **Countrywide Financial** (`www.countrywide.com`) is the leading mortgage lender in the United States. Its Web site is easy to navigate, and finding information is trouble-free.

- ✔ **GMAC Mortgage** (`www.gmacmortage.com`) offers an online mortgage path that can assist you in determining which loan type is best for you. Additionally, you can receive a free homeowner's insurance quote.

- ✔ **Wells Fargo** (`www.wellsfargo.com/mortgage`) offers online tools, products, and online assistance related to home buying, first-time home buying, finding the right loan for you, and other home-buying tools.

Top-rated online mortgage loan aggregators

Loan aggregators can save you time and money by signing up a large group of consumers to bargain on their behalf for the lowest possible price for loans. That is, the firm aggregates many smaller customers into one large customer for the purpose of negotiation. You don't have to leave work early to meet with a lender, and when working with a loan aggregator, the application or origination fees are often waived. However, third-party fees may be included in the estimates for closing costs. Make sure that you find out exactly what the lender's fees (loan application, origination, document preparation, processing, and underwriting) are before you make any commitments.

Loan aggregators make it easy to comparison shop several loans at one time. Moreover, you can even look for that perfect loan at any time 24/7/365. The following is a short list of the top-rated online mortgage loan aggregators:

- ✔ **E-Loan** (`www.e-loan.com`) offers mortgage rates, preapproval, estimates of closing costs, and applications for a loan. This site features a glossary and links to helpful services, and you also can discover which loan type is best for you.

- ✔ **Lending Tree** (`www.lendingtree.com`) provides what may appear as too much information too soon, but don't let that turn you away. After wading through several Web pages, you can expect smooth navigating on this valuable Web site.

- ✔ **Priceline.com** (`www.priceline.com`) offers Priceline Mortgage, which includes guaranteed closing costs, preapproval, and loan application, in addition to other banking services and information.

Calculating your maximum mortgage amount

Lenders use several formulas to determine the maximum amount of a mortgage you can afford. First, the lender looks at your current gross income and the amount of your debt payments. For example, say that you and your spouse both work, and your monthly gross income is $8,000 per month. Currently, your auto and credit card payments are $800 per month.

Generally, lenders allow you 29 percent of your gross monthly income towards housing costs (which include mortgage payments, property taxes, homeowner's insurance, and private mortgage insurance, if applicable). For example, multiply $8,000 times 0.29 for a suggested maximum mortgage payment of $2,320.

The lender then looks at your suggested mortgage amount of $2,320 with your minimum monthly payments on other long-term debts, and if the total doesn't exceed 41 percent of your gross income (in this case about $3,280), then your mortgage is likely to be approved.

Your current debt ratio is $800/$8,000 — 10 percent. Lenders don't want to see your debt ratio greater than 41 percent of your gross income. If you're approved for your loan, your total debt is $3,120. Your new debt ratio is 39 percent ($3,120/$8,000). This is less than 41 percent, so the lender is likely to approve your loan. (These ratios are general examples and may not apply to all situations.)

Luckily you don't have to do the math to determine your maximum mortgage amount. Just about all online mortgage lenders include mortgage calculators at their Web sites. Also, the Internet provides many calculators to help you determine the maximum amount a lending institution will allow you for a mortgage loan under normal conditions. The following are a few examples:

- **Finance calculators and advice** (www.reficenter.com/calculators.htm) offers a collection of articles, calculators, and service providers listed on one Web page. Find Mortgage Calculators, and then click on "How Much Will Your Payments Be?"

- **Mortgage calculators** (www.mortgage-calc.com) provides mortgage calculations and information for homebuyers. The online calculators offer quick and easy access to mortgage calculation for your home-buying needs.

- **Home Buyer's Information Center** (www.ourfamilyplace.com/homebuyer/mortcalc.html) supplies an easy-to-use online mortgage-payment calculator in addition to home-buying advice.

Making a point about points

You may have heard how some borrowers pay points to reduce their monthly payments. A *point* is a cash increment equal to 1 percent of the loan amount. Each point customarily is worth .25 percent interest on the loan. Paying 2 percent of the loan amount at closing (upfront) can reduce your loan's interest rate by 0.5 percent. Paying points can reduce your payments enough so that your monthly payments are below or equal to the amount needed for lender approval.

Overcoming the Down-Payment Hurdle

Home affordability includes several factors. The first one on the list is the down payment. If you don't have enough money for a down payment that's 20 percent of the home's value, don't be discouraged. If you qualify, many lenders can offer you a mortgage that's equal to 100 percent of the purchase price or even 103 percent of the purchase price. Lenders underwriting mortgages with down payments as little as 3 percent isn't uncommon.

Large or small down payment?

Two schools of thought figure into determining how large a down payment you need to make. The first theory is that small down payments result in your having cash for emergencies, landscaping, furniture, and home improvements. You can invest the money you don't use for a down payment in financial securities that can provide higher profits when your home is appreciating at a rate that's less than the stock market. Another advantage is more interest deductions on your income taxes.

The second theory is that homebuyers who make large down payments earn lower interest rates from lenders. For people with variable incomes, that approach may be a good one, because the mortgage always is affordable; moreover, no additional PMI costs are charged.

One source of a down payment is tapping into your 401(k) retirement account. You can repay the loan over five or more years, with interest. Most 401(k) plans enable you to borrow up to $50,000 of your balance or 50 percent — whichever is less.

No- or low-down-payment loans

Not being able to save enough cash for a hefty down payment frequently prevents many families from purchasing a home. To help increase homeownership, the government sponsors several no- and low-down-payment plans. The following are a few examples:

- ✔ **VA loans:** These loans are geared for eligible veterans and reservists. They enable them to purchase a home with a maximum price of up to $203,000 with no down payment. Qualification guidelines tend to be more flexible than FHA (see later bullet point for details) or other conventional loans. For more information about eligibility, see www.home loans.va.gov/eligibility.htm.

- ✔ **RHS loans:** These loans are provided by the U.S. Department of Agriculture, Rural Housing Services for farmers, and others buying property in rural areas. For more information, visit the Department of Agriculture Web site at www.rurdev.usda.gov/rhs/index.html.

- ✔ **FHA loans:** These loans are provided by the U.S. Department of Housing and Urban Development (HUD) and Federal Housing Authority (FHA). They have no eligibility restrictions. Private lenders make HUD-insured FHA residential mortgage loans. With FHA insurance, you can purchase a home with a down payment of as little as 3 percent of the purchase price. FHA loans have maximum loan limits that vary by geographic location.

- ✔ **State and local government loan programs:** Many state and local governments provide special loan programs that offer below-market interest rates to qualifying individuals. Some programs include help with closing costs. Many individuals are surprised by the high level of income that's acceptable to participate in these programs. Given the nature of these programs, expect plenty of paperwork (which can be time-consuming). But the result — owning your own home — makes it worth the time and effort.

Using a little creative financing

Here's another way to purchase a home with little or no down payment. The Multiple Listing Service (MLS) offer hundreds of thousands of homes for sale throughout the country. What the MLS doesn't advertise is which of these homes are available with no down payment or a low down payment. That's right, with a little creative financing, you often can fashion a no- or low-down-payment offer that's advantageous to both the seller and the buyer. The following are a few examples:

TIP

✔ **Assuming someone else's mortgage:** Many mortgages are assumable. If you don't want to qualify for your own loan, you can often purchase the home by assuming the seller's loan. Additionally, the loan may have a low interest rate and other advantages.

If the loan is nonassumable and in default, the lender may still be motivated to accept your request. In this way, the lender avoids foreclosing on the property.

✔ **Seller-take-back:** If the seller is motivated to get out of town fast, he or she may be interested in a seller-take-back purchase. Suppose the home price is $100,000 and the mortgage is $70,000. The lender lets you assume the 30-year fixed mortgage. You now owe the lender $70,000 and the seller $30,000. The seller gives you a second mortgage, or a *seller-take-back* for five years (as an example) at an interest rate that's below the market rate.

✔ **Renting with an option to buy:** In this situation, you rent the home for a predetermined period of time with an option to buy at a mutually agreed-upon price. Some or all of your rental payments may be applied to the purchase price. The purchase price is locked in at what may become a very favorable level.

✔ **Equity sharing:** Sometimes called a *shared appreciation mortgage* (SAM), *equity sharing* is when you make monthly payments at a below-market interest rate, and you agree to share with the lender a portion (usually 30 percent to 50 percent) of the appreciation in your home's value, either when you sell or transfer the home or after an agreed-upon number of years have passed.

Checking out gift-assistance programs

In addition to the creative financing tactics outlined in the preceding section, several nonprofit organizations provide homebuyers with gift assistance. Although sellers can't provide buyers with a down payment to purchase a home, nonprofit organizations are able to give money to buyers. These gifts are from funds provided by sellers, home builders, and others. Many gifts don't have to be repaid, but others do. Your lender can tell you which nonprofit organizations comply with HUD requirements and are on the up and up. The following are a few gift-assistance programs you can find online:

✔ **Gift America Program** (www.giftamerica.org) is a nonprofit organization that provides a cash gift to the homebuyer for a down payment (after the mortgage application has been approved but prior to closing). From the proceeds of the sale, the seller makes a contribution back to GiftAmerica to replenish the funds GiftAmerica used to provide the gift to the buyer.

✔ **Nehemiah Program** (www.getdownpayment.com/buyers/index.asp) is a down-payment assistance program for buyers of new homes. Gifts either range in value from 1 percent to 6 percent of the home's sale price or are a flat amount. Gifts are contributions and processing fees from homebuyers, lenders, builders, and sellers who use the Nehemiah Program. The gift doesn't need to be repaid.

✔ **RealtyAmerica.org** (`www.realtyamerica.org`) is a nonprofit organization with a gift program that provides buyers with money for a down payment or closing costs. Gifts can be up to 5 percent of the purchase price of the home. Gifts greater than 5 percent require special consideration. The gift program isn't restricted to first-time homebuyers, and funds don't have to be repaid.

Spotting Special First-Time Homebuyer Deals

First-time homebuyers are in a category all their own. Many government entities and organizations, in an effort to increase homeownership in the nation, created a variety of first-time ownership programs and deals. For example, first-time homebuyers can withdraw up to $10,000 without penalty from an Individual Retirement Account (IRA). You have to pay taxes on the amount you withdraw, but it's a good source for a down payment. Even if you don't have an IRA to tap into, three other types of first-time-homebuyer programs can be used:

✔ **Down payment assistance programs:** These programs often are sponsored by state and local governments to provide first-time homebuyers with the money for a down payment. These funds are grants that you may have to repay or that may have several restrictions. For example, repayment may be required when the home is sold or the borrower moves within a predetermined time period. These programs can also include deferred payments that are second mortgages, loans at below-market interest rates, or any combination of the previously listed items.

✔ **Mortgage credit certificates:** Lenders offer these credits in partnership with the Internal Revenue Service (IRS). Interest payments are nontaxable; therefore, the mortgage credit certificate shows employers that taxes shouldn't be deducted from the homebuyer's paycheck, which, in turn enables homebuyers to make larger house payments.

✔ **Subsidized interest rate loans:** Many states offer these loans to first-time homebuyers. Contact your state's housing finance agency to discover whether you're eligible for a special loan program, closing cost discount, or any other type of benefit that isn't included in a conventional loan. For example, at `www.bankrate.com/brm/news/mtg/20001102b.asp`, Bankrate offers hyperlinks to the housing finance agencies in all 50 states.

The Internet lists many city, local, and state entities that offer first-time homebuyers special programs that pay for the homebuyer's down payment or that offer lower-than-usual interest rates. Ameridream (www.ameridream.org) is a nonprofit organization administered by HUD that's geared toward first-time homebuyers. The organization offers assistance to first-time buyers of single-family homes valued up to $322,700 and multifamily homes valued up to $620,500. Gifts typically range from 2 percent to 6 percent of the home's sale price. Gifts can be used toward down payments or closing costs. The amount of the gift you may receive depends, in part, on the maximum allowed by the lender. The average gift is $7,500, and the maximum gift amount is $10,000.

Qualifying for Your Dream Home

The two ways you can get the nod for a home loan are *loan prequalification,* which you can receive almost instantly over the Internet, and *loan preapproval,* which requires a loan underwriter. For loan preapproval, you complete your loan application online and follow up with documentation supporting your application. The turnaround time generally is within 24 hours.

Keep in mind that neither loan prequalification nor loan preapproval is the same as loan approval.

Loan prequalification

To gain a competitive edge in a hot real estate market, it's often wise to be pre-qualified before you make an offer. A prequalification letter is important when you interact with real estate agents and sellers because it indicates that you're financially stable and likely to qualify for the necessary loan. *Mortgage loan prequalification* is the process by which you indicate the type and size of the loan you're seeking. You can be prequalified online through many Web sites and instantly receive your prequalification letter, but you need to provide some personal information, including your salary, any other income, your assets, and your debts. These Web sites offer mortgage loan prequalification:

- ✔ **eMortgages.com** (www.emortgages.com) is a California-based company that offers an online Prequal Calcu*Letter* that's both a prequalification calculator and a tool that generates a prequalification letter. The results are based on the borrower's having excellent credit.

- ✔ **Mortgage101.com** (www.mortgage101.com) provides all that you need to prequalify for a mortgage. On the home page, click on the "Prequalify Now" tab.

Getting online loan preapproval

Online preapproval requires a loan underwriter to examine your financial resources and debt to determine whether the mortgage is a good investment for the lender. Your credit rating is the foundation of this part of the mortgage process. To be preapproved for a mortgage, you may have to provide the lender with some or all of the information in the list that follows, including your

- ✔ **W2 ʼrms:** W2 forms from the last two years or a profit-and-loss statemen ̣ if you're self-employed.

- ✔ **Pay stubs:** One to two months' worth of pay stubs. If you're self-employed, provide two to three months' worth of bank statements.

- ✔ **Cash for the down payment:** The underwriter needs to know how much cash you have available for a down payment.

- ✔ **If applicable, submit a gift letter:** A *gift letter* is a document stating the amount of money you expect to receive as a gift toward the down payment or closing costs.

- ✔ **Cash for closing costs:** The underwriter needs to know how much cash you have for closing costs.

- ✔ **Current household income:** This amount includes wages, royalties, bonuses, tips, and irregular income.

- ✔ **Job status:** You need to know how many years you've been with the same employer, your employer's address, and your job description. Some financial institutions factor in your educational background and other nontangible attributes. Here's how one lender calculated my job status when I was refinancing my home: My lender included a Web page stating that my book, *Investing Online For Dummies* (Wiley), was the top-rated book about online investing at Barnes & Noble.

- ✔ **Net worth:** The amount of your assets less the amount of your liabilities. You may want to include your whole-life insurance policies, the appraised value of collections, and other assets.

- ✔ **Tax returns:** Provide tax returns for the last two years.

- ✔ **Financial institution statements:** Bank, brokerage, and related financial institution statements for the last three months.

Some lenders require originals of these materials to verify your financial standing, and as a result, collecting your financial information frequently takes more time than the lender does evaluating it for preapproval. You usually can get mortgage preapproval within 48 hours at many online mortgage-lending Web sites.

Loan preapproval illustrates that you're *credit-approved* for a certain amount of money subject to an acceptable appraisal of the home you select and verification of the documentation you supplied to your lender. Preapproval goes a long way for first-time homebuyers who have no equity and for self-employed individuals who may look bad on paper because they have no regular income. A disadvantage of preapproval is that it shows the seller exactly how much you can spend for a house. Whenever a bidding war erupts for the home, this information can be used against you. That is, you may pay more for the home than you expected because your preapproval information shows you can afford to pay more.

Getting prequalified or preapproved for a loan nevertheless gives you a competitive edge when dealing with realtors and sellers. The online mortgage preapproval forms are usually shorter versions of the lender's long application. Theses two sites provide examples:

- ✔ **ABN AMRO** (www.abnamro.com/com) provides a complete online mortgage origination process. For certain types of mortgages, you can instantly receive online loan approval.

- ✔ **IndyMac Home Bank Lending** (www.indymac.com) offers rates based on credit ratings and provides a list of rates, fees, and other expenses so you can do some comparison shopping. You can instantly print a preapproval letter to show to your real estate agent.

Now for the scary stuff: The role of your credit report in the mortgage process

You need to show the lender how you intend to pay the down payment and closing costs. The lender, in turn, investigates your financial profile. Knowing what lenders look for in your credit report and how you can improve your credit score can assist you in working with a mortgage lender. Credit reports are kept by the three major credit agencies: Experian (www.experian.com), Equifax (www.equifax.com), and TransUnion (www.transunion.com).

Credit reports show your demographic information (name, address, years at that address, and employer). Other information includes all your open lines of credit, including *revolving* (where the credit balance changes each month) or *installment* (payment for a set loan amount), student loans, mortgages, and so on. Individuals who habitually pay their bills late are downgraded by lenders because they represent more risk. (For more about credit reports and how you can improve your credit score, see Chapter 3.)

Credit reports are also used for determining certain ratios of debt to income. As a general rule, lenders require your monthly housing costs (mortgage payments, property taxes, homeowner's insurance, and private mortgage insurance) to amount to no more than 29 percent of your gross monthly income. Additionally, lenders don't like debt ratios that are greater than 41 percent. (The *debt ratio* is the amount of your monthly debt divided by your monthly income.) *Note:* These ratios are general examples and may not apply to all situations.

If you have a high debt ratio, you do have some ways to work around this situation and gain loan approval. If you have a high debt ratio, you can often qualify for a home loan if the amount of the mortgage payment is equal to your current rent or mortgage payment. If you're making a large down payment, lenders frequently downgrade the importance of a high debt ratio. Sometimes, if you have a high debt ratio, you can qualify for a different loan product. For example, you may not qualify for a 30-year fixed loan, but you qualify for a 30-year ARM with a lower rate.

Sometimes your loan application isn't approved even if you have an average to excellent debt ratio. You may be disqualified because you have a poor credit history, previous bankruptcy, or mortgage default on your credit report. You could be disqualified because your income is based on self-employment, commissions, or some other variable source. Additionally, you could be disqualified because you don't have enough cash reserves. For example, not enough cash to offset three mortgage payments in case of some unforeseen event.

These Web sites provide helpful information about how you can qualify for the loan you want:

- **Nolo Encyclopedia** (www.nolo.com/lawcenter/ency/article.cfm/objectID/CFEE8F98-D0D8-4D64-A040221D061458E5) offers an in-depth article about credit scoring and what you can do to improve your score.

- **CBSMarketWatch** (marketwatch.consumerinfo.com/cdtscore.asp) provides a helpful article titled "What is a Credit Score?" that details the elements that make up your credit score.

- **About** (homebuying.about.com/cs/mortgagearticles/a/debt_to_income.htm) shows you the math for conventional loan debt limits. Get explanations about the 28/36 debt ratios that lenders examine.

- **Federal Reserve Bank of San Francisco** (www.frbsf.org/publications/consumer/creditreport.html) offers a useful guide titled "Your Credit Report: What It Says About You." Read this guide to find out about the ins and outs of credit reporting.

Don't Forget Those Inspections

Home inspections are usually optional. For the most part, nobody is going to tell you that you have to have your prospective home inspected, but hiring a professional to inspect the property before you sign on the dotted line always is a good idea. Sellers also can use home inspection reports to get a house ready for sale. The cost of home inspections ranges from $150 to $500. Depending upon where you live, you may want to consider a specialized home inspector, who can

- ✔ Check for evidence of termites and other pests. Additionally, you'll discover whether the home has any existing pest damage.

- ✔ Test for radon. In some areas of the nation, radon tests may be required or part of the physical inspection of the house.

- ✔ Check for cracks in ceilings and walls caused by water damage, especially in older buildings. Cracked cement driveways in newer homes can indicate a water drainage problem.

- ✔ Determine whether the walls, floors, or ceilings contain any asbestos. Expert home inspectors additionally can identify walls that are covered with lead-based paint.

The standard home purchase contract includes many items that a home inspector needs to check. A short list of online sources for home inspectors follows:

- ✔ **American Society of Home Inspectors** (ASHI — www.ashi.com) has provided home inspectors with education, resources, and professional networking opportunities for 28 years. To find a home inspector near you, enter your zip code on the home page.

- ✔ **Home Inspections USA** (www.homeinspections-usa.com) is a national directory of home inspection companies. Click on your state. The next page shows a listing of inspection companies that do business in you state. Click on a company that interests you for a review of the firm, a listing of its locations and services offered, the estimated cost of an inspection, the average time needed to complete an inspection, and contact information for the home inspection company.

- ✔ **National Association of Home Inspectors** (www.nachi.org) is a professional association that offers links to its members. On the home page, click on "Featured Inspectors." You then can search for a home inspector by zip code or city and state.

It's Not Over Until You Pay the Closing Costs

After acquiring the down payment for your dream home, the next hurdle is paying closing (sometimes called settlement) costs. Closing costs are often confusing. Closing costs are one-time fees and expenses that are paid by the buyer and the seller to complete the transfer of ownership. Closing costs can range between 2 percent and 7 percent of the purchase price of your home.

The first hurdle to home buying is overcoming the down-payment expense. The second biggest hurdle is making sure that you have enough cash for closing costs. Many first-time homebuyers are surprised when they discover that closing costs must be paid before they can move into their new homes.

Table 14-1 describes the closing expenses and fees you could expect if you purchased a $500,000 house in El Dorado Hills (Sacramento County), California. Some lenders use jargon to hide extra charges. For example, one lender may not charge an application fee (usually between $200 and $250) but may tack on a document preparation fee at the closing. Savvy consumers know that many of these fees can be negotiated. If you see that you're being charged higher-than-average prices, don't hesitate to ask for a charge to be removed or discounted. The Motley Fool at `www.fool.com/homecenter/deal/deal04.htm` provides a glossary that defines different closing-cost fees and expenses. You can use this glossary to determine whether you're being charged twice for the same service.

Table 14-1 also explains fees paid to third parties. Some of these costs can be lowered when the lender allows the borrower to select his or her own team. For example, the lender needs to have an approved-provider list of appraisers, settlement attorneys, and closing service providers. Most lenders allow you to select your title insurance company. In many cases, you can get a better deal if you shop around.

Government fees are nonnegotiable. Statutory costs are paid to the state for transfer taxes, recording fees for the deed, and other state and local fees. The amounts of these fees usually are based on governmental regulations, such as when real estate taxes are due and the time of the month when the loan closes.

Table 14-1	Example of Closing Costs for a $500,000 Home	
Estimated Lender Fees	*Description*	*Amount*
Points and Processing Fees	Processing/Document preparation/ Underwriting	Varies
Total Lender Fees		Varies
Third-Party Fees	Homeowner's insurance	Varies
	Real estate agent's commission	Varies
	Real estate taxes	Varies
HUD #		
0819	Courier/ exp mail lender	$35.00
1107	Escrow attorney	$1,337.00
0811	Flood check	$25.00
1106	Notary	$95.00
1201	Recording	$85.00
0810	Tax service	$60.00
1302	Termite report	$90.00
0804	Credit report: (Your credit is reported to the lender.)	$35.00
0803	Appraisal	$390.00
1102	Abstract/title	$150.00
1109	Title insurance	$949.00
1113	Title insurance endorsements	$80.00
Total Third-Party Fees		**$3,328.00**

The Internet provides access to many closing-costs calculators and title company Web sites (if you're shopping). Here are a few examples:

✔ **Chicago Title** (www.ctic.com) offers consumer information about what title insurance is. You can discover why title insurance is important and how not having a good title — one that's free and clear of any claims — can possibly affect your ownership in the future.

- **Countrywide Home Loans** (`www.countrywide.com/calculators/closecosts.asp`) offers an online calculator that provides the amount of closing costs you can expect in a given location, based on the purchase price and the loan product used to purchase the home.

- **HUD Settlement Cost Booklet** (`www.hud.gov/offices/hsg/sfh/res/sfhrestc.cfm`) is an unbiased account of what you can expect at closing. You find definitions of specific settlement costs, a sample HUD-1 settlement statement, and a calculator to help you determine how much you need for closing.

- **Stewart Title** (`www.stewart.com`) is a technology-driven global real estate information company that provides title insurance. Stewart provides title insurance and related services through more than 7,000 issuing locations in the United States and several international markets.

Many of your closing costs are tax-deductible. Find out which ones are so you can write them off. You can get started by using information provided by online IRS publications at the Department of the Treasury, Internal Revenue Service located at `www.irs.gov/formspubs/index.html`.

Chapter 15

Buying Your Dream Car Online

· ·

· ·

For most people, making a car purchase is the second largest purchase they'll make next to purchasing a home. Cars and leases can be financed through a finance company, bank, credit union, or even through the Internet. The Internet changed the dynamics of car dealerships. The number of cars sold on the Internet, according to J.D. Power & Associates, was less than 1 percent of the total auto sales in 2000. However, more than 60 percent of all car buyers use the Internet to research cars and compare prices.

Car buyers can, for example, go to the National Automobile Dealers Association Web site at www.nada.com to view the suggested retail price of the car they want. Next Internet users can go to Edmunds (www.edmunds.com) to discover the dealer's invoice price. Gaining this information empowers consumers more than ever before. Further empowering you to get the absolute lowest price possible, this chapter shows you how to select the vehicle that's right for you, how to use online calculators to determine how much car you can afford, and how to compare advantages and limitations of leasing or buying a car. This chapter also covers some of the finer points of getting a good deal on a lease, offers a few warnings about the fine print, and shows how the Internet can help you gracefully exit a lease that just doesn't fit anymore.

The three ways of actually purchasing a vehicle online also are described in this chapter. The first approach is paying the price you see. Saturn dealers, for example, say the price that shows is the price that counts. The second approach is negotiating over the Internet or via e-mail, meaning you don't have to visit the dealership until you're ready to sign the paperwork and pick up the car. The third way is purchasing a prenegotiated car that guarantees a low price. I also cover rebates and how they may or may not result in the best deal and show you how to compare new and used cars and why the used-car market is a great place for a hot, money-saving deal.

Choosing the Right Vehicle

When purchasing a car, identifying your current and future needs is important. If you telecommute and drive only 3,000 miles per year, for example, you often don't care about what the social status of your car implies. Your only interest is likely the car's reliability. On the other hand, if you have an hour-long round-trip commute to the office and travel to different local customer locations every day, you may drive about 30,000 miles per year. In this situation, you're probably using your car as a status symbol when taking clients out to lunch or to project an image of success, so you may be concerned as much about flash and dash as you are about reliability.

Before purchasing your dream car, don't forget to establish

- **Your budget:** Determine how much car you can afford. Longer car loans have lower payments but result in paying more financing fees.

- **An acceptable price range:** Be an educated consumer. Discover the price range of the car you want to purchase by checking online consumer guides, car ads, and manufacturer Web sites.

- **Your financing:** Gain an understanding of the terms and conditions of the different types of car financing. Don't be afraid to shop for great financing. Comparison shop for a good car loan from banks, finance companies, and credit unions.

- **The car's fuel economy:** Fuel-efficient cars are important for the economy and you. The better your car's fuel economy, the better it is for your savings account.

- **Whether you want to lease or buy:** Know the difference between leasing and buying. Uncover the different types of car leases.

- **Your credit history:** Make sure you know your credit history and how it can affect your ability to negotiate.

When purchasing a new car, taking fuel economy into consideration is important. A car that gets more miles to the gallon is good for your savings account and for the environment. The Green Vehicle Guide located at www.epa.gov/emissweb helps you search for a car that gets the best fuel economy, and a Web site called Fuel Economy.gov, located at www.fueleconomy.gov/feg/savemoney.shtml, shows you comparisons of the miles-per-gallon ratings of different car models manufactured since the mid-1980s.

Before purchasing a new car, most car buyers research the Web to get expert reviews, test-drive reports, information about discontinuing and upcoming models, and pricing information about the car you selected and its available option packages. The following are a few of the best Web sites online to begin your research:

- ✔ **Cars.com** (www.cars.com) partners with 175 newspapers, television stations, and their Web sites and aims to be a one-stop shop for people looking to buy or sell a new or used car. The site places vehicle listings from approximately 6,700 dealers alongside nationwide classified advertising and private-party listings, offering consumers new and used cars online. Cars.com combines inventory search tools and new-car configuration with pricing information, photo galleries, buying guides, side-by-side comparison tools, and original editorial content and reviews.

- ✔ **New Car Test Drive** (www.nctd.com) offers many views of each car, in-depth descriptions, and editorial reviews. This company is privately owned but isn't tied to any manufacturer, so you can rest assured that its more than 2,000 online evaluations are unbiased. Make sure you try the test-drive checklist and price-comparison features.

- ✔ **Road and Track** (www.roadandtrack.com) is the original automotive enthusiast's magazine. The magazine's technical expertise and comprehensive road tests are balanced with the experiential and sensual aspects of the driving experience. You can find feature articles, forums, a buyer's guide, and information about auto shows. You can subscribe to the hard-copy monthly magazine ($12 for 12 issues or $22 for 24 issues).

- ✔ **PriceQuotes** (www.pricequotes.com) works like a mega search engine, comparing six auto-buying resources: Invoice Dealers, AutoUSA, AutoNation, Autobytel, AutoWeb, and Car.com. Enter the car you want, your contact information, payment method, and when you want the car. If the car you want can't be found within approximately 50 miles of your location, you won't receive any contact information for a dealership. If your search is successful, up to three dealerships receive your request and contact you via phone or e-mail.

Getting the Best Price

Buying a car is a huge financial commitment. With tens of thousands of dollars at stake, you need to do all you can to get the best price possible for the vehicle you have in mind. Don't spend endless hours traveling from one dealership to another searching for the best deal. Using the resources on the Internet, you can determine how much of a car you can afford, become an educated consumer, and get the best price for a car.

Deciding how much car you can afford

How much can you afford to spend on a car? Most Americans love cars. The latest, the fastest, and the brightest all seem to be what consumers want regardless of the price of the car or the price of gas. General guidelines exist, but no hard and fast rules govern how much you need to spend on a car. If you need to finance a new or used car, you have to consider the amount of the down payment and how much of a car payment you're willing to pay every month. Keep in mind that your car needs to fit comfortably in your overall budget. Loan officers frequently use a general rule that estimates your monthly car payment should never exceed 15 percent of your monthly after-tax income. The three Web sites in the following list offer similar advice:

- ✔ **FinanCenter.com** (www.financenter.com) offers a number of automobile-related calculators. Just select the "How Much Car Can I Afford" calculator. You can try out several "what if?" scenarios by increasing or decreasing your down-payment amount and adjusting other factors.

- ✔ **Nolo** (www.nolo.com) offers an automobile affordability calculator. On the home page, click on "Consumer & Travel," click on "Calculators," and then on "How much car can I afford?" Use this online calculator to determine the most expensive car you can buy.

- ✔ **Bankrate** (www.bankrate.com) offers a "How much car can you afford?" calculator. Bankrate, not surprisingly, takes the view of a loan officer when calculating the maximum sticker price you can afford, based on your monthly budget and the loan terms you select.

The ins and outs of invoice pricing

New car prices can be negotiable and are required by law to carry a manufacturer's suggested retail price. The manufacturer's sticker price is called a Monroney label and is attached to one of the car's windowpanes. The sticker price includes the *base price* of that model (including all standard equipment), manufacturer-installed options, transportation or freight charges (sometimes called destination delivery charges), and the total manufacturer's suggested retail price (MSRP). You also discover details about fuel efficiency on the sticker.

The negotiated final price needs to be between the invoice price and the sticker price. How much you actually pay for the vehicle often depends on market demand. In other words, how much consumers are willing to pay for a particular car.

To find the *invoice price* (what the dealer paid for the vehicle) check out:

- **Edmunds.com** (www.edmunds.com), which offers consumers the invoice price of new and used cars. Edmunds' True Market Value tool enables you to see what others in your geographic area are paying for the car you desire.

- **Intellichoice.com** (www.intellichoice.com) shows the invoice price and the suggested retail price and then makes an intelligent guess at the car's final target price.

To find the suggested manufacturer's retail price (the sticker price), see

- **Kelley Blue Book** (www.kbb.com), which is one of the most useful car Web sites online. You'll find every vehicle and configuration of options that are possible to buy. That critical manufacturer's sticker price information is free.

- **National Automobile Dealers Association Guides** (www.nadaguides.com), which is a directory of value that's comparable to MSRP.

Some dealers may use other stickers that include additional charges, such as dealer-installed options and an additional dealer markup. Some manufacturers prohibit the addition of dealer charges for preparation. After all, for the most part, dealer preparation is just checking to make certain that all the car's bits and pieces are included in the price and adjusted correctly.

Strengthening your bargaining position

Here are a few buying tips to help you be a better negotiator and get the best deal possible.

- **Timing is everything.** Early autumn often is the best time to purchase a car. Dealers are anxious to make room for the next year's models, so they're willing to sell at a discount. Dealerships frequently have monthly and weekly sales quotas, which means that purchasing a car on a Saturday night after the 25th of the month can encourage a salesperson to slightly reduce his sales commission to lock down a sale to reach his quota.

- **Don't be in a hurry.** Make certain that you have plenty of time to negotiate. Prepare a checklist of features and options you want. Don't pay for options you don't have on your list; look for a car that's set up the way you want it.

- ✔ **Don't forget the warranty.** Warranties are another way for automobile companies to compete. Automakers offer a wide variety of differing warranties for new cars.

- ✔ **Check out rebates and incentives.** Many auto manufacturers offer rebates and other incentives on new cars. Read the fine print of the rebate being offered because it may or may not apply to the model of the vehicle you selected. Remember to keep the rebate and car price separate. Negotiate for the lowest price on the new car, and then deduct the rebate from the final car price. Whenever the incentive is a package deal that includes financing, make sure what you're receiving is the best deal for the car.

- ✔ **Avoid the four-square sales strategies.** Salespeople often use a four-square technique to manipulate the numbers. Here's how it works: The four-square method begins with the salesperson dividing a piece of paper into four separate sections for the car price, the trade-in value of your current car, your down payment, and the monthly payment. Each of the four quadrants is negotiated separately. Numbers are crossed out with new numbers quickly written in, making the result look like you made a great deal, when in fact, all you did was let the salesperson know the most you're willing to pay.

Treat car buying like three separate transactions. First, purchase the best car possible for the least amount of money. Second, acquire a loan with the lowest annual percentage (interest) rate (APR) available. Third, trade in your car for the best price.

Taking advantage of rebates and incentives

According to *BusinessWeek*, automakers spent an average $3,775 per vehicle on incentives during January 2004. Keep in mind that the total cost of the car depends on manufacturer's incentives. Let the dealership know in advance that you're aware of the rebate, but don't include the rebate in any of your negotiations. Subtract the rebate only after you've agreed on a final car price. Incentives can include:

- ✔ **Cash-back rebates:** The APR of an auto loan approved by a bank, credit union, or thrift may be low (or lower than what you've been offered by the automaker). When that's the case, take the cash-back rebate. Taking a rebate is better if you plan to keep the car for only two or three years.

- ✔ **Cut-rate financing:** Auto manufacturers still are offering 0.0 to 2 percent APR financing. Your earnings muscle and credit history must be top-notch to qualify for these low APR rates. Some industry experts say that only one-third of the car buyers who apply for cut-rate financing actually receives credit approval.

✔ **Option-package discounts:** Make certain that you know the invoice prices of options packages on the vehicle you're considering before you communicate with the dealership. Knowing which options you want before you start negotiating also is important. Paying for options you don't want isn't getting a good deal.

In a situation where the auto manufacturer is offering either a rebate or a financing incentive, you need to compare these incentives to a good old-fashioned low-interest loan you can acquire from your bank or credit union. Check the online calculator at SmartMoney.com (`www.smartmoney.com/autos/?nav=droptabs`) to determine whether a cash rebate or lower financing is best for you.

Financing Your Car

Having your financing in hand when you go car shopping is a good idea because that way you know your limits. Additionally, by taking the financing out of the equation when negotiating with a dealer, you're making the whole process more straightforward. You're more likely to get a good deal when negotiating based on the price of the car rather than monthly payments, which, again, is that trick some salesmen use to their benefit.

You must make many decisions about financing your car, including answering these questions:

✔ **Should you finance or pay cash?** When you pay cash, you save finance charges by not taking out a loan for your car. However, you may not want to lose the flexibility that comes with financing a car purchase or deplete your emergency funds by paying so much cash for a car.

✔ **How much down payment do you pay?** If you make a higher down payment and finance your car for a shorter period of time, you don't have to dole out so much cash, and the amount you save can be reinvested in an interest-bearing account.

✔ **How much will you pay each month?** The amount of your monthly payment depends on your loan amount, loan term, and the interest rate of your loan.

✔ **How long do you keep your car?** Depreciation of your car's value affects its book value. If you buy a new car frequently, you may owe more on your car than you receive when you sell it or trade it in for a new car. Industry experts note that new cars depreciate between 30 percent and 40 percent in the first two years after they're made.

Shopping for car financing in advance can mean a better car loan. Compare the APRs of different loans. If all other things are equal, the car loan with the lowest APR is the best deal.

Direct lending

Vehicles can be financed through banks, credit unions, or other similar financial institutions. This type of financing is called direct lending. *Direct lending* is when the purchaser agrees to pay the amount financed, plus a predetermined finance charge during a specified period of time. According to a Kelley Blue Book (www.kbb.com) survey, 54 percent of car buyers are seeking direct financing. Additionally, 13 percent of all car buyers obtain their financing online. The following are a few online sources for information about auto loans:

- ✔ **Bankrate.com** (www.bankrate.com) reveals what the current APR is for an auto loan.
- ✔ **E-Loan** (www.eloan.com) enables you to shop several lenders for your auto loan at one Internet location.
- ✔ **Lending Tree** (www.lendingtree.com) enables you to shop several lenders for the best rates at one online location.

Dealer financing

Dealerships also offer financing. *Dealership financing* is when the dealership and buyer enter into a contract in which the buyer agrees to pay the amount financed, plus a predetermined finance charge during a specified period of time. The dealership may retain the contract but usually sells the loan to a bank, finance company, or credit union, which, in turn, services the account and collects payments.

The finance and insurance departments of the dealerships require you to complete a credit application, and with your permission, obtain a credit report and your credit score (see Chapter 3 for details). Your credit history, current finance rates, competition, market conditions, and special offers affect your APR. The APR is the amount of interest you pay for your car loan. The higher the APR, the more expensive the car loan.

Information that you need for your credit application includes

- ✔ Driver's license for identification.
- ✔ Employment and salary information, including paycheck stubs. If you're self-employed, you may need to bring bank statements.

- ✔ Information about other sources of income such as alimony, child support, or retirement income.
- ✔ Information about bank, brokerage, and credit accounts — for example, the account numbers of your credit cards.
- ✔ Personal references with addresses and telephone numbers.

When finalizing your budget, don't forget to add car insurance (see Chapter 18 for details).

Next you need to look at the terms, conditions, and costs of your car loan. For example, Table 15-1 shows a comparison of a three-year auto loan to a five-year auto loan. In most cases, the longer the loan's term, the lower the monthly payments and the higher the finance charges. Currently, the difference between a three-year and a five-year auto loan is about 0.25 percent. For the sake of argument, say that the interest rate is the same for both the three-year and the five-year auto loans. The monthly payment for the five-year loan is $406 compared to $627 for a three-year auto loan. Although the low monthly payment seems attractive, the cost is high. Total interest payments for the five-year loan are $4,332 compared to $2,562 for the three-year loan. Bottom line: The longer the loan, the higher the financing costs. In this example, the total difference is $1,770.

Table 15-1	Comparing Loan Terms	
	3 Years (36 Months)	*5 Years (60 Months)*
Amount Financed	$20,000	$20,000
Contract Rate (APR)	8%	8%
Finance Charges	$2,562	$4,332
Monthly Payment Amount	$627	$406
Total Payments	$22,562	$24,332
Down Payment	10%	10%

Note: *All dollars are rounded in this example.*

The Big Dilemma: Leasing or Buying?

Leasing is a fast and easy way to get a car with little or no down payment. Monthly lease payments usually are less than loan payments for a new car. Additionally, you'll encounter less paperwork, inspections, and registration hassles when leasing a car. Leasing appeals to individuals who use cars for business, need a car for a limited period of time, trade in their cars at regular intervals, want to know their monthly costs in advance, or want to invest their cash in different activities. Leasing, however, has its share of limitations and disadvantages. Table 15-2 provides a brief overview of the comparison between leasing and buying.

Table 15-2	Comparison of Leasing versus Buying
Leasing	*Buying*
Monthly payments are applied to depreciation, not the purchase price of the vehicle.	Monthly payments are applied to purchase of vehicle.
Monthly lease payments are significantly lower than car loan payments.	Monthly payments include financing charges.
A down payment often isn't required.	Down payment usually is required.
After the lease period is over, you need to lease another vehicle.	When the car loan is paid, you own the car.
Exiting the lease early usually requires coming up with a large amount of cash. Early termination penalties vary.	You can modify your car any way you want. Don't hesitate to put on those fancy hubcaps.
You must predetermine how many miles you drive per year.	No mileage restrictions; however, higher mileage reduces the trade-in value of the car.
Your vehicle usually is covered by the manufacturer's warranty for the duration of your lease.	Car loans usually extend past the warranty period, so you'll be responsible for repairs.
You have to pay for any excess wear and tear.	Although you have maintenance and upkeep requirements, performing routine tasks is a good idea.

Be sure to calculate the differences between purchasing and leasing by referring to the Internet. The following are a few Web sites that can help you with your decision-making:

✔ **Edmunds.com** (www.edmunds.com) provides comparative data on leasing versus purchasing a specific auto or truck and shows you "10 Steps to Leasing a New Car."

✔ **FinanCenter.com** (www.financenter.com/products/calculators/auto) offers a calculator that assists you in deciding whether leasing is preferable to borrowing to buy a vehicle. The calculator assumes that you don't exercise the purchase options at the end of the lease. With a car loan, you own the vehicle when the loan is paid off.

✔ **SmartMoney.com** (www.smartmoney.com) offers an auto buy-versus-lease calculator. At the home page locate Personal Finance and click on "Autos." Next click on "To Buy or Lease." Scroll toward the bottom of the page and enter the price of the car, your down payment, monthly payment or lease, rate of return from your investment portfolio, and value of car at the end of the lease. The online calculator makes a recommendation.

Purchasing Your New Car Online: The Auto Show Comes to You

When you purchase your car online, it doesn't come wrapped in brown paper and isn't delivered by UPS the next day. You have to interact with a dealership or owner and sign paperwork before you get your car. You now can research cars online to find out the dealer's invoice price and the manufacturer's suggested retail price. Additionally, you can customize your online car selection and even have the dealer deliver the car to your home or office. Among the several ways that you can purchase a car via the Internet are

✔ **No-haggle pricing:** You see what you get and for how much. If you think you have better things to do than haggle with a salesman about the price of a car, you may want to consider purchasing your new vehicle from a company like Saturn. Automaker Saturn's pricing policy is you pay the sticker price and that's the end of it

✔ **Negotiating your price online:** Using several online Web sites, you can get a price quote for the year, make, model, and options you desire. You can negotiate a lower price entirely online or via e-mail without going to the dealership at

• **Autobytel** (www.autobytel.com), which lets you compare a dozen or more cars at the same time and get a local dealer's price quote. Use the Web site's calculator to estimate your monthly car payment.

- **Yahoo! Autos** (autos.yahoo.com), which provides consumers with a way to search for and find comprehensive automotive content online. Features such as a personalized search section and recommendations based on the most researched cars can assist consumers in better managing the buying, selling, and research process.

- **Edmunds.com** (www.edmunds.com), which supplies research for new and used cars. Discover the dealer's invoice pricing for a new car, the trade-in value of your current car, and the true cost of owning a car.

- **Kelley Blue Book** (www.kbb.com), which is the online version of the offline publication of the same name. At this Web site, you'll find the MSRP for a new car, the value of your trade-in, reviews, financing, and lemon checks.

- **CarsDirect** (www.carsdirect.com) is a multibrand online car buying service, providing new and pre-owned automobiles and related products and services. The staff at CarsDirect haggles for low car prices for you.

✔ **Online prenegotiated pricing:** This method offers no upfront price haggling. A staff of pricing experts prenegotiates all prices. Many Web sites offer a low price guarantee to help ensure that you're paying below the manufacturer's suggested retail price.

Choosing a Used Car Online

If you're wanting to buy a used car, the Internet is a great place to shop. You'll find lengthy descriptions and plenty of interior and exterior photos of vehicles for sale on the Web. Some photos highlight dings that wouldn't appear in newspaper ads. According to *The Wall Street Journal,* last year 43 million used cars were sold in the United States. *Ward's Dealers Business* states that used-car sales last year amounted to $370 billion. In 1998, only 14 percent of used-car buyers used the Internet to shop for vehicles, but in 2003, that number increased to 47 percent.

A fellow researcher purchased his used car using the Internet. He wanted a certain year, make, and model of a car. Low mileage was a deciding factor, but any interior or exterior car color was okay. If he couldn't find the used car he wanted, he decided he'd purchase a new but less luxurious new-car model. Using the Internet, he searched for the used car within a 100-mile radius of Washington, DC. Not finding any results, he expanded the search to Kansas City, Missouri, and found his dream car. The researcher raised a few key questions about the car and asked the owner to take it to a dealer for a full inspection (cost $125). The dealership gave the car a clean bill of health. The researcher then sent the seller 10 percent of the purchase price as a deposit via Federal Express. That weekend, the researcher caught a cheap flight to Kansas City and handed the seller a cashier's check for the remaining balance due on the car. The researcher and seller completed their paperwork in less than an hour. At that time, the researcher happily drove the car 1,200 miles to his home. The price of the car (including the car inspection, air fare, and related transportation expenses) was well below what he would've spent buying a new but less desirable car.

Where to shop?

Many local dealerships offer their used-car inventories online. These Web sites have search capabilities for picking the make and model of car you're seeking. Large, national online retailers of used cars can be found at the Web sites that follow:

- **Cars.com** (`www.cars.com`) is the largest online classified-listing service with 2.2 million used cars. Cars.com pulls vehicle listings from thousands of dealer inventories and classified ads nationwide, offering consumers the best selection of new and used cars. You can find pricing information, photo galleries, buying guides, side-by-side comparison tools, original editorial content, and reviews.

- **AutoTrader.com** (`www.autotrader.com`) offers a large selection of used vehicles, buying and selling tips, car reviews, vehicle pricing and safety information, and help with financing, insurance, and warranty programs. If you're not exactly sure which type of car you're looking for, you can perform side-by-side comparisons.

- **eBay Motors** (`pages.motors.ebay.com/index.html?sspagename=ml01`) is a mighty online used-car force. Last year eBay Motors played host to more than 300,000 used cars. Auto sales accounted for $100 million of eBay's total $1.2 billion revenue.

Are you sure you want a used car?

Purchasing a used car rather than a new one can be a good financial decision depending on your circumstances.

When comparing the purchase of a new car to the purchase of a used car, a number of advantages and limitations become evident. Table 15-3 summarizes the advantages of owning a new car versus the advantages of owning a used car.

Table 15-3	Comparing New and Used Cars
New Car	**Used Car**
Includes the latest safety features, such as air bags, child seats, and structural reinforcements.	Can dramatically reduce the cost of owning and operating a car.
Includes new technology such as Global Positioning Satellite (GPS) navigating computers and TVs so children can be entertained on long trips.	Registration, taxes, and licensing fees are reduced.
No battle scars from past accidents or poor choices (such as low-quality tires) of previous owners	New cars depreciate 30% to 40% in the first two years. If you purchase a used car, the previous owner takes the loss.

Summing it up, used cars cost less than their new counterparts, and that's a big plus, but you need to be willing to assume the wear and tear that someone else has inflicted on the car. And you'll have to be willing to live without a full new-car warranty.

The Internet and car inspections

When you purchase a used car, you want to make certain that the used car you're buying is accurately represented. You can use the Internet to help you gain peace of mind. The Internet can assist you in getting an online vehicle history report from Experian Automotive (www.autocheck.com) or CarFax report (www.carfax.com). These vehicle history reports include such items as a maintenance history, any previous accidents, and odometer fraud. Be sure to ask the seller for the vehicle identification number (VIN) when you shop. VINs can be found on dashboards, driver-side door jams, and title documents. You can order a CarFax Report online for $20. If you're researching several used cars, you may want to pay $25 for an unlimited number of CarFax reports. You'll receive your reports within five minutes of requesting them.

One way to make sure that you aren't being taken for a ride (especially when you aren't close enough to test drive a vehicle you may want) is to hire someone to do the test-driving for you. For example, SGS Automotive (sgs-ebay.sgsauto.com) inspects vehicles seven days a week for approximately $100. Inspections usually take two days, depending on the location. The report is available online within 24 hours of the completion of the 30- to 45-minute inspection. The seller of the vehicle gives his or her permission for the inspection (or the owner may be present for the inspection). The inspection includes a test drive, the vehicle registration, and proof of insurance. After you order an inspection online, you're transferred to PayPal (`www.paypal.com`) to arrange for payment (for more information about making payment through PayPal, see Chapter 5). After approval, you're transferred back to a representative to order the inspection. SGS takes over from there. SGS employs more than 1,400 inspectors and completes more than 17 million inspections annually across the (all 50) United States.

Pre-owned certification programs

One reason for the increase in used-car sales is the booming leasing market. When leased vehicles are returned, their values are often below the residual values calculated at the time of the lease. These lease losses drive down used-car prices and make used cars a bargain for used-car shoppers. These off-lease vehicles have helped create many certified used vehicle programs. Many individuals who in the past never would've considered purchasing a used car now are buying certified used vehicles. Last year, 1.3 million certified used vehicles were sold.

Certified programs offer used-car buyers some assurance about their purchases. Don't forget that not all certified programs are alike, so you'll need to use your best judgment when evaluating a pre-owned car. For example, you need to take these factors into account:

- **Inspection:** Intellichoice (`www.intellichoice.com`) has created a list of 141 items that need to be checked on a used car. You need to find out how many of these items are covered in the certified program you're checking out.

- **Warranty:** A warranty can be evaluated in two ways. The first concerns the *total warranty,* or what's left of the original total warranty and your effective coverage. The second concerns the *net warranty,* or an additional warranty gained by purchasing though the certification program.

Recognizing and avoiding lemons

Some states require titles issued by their respective departments of motor vehicles (DMVs) to state whenever a vehicle was returned to the manufacturer as a lemon. For example, in California, a *lemon* is defined as a car that the dealer has in the shop for repairs for more than 30 days during the first year or is unable to be repaired after four attempts. According to California law, if either of these conditions occurs the car automatically is classified as a lemon. Unfortunately, some of these cars still are sold as ordinary cars.

The American Automobile Manufacturers Association (AAMA) is trying to get legislators to identify lemons so that even the small percentage of people who are exposed to them don't have to worry about the quality of the car they're purchasing. If you think you've purchased a lemon, send your complaint to your state department of consumer affairs. The following are several examples:

- **New Jersey Office of Consumer Affairs** (www.state.nj.us/lps/ca/ocp.htm), which provides contact information and an online complaint form.

- **Tennessee Department of Consumer Affairs** (www.state.tn.us/consumer/lemon.html), which offers guidelines for what to do if you purchase a lemon.

- **State of Hawaii Department of Consumer Affairs** (mano.icsd.hawaii.gov/dcca/rico/lemonlaw.htm), which provides an online Lemon Law Handbook and complaint forms.

Part V
Protecting Your Money Online

The 5th Wave · By Rich Tennant

"My portfolio's gonna take a hit for this."

In this part . . .

Find out how to protect your data, spot viruses, fight spam, and avoid online scams in this part of the book. Protect your assets by using Web-based insurance calculators to determine how much insurance you need, compare online quotes, and use the Internet to get the best insurance for the least amount of money.

Chapter 16

Keeping It Personal: Securing Your Data

In This Chapter

▶ Protecting your data

▶ Preventing unwanted visitors with firewalls

▶ Keeping your e-mail address unlisted

▶ Outsmarting spyware and adware intruders

▶ Avoiding spam

▶ Protecting your privacy and avoiding identity theft

More Internet users are using Internet connections at higher speeds than ever before. High-speed connections enable home computers to become just as powerful as (and in some cases more powerful than) business computers. High-speed connections used with home computers (cable modems, digital subscriber lines, or T1 lines) frequently have fixed Internet protocol (IP) addresses that can be targeted by hackers and virus writers who search for easy prey that gives them a low likelihood of being prosecuted if they're discovered. No disrespect to home Internet users, but even large companies have a hard time prosecuting these cybercriminals.

Computer hackers can view, change, corrupt, or destroy data on your computer. Intruders don't care who you are or where you're located. Hackers can change the content of documents or gain control of your software programs from remote locations. They may be teenagers using malicious code (any code that's intentionally included in software or hardware for an unauthorized purpose) that's often downloaded from the Internet or sophisticated criminals using cutting-edge technology to sniff out computers with vulnerabilities. An attack can happen at any time and with just one click.

In this chapter, you not only find out about different types of viruses, worms, and Trojan horses that can infect your computer, but you also discover what you can do to fend off and prevent future threats. You'll discover free, online, antivirus-scanning Web sites and view a comparison of the leading antivirus software programs. You'll likewise explore hardware and software firewalls and gain an understanding of how these gatekeepers can put a stop to unwanted traffic. You'll also be shown online random password generators that can help you make certain that your password remains a secret.

I show you how to travel the Internet highway without leaving a trail to which spammers attach unwanted e-mail offers. You'll be introduced to free and low-cost e-mail accounts and shown how Web mail works. Web mail is great whenever you want to receive e-mail but have limited Internet access because you're on the road or for some other reason. In this chapter, you uncover how cookies help you make multiple online purchases and see how marketers track your actions so they know just what sort of advertising elicits a response from you. You'll also find out how to combat spyware and adware so you don't have to put up with annoying pop-up ads and unwanted e-mail messages. And if you don't think that's enough, check out my in-depth look at how you can protect your privacy from spammers and potential identity thieves.

Data Protection Pointers

Internet users have become so accustomed to *viruses* (pieces of programming code inserted into other programming to cause some unexpected and usually undesirable event, such as lost or damaged files) that the announcement of a new outbreak barely raises a collective eyebrow — until your computer is infected by one.

Your first line of defense is antivirus software and a good firewall for the more than 250 viruses that currently are on the horizon and some 23,000 old viruses, worms, bits of malcode (short for malicious code), and *Trojan horses* (destructive programs that masquerade as benign applications) that are still trying to invade your computer. As a result, everyone needs to protect their data from *hackers* (individuals who attempt to gain unauthorized access to computer systems for the purpose of stealing and corrupting data), *spammers* (people who spread electronic junk mail or junk newsgroup postings), and *eavesdroppers* (folks who pry and poke around in your online business), and your first line of defense is antivirus software used in conjunction with a good firewall.

Antivirus software is an application program that protects your computer from viruses, worms, Trojan horses, and other types of unwanted, invasive, and destructive programs. You may already have antivirus software installed on your computer, or you may need to purchase and install it. Unwanted programs can make your computer run slowly or track your private movements on the

Internet. Problems created by unwanted invaders can include malicious acts, such as deleting your files, accessing your personal data, or turning your computer into a zombie so a hacker can use it to launch a denial of service (DoS) attack against other computers. (A *DoS attack* is a type of attack on a network that's designed to bring the network to its knees by flooding it with useless traffic.)

Getting a hold on viruses and worms

Unfortunately, Internet villains can be efficient, designing viruses that are anything from a petty annoyance (such as a banner that calls you a jerk) to devastation (deleting your operating system). What makes a virus effective is that it needs only to remain undetected just long enough to reproduce and spread to new hosts. Knowing this weakness, virus writers have grown more efficient than ever, and yet many computer users still are surprised when they find out the length of time that's transpired since their computers originally were infected. This ability to remain undetected makes tracking virus writers or hackers who purposely infect host computers extremely difficult.

Just like a terrible cold, viruses like to spread

A computer virus relies on humans to spread its infection to other computers. Viruses can spread by themselves from one file to another on a single computer, quickly infecting an application program or slowly infecting individual documents.

Viruses also are referred to as *malcode* (short for malicious code), a dialect of computer language that can insert itself into a program, file, diskette, or portion of a hard disk where it can replicate into executable programs. *Executable programs* include programs that end with *.com*, *.exe*, *.sys*, or *.dll*. So if you see one of these files in your e-mail inbox, don't open it. The goal of each virus is twofold:

- **Finishing its mission:** The mission of a virus can range from reformatting your hard drive to corrupting *MS Word* files, and so on. To finish its mission, the virus clones itself over and over again using unsuspecting humans to give it a helping hand.

- **Attaching to other programs:** Each virus tries to transfer itself to other programs, infecting them with the same virus. Computer viruses are easily transported or transmitted via diskettes, e-mail attachments, file sharing on a network, and the Internet.

Endless worms

A *worm* is designed to repeatedly copy itself as it moves from one computer to another. Networks and e-mail are the primary means of transportation for worms, which can spread to many computers on the network without the help of humans. As such, worms are more lethal than viruses because they don't need a helping hand from humans.

Worms can slowly consume all the resources on your computer. For example, a worm gets into memory and starts filling it with nonsense data. With less memory, the computer processes legitimate data slower than usual. Another example are worms that consume bandwidth by talking with one another. *Bandwidth* is the amount of data that can be transmitted in a fixed amount of time. If the majority of bandwidth is consumed, your computer works slower than usual.

Self-replicating worms likewise can exploit loopholes in Internet protocols. *Internet protocols* (called IPs) are part of the mail system used by the Internet. IP specifies the format of packets and the addressing scheme. Most networks combine IPs with a higher-level protocol called *Transmission Control Protocol* (TCP), which establishes a virtual connection between a destination and a source. After worms are released, they pretty much act on their own. For example, as an experiment in 1988, Robert Morris, Jr., released a worm that eventually shut down approximately 10 percent of the Internet during only a short period of time.

Hiding malicious programs in Trojan horses

Trojan horses, which also go by the name of *routines,* are programs that are concealed in software and installed on computers without the knowledge or consent of computer owners. Trojan horses aren't viruses but are programs that can carry viruses or worms. A Trojan horse looks like a program that appears to do a useful service. For example, the Trojan horse can be something like a downloadable antispam program, calculator tool, or solitaire game. Although the free antispam program appears to be doing what it's designed to do, it secretly serves another function. That's why Trojan horses often are called back door programs. The Trojan horse can be attempting to reformat your hard disk drive or sending your personal passwords to a hacker.

Using free online antivirus scanning

You can use free, online antivirus scanning to keep your computer safe. Online anti-virus scanning can help you detect and destroy viruses, worms, and Trojan horses. Although you won't be able to customize the scan, you will be certain to get the latest in antivirus updates. Start by trying any of the following:

✔ **Trend Micro's HouseCall** (`housecall.antivirus.com/housecall/
start_corp.asp`) is a personal favorite. HouseCall demonstrates the
power of Web-based technologies that Trend Micro is developing to
make deployment and management of virus protection in corporate set-
tings fast and easy. HouseCall scans the drives you select and (if you so
choose) enables you to clean or delete infected files.

✔ **McAfee FreeScan** (`us.mcafee.com/root/mfs/default.asp`) can
assist you in detecting thousands of viruses on your computer. FreeScan
searches for the latest and greatest viruses and displays a list of infected
files. If FreeScan finds infected files, you're given links to more information about how to clean your computer.

✔ **Symantec Security Check** (`www.symantec.com/product/index_home
comp.html`) examines your computer for any known virus or Trojan horse.
Click on the Symantec Security Check button in the center of the page.
The scan doesn't include compressed files, and the program doesn't fix
infected files, but it does provide a detailed analysis of your results.

Selecting the right antivirus software

You don't want any viruses, worms, or Trojan horses trying to invade your
computer, so when you're selecting antivirus software, be sure that it's easy
to install, verify that your system is compatible with the requirements of the
antivirus software, and confirm that you can easily update the antivirus program. Table 16-1 compares the top three antivirus programs.

Table 16-1	Comparison of the Top-Rated Antivirus Programs		
Attribute	**Antivirus Program**		
	Norton Anti-virus 2004 Professional (`security.norton.com`)	**McAfee Virus Scan Professional 8.0** (`us.macafee.com`)	**PC-cillin Internet Security 2004** (`www.trend micro.com`)
Price	$14 to $79	$27 to $59	$38 to $49
Ease of use	Good for first-timers. Easy to use, set, and forget.	Simple interface. Easy to use, set, and forget.	Easy to use, set, and forget.
Includes a firewall	No	No	Yes

(continued)

Table 16-1 *(continued)*

Attribute	Antivirus Program		
	Norton Anti-virus 2004 Professional (security. norton.com)	**McAfee Virus Scan Professional 8.0** (us.macafee.com)	**PC-cillin Internet Security 2004** (www.trend micro.com)
Includes anti-spam tools	Yes, but you may want to back up with spyware.	Yes, but you may want to back up with spyware.	Yes
Performance	Scans e-mail and computer for viruses, worms, Trojan horses, and malcode. Can scan scan compressed files.	Scans e-mail and computer for viruses, worms, Trojan horses, and malcode.	Scans e-mail and computer for viruses, worms, Trojan horses, and malcode.
Customer support	Yes	Yes	One-year free telephone support
Updates	Free and easy online updates available for one year. Provides warnings if you don't update.	Free updates available for download online for one year. **Note:** Available in boxed and subscription versions. After one year, subscription version won't work if you don't upgrade.	Free updates available for download online for one year.

Connection Protection for Your Data

As the World Wide Web matures, it includes more and more graphics, so Internet users want faster and faster service. As a result, the Internet connections of more and more users are being left open to the Web via cable modems, digital subscriber lines (DSL), or T1 (high-speed commercial telephone) lines. In most cases, these continually open connections mean that a high-speed user has only one IP address. As a basis for comparison, Internet dial-up users receive a new IP address every time they log on to the Web.

Having an uninterrupted connection to the Internet is a little like leaving your front door open. Sooner or later someone tries the door handle and is rewarded with access to all the data on your computer, which can include

Social Security numbers, credit-card numbers, and passwords. If you use *Turbo Tax* (an income tax return preparation program) and save your past IRS tax forms on your computer, intruders may get an unfettered view of your financial position.

The best way to thwart unwanted incursions on your privacy by eavesdroppers is to purchase Internet security software that includes a firewall. A firewall analyzes information flowing between you and the Internet, restricts access by unknown parties, and prevents hackers from getting a look at your data or turning your computer into a zombie that spreads denial-of-service attacks to targets selected by hackers.

Two types of firewalls are available. The first is a hardware firewall. *Hardware firewalls* keep attacks outside your PC. If an attack begins to overwhelm a hardware firewall, it automatically shuts down, and then nothing gets into your PC. The second is a *software firewall,* which protects your system and constantly logs attacks.

Hardware firewalls

Hardware firewalls are good gatekeepers for inbound traffic. Even so, you still need a software firewall to catch outbound traffic like spyware, malcode, and other viruses that can use your PC to send e-mail messages without your knowledge or approval. The following are a few of the top-rated hardware firewalls:

- **D-Link DI-624** (www.dlink.com) combines easy installation with advanced security options, making it a good choice for homes and offices. Priced between $59 and $104.

- **Netgear Pro Safe Firewall/VPN Model FR114P** (www.netgear.com) includes a Smart Wizard that quickly connects to your ISP. This firewall includes an easy-to-use, Web-based configuration screen and an install assistant to reduce setup time. Priced between $74 and $94.

- **Linksys Firewall Router BEFSX41 EtherFast Cable/DSL Firewall Router** (www.linksys.com) is designed to protect computers from the *ping of death,* a malicious program that bounces a request off of another computer over a network; *SYN floods,* a flooding of the SYN queue that makes opening a new connection impossible; *LAN attacks,* attacks on your local area network (LAN); *IP spoofing,* any of several methods for changing an IP address to one acceptable to a firewall, so as to trespass on an internal network; and other *DoS attacks,* actions that prevent any part of a system or network from functioning properly. This firewall also supports URL filtering and time filtering, blocks Java, Active X, and cookies, and is easily configurable through a Web browser from any networked PC. Priced between $70 and $120.

Software firewalls

A software firewall is a security system that acts as a shield between your computer and the outside world. An effective firewall can prevent your personal computer from becoming infected by viruses, worms, or Trojan horses by using a proxy server and Internet ports. A proxy server is an Internet server that acts as a firewall, mediating traffic between a protected network and Internet ports. *Internet ports* are logical, not physical, addresses within a domain. By convention, servers on TCP/IP networks monitor (and are expected to be found at) certain access points called ports. When default ports are used, a port number (such as 80 for an unsecured Web server) doesn't need to be specified.

Windows XP includes a firewall by comparing inbound traffic to outbound traffic and discarding inbound traffic that doesn't match. Firewalls are based on the theory that if you didn't originate the request for data, it must be an attack. Unfortunately, Windows XP has a few other flaws. For example, spyware and other malcodes that are already on your computer aren't stopped. Additionally, hackers create new ways of attacking computers each day. Consequently, it's a good idea to install a firewall even if you have Windows XP.

Listed below are several freeware and license firewall programs. You may want to download the free firewall programs before purchasing the licensed versions.

✔ **Zone Labs ZoneAlarm** (`www.zonelabs.com`) is a an easy-to-use firewall that blocks hackers and other unknown threats. Features include intrusion blocking by systematically identifying hackers and blocking access attempts. Stealth mode automatically makes your computer invisible to anyone on the Internet. ZoneAlarm automatically decides whether to allow or deny Internet access to individual programs. ZoneAlarm is free for individual and not-for-profit charitable-entity use (excluding governmental entities and educational institutions). Here's the link to the free download for Zone Alarm Firewall Protection `www.zonelabs.com/store/content/company/products/znalm/freeDownload.jsp?lid=zaskulist_download`.

✔ **Norton Internet Security Suite 2004** (`www.symantec.com/sabu/nis/nis_pe`) includes the whole nine yards (antivirus, parental controls, privacy protection, and antispam features for *Eudora, Microsoft Outlook,* and *Outlook Express.*) The program is almost as friendly and feature-packed as *Norton Personal Firewall 2004,* but it lacks Norton's privacy-protection features. The price to purchase a package or download is $69.95. If you're upgrading, a $30 rebate is available. *Norton Internet Security Suite 2004* includes free *trialware* that you can immediately download; however, in return for this giveaway, you agree to receive periodic follow-up e-mails that contain unsubscribe information.

✔ **Free Version of the Sygate Personal Firewall** (`soho.sygate.com/products/spf_standard.htm`) is offered free for your personal use. *Sygate Personal Firewall 5.x* provides a user-friendly interface and is designed to protect your desktop PC from hackers, Trojan horse programs, and DoS attacks. One included feature is protection from malcode intrusions. *Sygate Personal Firewall Pro 5.0* is designed for advanced users and organizations that need more than one license. Prices start at $39.95.

If you don't have any Internet security software, purchasing a package that includes a firewall and antivirus software may enable you to get the biggest bang for the buck. For more information and to stay updated about the latest firewalls, check out the following Web sites:

- **AntiOnline** (`www.antionline.com`) is a community of security, network, and computer professionals, students, and keen amateurs who visit the Web site to find out about online security. AntiOnline offers antihacking, antivirus news, and tips and information about new products. Gaining full use of the Web site requires you to register, but it's free.

- **Firewall Guide** (`www.firewallguide.com`) provides easy access to basic information about protecting home computers and networks from Internet outlaws by using firewall, antivirus, anti–Trojan horse and antispyware software in addition to hardware firewall routers.

- **Shields Up!** (`grc.com/x/ne.dll?rh1dkyd2`) shows how the Windows networking technology that connects your computer to the Internet may be offering some or all of your computer's data to others without your knowledge or explicit permission. Software developer Steve Gibson illustrates the dangers and shows what you can do to defend yourself.

SSSH! Keeping Your Passwords Secret

While you sit in the comfort of your home or office, you're likely to feel that having a password on your computer isn't necessary and is just another waste of time. Visualizing someone accessing your computer while you're away from your home on vacation or away from your desk on a business trip at some future point is difficult.

That's definitely the wrong mind-set. All your personal financial data (that's what this book is about, after all) needs to be protected by a password. Some individuals can sit at your desk (physically or from a remote location) and in only a matter of a few minutes identify your password. That's because people often use birthdates, names of children, or favorite football teams as passwords. Some individuals actually even keep their passwords on sticky notes under their desk blotters.

One easy way to increase the security of your computer is by changing your password every 30 to 60 days. Regularly changing a password can deny an intruder's access to your computer. Frequently changing your passwords helps you ensure that unauthorized users can't access your computer or system. Don't forget to change the passwords on any data files or programs that may require a password.

If you're lacking in the art of creating a password, you're not alone. Several online services provide free random password generators. A free random password generator is a small application program that in an ideal world generates a password that nobody could guess. Check out the following and select the one you like the best:

- **Security Guide for Windows** (www.winguides.com/security/password.php) enables you to create random passwords that are highly secure and extremely difficult to crack.

- **RoboForm** (www.roboform.com/?affid=goopg) uses artificial intelligence to create passwords. This Web site works well and doesn't burden you with useless ads. Hoorah!

E-Mail: It Isn't Private

When you use your e-mail accounts, unless you employ devices, such as message encryption, anonymization of your messages, or a virtual private network (VPN), you must assume that someone (anyone) can read your e-mail messages. A good example of this vulnerability occurred in 2003 when administrators of Microsoft's Passport.net service discovered a service hole that allowed hackers to view the passwords of HotMail users for one complete week.

Using an anonymizer is a good way to prevent others from getting into your e-mail. *Anonymizers* frequently prevent identity theft, shield your IP address, and enable you to visit chats, newsgroups, and otherwise surf the Internet without leaving a trail for spammers and direct-mail advertisers to follow.

Anonymizers provide Internet users with full-time privacy by encrypting all traffic to and from your computer. Doing so prevents online snoops from tracking your surfing habits and then using that personal information for undesirable purposes. Having a firewall doesn't provide you with the type of privacy an anonymizer program does.

At Anonymizer (www.anonymizer.com), take the free Privacy Test. On the home page click on "Take Our Privacy Test" under the "Home & Office/Free Tools" menu. Test results show your IP address, operating system, browser name, location, number of sites visited, and your referrer page. Even information from your *MS Word* clipboard is exposed. The name of your computer may be protected, but Anonymizer can place a sample cookie on your computer to demonstrate that others who may not be so friendly can do the same. Cookies, for example, can be used to track your buying behavior on the Internet.

The following are highly rated anonymizer programs:

- **Anonymizer** (www.anonymizer.com) makes it possible for you to surf the Internet safely, blocks pop-ups, helps stop spam by blocking e-mail address harvesting, and filters and blocks cookies, banner ads, tracking bugs, and more.

- **Primedius** (www.primedius.com) helps you keep your Internet address unlisted, automatically detects spam, protects your e-mail from viruses, kills pop-ups and ads for a better Web experience, and offers secure e-mail and online storage.

- **Steganos** (www.steganos.com) helps you become anonymous on the Internet with the click of a button. It includes an "Internet Trace Destructor," which deletes all information about your online activities left on your hard disk after an Internet session.

The Dark Side of Cookies (And It Isn't Chocolate)

Cookies and spyware can be used to harvest your personal information and private data surreptitiously. *Cookies* are small text files (not programs) that are stored on the Internet user's hard drive. When an Internet user contacts the Web server of an organization, for example, and requests a document, the Web server of the organization sends the requested document and a cookie to the user. If the Internet user is shopping, the cookie helps the Web server remember who's shopping and what's been selected for the shopping cart.

Cookies usually take up only about 50 to 150 bytes of space, and they're always less than 4 kilobytes. As a general rule, a Web server is limited to only 20 cookies per individual, and users are limited up to 300 cookies on their computers. In general, the two types of cookies are

✔ **Session cookies:** *Session cookies* are sometimes called *transient cookies*. Session cookies are stored in temporary memory and are deleted when users close their Internet browsers. In other words, session cookies exist only during an Internet session.

✔ **Persistent cookies:** *Persistent cookies* reside on the Internet user's hard disk drive and recognize the user when he or she returns to a Web location after an initial session. Persistent cookies are used to personalize your online experience, recognize you when you return for a second shopping trip or visit, and can live on your hard disk drive for months or even years.

Many Web-based businesses, such as Amazon.com, permit customers to reuse information they provide by writing it on another cookie, which is stored on the enterprises' Web servers. The information then is used for *one-click shopping*. To use one-click shopping, the customer enters a customer identification number (often an e-mail address) and a password. Then credit-card information and billing and shipping addresses already provided by the customer are quickly accessed to complete a transaction.

Internet users can decide whether they want to accept or reject cookies. *Internet Explorer 6.0* makes it possible for you to automatically decline *all* cookies. Although crumbling all of your cookies this way is another means of maintaining your privacy, doing so isn't practical. You can set your Internet browser to "Always confirm before setting a cookie." Unfortunately, many Web pages include two or three cookies. So that means when you're using the Internet for several hours per day, confirming the use of each and every cookie is almost impossible (and highly annoying). Therefore, frequent Internet users limit their cookies by either opting out at a media network such as Web sites like Double Click (doubleclick.com) or using a cookie-management software application, such as Cookie Crusher (www.thelimitsoft.com/cookie). For more information about cookies, check out

✔ **Cookie Central** (www.cookiecentral.com), which is a comprehensive resource on Internet cookies, explaining what they are and how to block or stop them.

✔ **CookiePal** (www.kburra.com), which features *Cookie Pal 1.7* software that helps users maintain their privacy by keeping track of their cookies. Try it for 30 days, and if you like it, buy it for $15.

✔ **Cookie Crusher** (www.thelimitsoft.com/cookie), which acts as a real-time cookie manager. *Cookie Crusher* classifies, accepts, or rejects cookies in addition to making it possible for you to turn persistent cookies into session cookies.

Outsmarting Spyware Intruders

Threats to privacy and confidentiality are the fastest-growing online security problem for Internet users. ISP EarthLink (`www.earthlink.net/spyaudit`) claims that during the first three months of 2004, it uncovered 28 spyware programs on average for each PC it scanned with its Spy Audit program. Many experts believe that adware and spyware problems are growing faster than viruses. *Spyware* is defined as software or hardware that's installed on a computer without the user's knowledge or consent. Generally, spyware programs are divided into these two categories:

- **Surveillance spyware** often is disguised as an e-mail attachment or free software product. These forms of spyware programs monitor your every move. A spyware program can monitor chat-room dialogue and e-mail logs in addition to logging your keystrokes, monitoring your encrypted log file for later retrieval, and placing Trojan horses onto your computer.

- **Advertising spyware** doesn't ask for your consent when it's installed on your system. Commonly known as *adware,* this form of spyware includes pop-up ads, and it can share your personal information with other Web sites, thus enabling marketing firms to create a personal profile about you that can be sold to other companies.

Combating adware

Adware often capitalizes on the use of persistent cookies that can enable marketers to track your online behavior and thus gain an understanding of what Internet content interests you, based on your previous Web site visits. You may, for example, view several Web sites that have ads for CDs but never click on ads that offer discounts on baby strollers. With this type of information in hand, advertisers can use your and others' Internet behavior to create ads that match your preferences.

Adware uses *tracking cookies* that virtually stalk Internet users because they're cookies that aren't exclusive to the original Web site at which the user's computer encountered them. Ads containing tracking cookies can be downloaded from separate, third-party web servers whenever the Web page is requested. Use of these tracking cookies lets spammers discover whether your location is active.

The usual suspects for purveying spyware

Internet users who frequently use *peer-to-peer* (P2P) file-swapping programs can expect to be infected with spyware. P2P is a process whereby computers can trade information without having to pass the information through a centrally controlled server. In other words, P2P uses networks that connect individual users with each other, allowing them to share files. IRC (Internet Relay Chat) rooms have allowed P2P file-sharing for many years, but it was Napster that made P2P networking wildly popular.

Kazaa (www.kazaa.com) is an example of a P2P company that lets users swap music, movies, and other computer files. Kazaa is often is cited as a suspected spyware carrier. In some cases, spyware is downloaded along with other components that you didn't realize existed until you discover that your browser has been highjacked or you start having problems. You may even find yourself asking "How come I can't reset my home page or search engine setting?" When you suspect your computer is infected with spyware, you may need a good antispyware program. You can download one of the top-rated antispyware programs in the list that follows to gain a little peace of mind and privacy:

- ✔ **Lavasoft** (www.lavasoftusa.com/support/download) is one of the Internet's most popular downloads for keeping your computer clear of adware and spyware. Download the program for free at Download.com (www.download.com).

- ✔ **Spybot Search and Destroy** (www.safer-networking.org/index.php?page=download) scans your computer for spyware, adware, hijackers, and other malicious code. Spybot Search & Destroy is free. You can make a donation via PayPal if you value the program.

- ✔ **WebRoot** (www.webroot.com/wb/products/spysweeper/index.php) believes that nine out of ten computers are infected with adware and spyware and understands that these programs can't be manually deleted from your computer without causing serious problems. *Spy Sweeper* is designed to delicately and completely eliminate adware and spyware. Try it for free; buy it for $29.95.

Canning Spam

Who can forget the Monty Python skit where the actors sing "Spam, Spam, Spam. Oh, glorious Spam!" Today, no one is in love with the kind of spam I'm about to explain. *Spam* is junk e-mail — the e-mail that increases each day. Internet analysts estimate that spam represents between 30 percent and 70 percent of all e-mail traffic. On the rare occasion when a spammer is caught for some reason, the punishment usually equates with a light slap on the wrist. Government legislation, it seems, has failed to outlaw spam. No federal laws outlaw spam, but legislation is pending in some states that requires that messages be identified as unsolicited commercial e-mail and that recipients of those messages must be told how they can opt out of the mailing list. Additionally, legislation is pending that also prohibits senders from using false routing information.

Avoiding spam on your own

One limitation of using a personal antispam filter on your desktop computer is that it doesn't travel with you. If you have to use an Internet cafe or business laptop, you may have to pay for the extra time that it takes for all of the unwanted junk e-mail to download. When that's the case, you'll want to use a few of the following techniques to avoid receiving unwanted e- mail:

- ✔ **Turn off the preview pane when retrieving your messages.** Many e-mail programs have panes or windows. Windows usually change as the result of the user clicking a tab or a button or choosing an item from a pop-up menu. If you don't open the preview pane or window to view e-mail messages, you can likely reduce the amount of spam you receive. (That is, just view the titles of your e-mail.) Spammers often send e-mail messages that include references to pictures or logs posted on their own Web servers. When you preview the message, the picture is retrieved from the spammer's Web site, which tells the spammer that you've read the message, creating what sometimes is called a *beacon* to your e-mail address.

- ✔ **Never reply to a spam e-mail message.** Not replying to spam includes not clicking on the unsubscribe button and not clicking on any of the links in the junk e-mail message because clicking on a link activates a beacon.

- ✔ **Avoid advertising your e-mail address on the Web whenever possible.** If you include your e-mail address, make sure that it must be manually copied to be useful to a sender.

- ✔ **Be cautious about handing out your e-mail address to Web sites, discussion groups, and newsletters.** If the privacy notice or your preferences don't explicitly state that your information won't be shared with others, your e-mail address will likely be passed on.

Putting antispam software to work

New antispam software tools are released regularly, but unfortunately, six-month-old products frequently are obsolete. Software programs that use *Bayesian filters* are the latest strategy in personal spam filters. Named for Thomas Bayes, an 18th-century nonconformist minister who developed the theory of probability, Bayesian or statistical filtering in personal antispam programs is a machine method of sorting good e-mail messages from junk e-mail messages. Bayesian filters are trained by users to recognize what the user believes are junk e-mail messages or spam. At the moment, most personal Bayesian spam filters don't integrate well with *Outlook Express* or other client programs. Additionally, most personal antispam programs that use Bayesian filters are for more advanced Internet users. Personal antispam programs like Symantec's Norton Anti-spam (2004) rely on user-defined addresses, outgoing e-mail, and heuristic analysis. *Heuristic analysis* basically means using common sense (or a set of rules) intended to increase the probability of identifying and then quarantining junk e-mail.

Many antispam programs are easy to set up. You can create a friends list from your address book and an enemies list that blocks junk mail you receive. One benefit of an antispam program is that it automatically quarantines all future mail from addresses on your enemies list. Some antispam programs, however, can be too aggressive, causing users to miss important e-mail messages about meetings, due dates, and so on. MSN HotMail, AOL, Yahoo!, and EarthLink offer customers a *prefiltering service* that automatically moves suspected spam messages into a quarantine folder and then deletes them after a period of time. Keep in mind that the accuracy of these prefiltering services is iffy. You may find yourself missing a critical e-mail message that ended up among stacks of suspect messages your quarantined-mail folder.

Many experts agree that when selecting antispam software, you may want to consider these features:

- **Compatibility:** Make certain the antispam program offers a variety of protocols. Protocols are a set of rules enabling computers or devices to exchange data with one another with as little error as possible. The most popular protocols are POP3 (a protocol that provides a simple, standardized way for users to access mailboxes and download messages to their computers), IMAP (a mail protocol that provides management of received messages on a remote server), and Exchange (Microsoft's integrated fax and e-mail program designed for Windows). Contact your ISP to discover which protocol you use, and then select the filter that supports that protocol.

- **Use a plug-in:** Select a spam filter that works within your e-mail program — a *plug-in* — so you don't have to download your e-mail twice and so you won't ultimately have to change your e-mail address.

- **Don't forget updates:** Be sure to choose a spam filter that provides regular or routine updates that you can easily download. You won't have to change spam filters because those devious spammers are using new techniques that leave you defenseless. Make sure you check the cost of updates. You may be surprised at how much costs have increased.

Table 16-2 compares the three leading personal spam filters. All three support *Outlook, Outlook Express,* and any POP client, and they all analyze and then divide e-mail messages into two categories, the ones from your friends and the ones from your enemies.

Table 16-2	Comparison of Personal Spam Filters		
Attribute	**Spam Filter**		
	Norton Anti-spam 2004 (www.symantec.com/anti-spam)	**SAproxy Pro** (www.statalabs.com)	**SpamCatcher** (www.aladdinsys.com)
Ease of Setup	Very easy to set up.	Some difficulty in setting up on *Outlook, Outlook Express,* or other clients.	Easy to set up.
Ease of Use	Can train Bayesian engine with the flick of a button.	Uses Bloomba Bayesian filter that's geared for advanced users.	Can slow down the speed of *Outlook Express.*
Customization	Supports HotMail. Also blocks ads & pop-ups. Features automatic updates.	Have to program Bayesian filter for best results.	Supports HotMail & Exchange.
Accuracy	Includes customizing filters. Can adjust aggressiveness.	Without Bloomba, works like any other personal spam filter.	Includes collaborative filtering. *Outlook* version works best.
Price	$39.95	$29.95	$29.99

Protecting Your Privacy

Phishing for your identity is a new type of online scam. *Phishers* use a variety of pretexts to obtain your personal information without your knowing it. For example, the phisher may claim to be from an online survey firm that wants to ask you a few questions. When the phisher gets the desired information (usually Social Security, bank, or credit-card account numbers), he or she contacts your financial institution and proceeds to pretend to have access to your account. Phishing by false pretext results in unwary Internet users actually volunteering their personal financial information.

Although some information about you already may be part of the public record, phishers break current laws by using false, fictitious, and fraudulent statements (false pretexts) to gain your customer information. Frequently, they use counterfeit, forged, or stolen documents from financial institutions. Figure 16-1 shows the fraudulent e-mail message of a phisher posing as Citibank to gain your personal information.

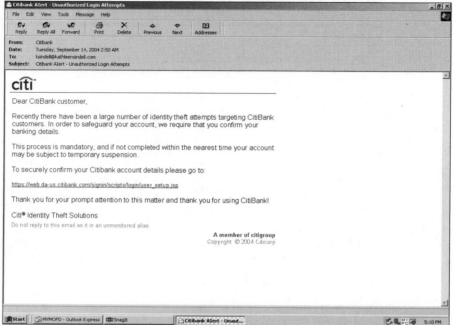

Figure 16-1:
Here's an example of a hacker using Citibank to phish for personal information.

Types of identity theft

Usually, phishers use the personal information they illegally gain to commit (or help someone else commit) identity theft. *Identity theft* is when someone hijacks your personal identifying information to open new charge or bank accounts, order merchandise, or borrow money. The kinds of information they seek access to without your consent are your Social Security number, driver's license number, credit-card number, or other identifying information. Their aim is to get away with committing fraud or other crimes. The four types of identity theft are

- ✓ **Financial ID theft:** The theft of your financial identity means using your personal financial information to apply for and receive telephone services, credit cards, loans, merchandise, cars, apartment leases, or other financial gains.

- ✓ **Criminal ID theft:** A criminal can supply arresting authorities with your personal information when stopped by law enforcement for a crime. Eventually, an arrest warrant is issued in *your* name.

- ✔ **ID cloning:** Your personal information is used to create a new life for the criminal. The criminal may be trying to establish a new identity (in your name, of course) for an illegal alien, trying to avoid outstanding arrest warrants, or even hiding from an abusive situation. Victims of identity cloning can be left with a poor work record and ruined financial history.

- ✔ **Business or commercial ID theft:** Businesses also can fall victim to identity theft. A criminal usually secures illicit credit cards or checking accounts in the name of the business, and the real business eventually is confronted by unhappy suppliers when they receive collection notices or the financial rating of the business is adversely affected.

The horrible results of ID theft

Individuals who experience identity theft must often spend large amounts of money and time cleaning up the mess that identity thieves have made of their lives. During the interim, identity theft victims can lose job opportunities, be turned down for educational opportunities, and be refused auto and home loans. Some victims may even be arrested for crimes they didn't commit. In many cases, individuals who experience identity theft are unaware that they're victims. They don't often gain an appreciation of just how big a problem identity theft is until bad things start to happen. The first tip off can be when an application for a mortgage or car loan is denied. Or collection agencies can begin dunning procedures for purchases you never made or because you've failed to pay large loans that identity thieves took out in your name. The treasure trove of information about identity theft that the Internet provides includes Web sites (for starters) for these agencies:

- ✔ **Federal Trade Commission** (www.consumer.gov/idtheft) explores how identity theft works and provides consumer information and complaint forms.

- ✔ **Identity Theft Resource Center** (www.idtheftcenter.org/index.shtml) is a nonprofit organization that is developing and implementing a comprehensive program against identity theft. The organization supports victims and has a public outreach program to increase awareness and understanding.

- ✔ **Privacy Rights Clearing House** (www.privacyrights.org/identity.htm) provides identity-theft fact sheets, links to online publications about identity theft, and stories from victims.

Avoiding identity theft

The National Fraud Center reports that the Federal Trade Commission (FTC) released a trade report on global competition and new technologies. The report points out that Internet technology is a growing threat to consumers because it enables clever criminals to develop Web pages at low cost to exploit an expanding number of consumers. The Federal Trade Commission Web site (www.ftc.gov/bcp/menu-internet.htm) provides consumer information about the Internet and e-commerce. The FTC can be contacted online and is interested in all types of Internet fraud and privacy issues. To file a consumer complaint online, go to www.ftc.gov/bcp/conline/pubs/credit/affidavit.pdf.

Here are five tips that can assist you in protecting yourself from unscrupulous fraudsters:

- ✔ Don't disclose any personal financial information.
- ✔ Make sure that you're using a secure server whenever you're making any transactions.
- ✔ Don't hesitate to ask for more information whenever you're uncertain about your purchase.
- ✔ If the information you receive is insufficient, contact the Better Business Bureau (www.bbb.org) or state department of consumer's affairs.
- ✔ Don't send money or sign a contract until you have all the information you need to make an informed decision.

Chapter 17

Facts about Online Frauds and Schemes

In This Chapter

▶ Verifying financial information on the Internet

▶ Looking into potential online swindles and deceptions

▶ Determining how you can protect yourself

▶ Honing your online skills to get the right information before deciding about an online offer

▶ Identifying the roles of consumer watchdog organizations on the Internet

▶ Grasping when and where to file a consumer complaint using the Internet

---

Knowing how to judge the reliability of Internet data can save you money, embarrassment, and heartache. This chapter explains techniques for judging what's real and what isn't. After mining the Internet, you need to judge the quality of the information you've gathered. Some ways of doing just that are determining whether the information is current, considering the source, and thinking about what the data provider has to gain. In addition to getting the information right, this chapter explores potential Internet swindles, including brokerage scams, investment schemes, charging unnecessary fees for credit cards and scholarship searches, charging high fees for credit-repair services, upfront fees for loans, and pyramid schemes. You'll also gain an understanding from the Federal Trade Commission (FTC) and other organizations of how you can protect yourself online.

In most cases, these preventive measures are heavy doses of common sense. In other words, just because you read it on a Web page doesn't mean that it's true. This chapter discusses fraud-prevention tactics such as being careful about what you download and being wary of endorsements from government agencies. You'll become aware of when to ignore e-mail, discover tips about avoiding financial-aid scams by reading the fine print and requiring financial disclosures, and uncover how to investigate a company before you invest. Best of all, I provide you with information about how to lodge a protest and where you can file your consumer complaints online.

Urban legends are good for storytelling because they mysteriously appear and spread almost spontaneously in many different forms. Usually an urban legend contains either humorous or horrific material. Most urban legends are false and normally get their life after an event that piques interest in them. The Internet is a nearly perfect medium for spreading popular urban legends. Tall tales quickly spread through instant messaging and chat rooms, by e-mail messages, or through online chain letters. A good example of an urban legend is that UPS uniforms are being purchased on eBay by possible terrorists. For the latest about this Net lore and these urban legends, go to About.com at `urbanlegends.about.com/library/blxatoz.htm`.

Is the Deal Real? Identifying Fraudulent Schemes on the Internet

Most people are honest and operate as responsible *Netizens,* but a criminal element exists in virtually every population. These folks are interested in their own personal gain at the expense of others, and their online activities can be defined as nothing less than fraud. *Fraud* is characterized as a deception designed to secure an unfair or unlawful gain. It also can be the deliberate misrepresentation of the truth for the purpose of gaining something of value.

Internet fraud is any type of scheme that uses one or more components of the Internet to get your hard-earned dollars into the pockets of online con artists. These online crooks are good at presenting what appears to be a legitimate front, but they do so at the expense of the dark shadows they cast on genuine e-commerce, giving it a bad name and undermining consumer confidence. Some of the typical frauds carried out on the Internet are

- **Online auction and retail scams:** Items for sale are purported to be original, unique, or of high quality, but what consumers receive are shoddy wares, imitations, or nothing at all.

- **Business opportunities:** These so-called business opportunities are often work-at-home schemes that promise you'll earn thousands of dollars per month. These frauds usually require upfront fees of $35 to several hundred dollars without providing any information about how to turn the venture into a viable business.

- **Get-divorced-quick schemes:** Some Web sites offer assistance in obtaining a quick divorce in a foreign country. Individuals pay as much as $1,000 or more for divorces in the Dominican Republic or some other foreign country without ever leaving the United States. Unfortunately, these divorces usually are shams regardless of the number of e-mail messages exchanged.

Follow the Money Trail! Evaluating Information on the Internet

In the early days of the Internet, much of its content was based on government experts and academics sharing high-level information. Individuals who were knowledgeable, in general, wrote what they knew and had the data reviewed by an editorial committee before posting it on the Internet. Through the years, the Internet has expanded to include information from individuals, not-for-profit organizations, and corporate entities. Although the majority of this information is straightforward, its reliability still requires you to exercise good judgment.

When evaluating the quality of Internet information, you need to remember who is sponsoring the Web site and what they have to gain, determine how old the data is, and verify it with offline sources before you sign any contract, make a commitment to purchase, or offer up your credit-card number online.

By now, I'm sure you're wondering just how you determine what's good, dependable information and what data aren't reliable, right? Evaluate Internet data the way you do any other kind of data. Data from nationally known news services, press releases from large corporations, and statistical information gathered by government agencies is likely to be of high quality and accurate. Other sources of Internet information, however, may not be as accurate. A couple of examples of how to judge Internet information include asking the following questions:

- ✔ **Does the author have an axe to grind?** Sometimes authors, the purveyors of the information, have a slant on a topic that's based on their political persuasions. If the source is a political or lobbying organization, then you need to check the opposing side of the story. When you do, your research results will be clearer and more accurate when they include both sides of the argument.

- ✔ **Are you expected to make decisions based on the face value of the information?** Information presented as fact by individuals is hard to accept at face value (without confirmation). Other information that's likely to be undependable comes from second- or third-hand sources. This intelligence needs to be verified by checking offline or with reliable online sources. For example, the names of corporate officers, business addresses, and telephone numbers that you find in an online telephone book need to be double-checked against another business directory if you plan on giving your personal financial information, credit data, or credit-card number.

Another way to verify numbers quoted in a mailing list or in Usenet correspondence is to ask the author for attribution. A *mailing list* is a group discussion conducted through e-mail messages. When a message is sent, each mailing list subscriber receives a copy of the message. *Usenet* is a worldwide bulletin-board system that includes newsgroups. Usenet can be accessed through the Internet or through many online services. Check the author's references and make certain that the sources actually exist because newsgroup authors have been known to falsify their sources — sometimes all of them.

Gone sour: The problem of stale information

Whenever possible, use the most recent data that's available. Any financial information that's more than six months old is likely to be out of date and inaccurate. Sometimes material found on the Internet isn't dated. When that's the case, check the content of the document for clues about when it was written. For example, if the author refers to a DOS platform as a "new technology" or "PC computers" as the latest innovation, you know that the article is probably more than ten years old. If you can't find the date of the source material, the conservative approach to this dilemma is not to use it. In other words, better safe than sorry.

Although going to the library, calling a corporation, and visiting a brokerage's regional headquarters are inconveniences, sometimes you can't sidestep those methods. For years, individuals used paper and shoe leather to complete their research. Even with the best technology in-hand, checking offline can't be avoided.

A little shoe leather goes a long way

A business associate of mine is a physician who sells medical supplies and equipment internationally. The countries where he does business are sometimes underdeveloped and use conduits located in the United States. My associate lives in Houston, Texas, and I live near Washington, D.C. He recently asked me to check the address of a potential customer who contacted him through the Internet. The company in question was touted as the largest of its kind "with a dominant presence in the nation's capital." When I visited the company's corporate headquarters, it was a rent-by-the-month office located on Pennsylvania Avenue. Based on the size of its small office, it was unlikely that the company's annual sales were anywhere near what they reported to my associate.

Taking investment advice and solicitations with several grains of salt

Personal online investing often is ripe for Internet swindlers. The National Association of Securities Dealers (NASD) warns about "hot stock picks" or other gossip that investors may hear about in newsgroups, in chat rooms, or by e-mail.

NASD tracks price and volume changes in some very low-priced stocks and correlates these numbers with increases in the number of Internet messages related to the underlying stocks. NASD has concluded that this higher-than-normal Internet traffic may consist of legitimate exchanges by investors sharing ideas about new companies, but it also has two other concerns:

- ✔ Messages can be planted by company insiders using aliases to hype a stock they plan to dump on the public.

- ✔ A brokerage firm that wants to get rid of its excess inventory can illicitly fabricate Internet messages to stir up investor interest.

Both practices are illegal. The Securities and Exchange Commission (SEC), located at www.sec.gov, offers this example scenario:

> According to a 1997 Securities and Exchange Commission (SEC) lawsuit, Charles O. Huttoe and 12 other defendants secretly distributed nearly 42 million shares of Systems of Excellence, Inc., known by its ticker symbol "SEXI," to friends and family. Huttoe drove up the price of SEXI shares through false press releases claiming nonexistent multimillion-dollar sales, an acquisition that hadn't occurred, and revenue projections that had no basis in reality. Huttoe also bribed codefendant SGA Goldstar to tout SEXI to subscribers of SGA Goldstar's online *Whisper Stocks* newsletter. The SEC sought and obtained court orders freezing Huttoe's assets and those of various others who participated in the scheme or received proceeds from the fraudulent activity. Six people, including Huttoe and Theodore R. Melcher, Jr., the author of the online newsletter, eventually were convicted of criminal violations. Huttoe and Melcher were sentenced to federal prison. Although the SEC has recovered approximately $11 million to date in illegal profits from the various defendants, it nevertheless warns that Internet investment tips should never be the basis for purchasing stock.

If you find an online investment opportunity that seems legit and decide to consider it, download and print a hard copy of the online solicitation for the investment you're considering. Required written financial disclosures about the company include the prospectus, annual report, offering circular, and audited financial statements.

The SEC doesn't require companies that are seeking less than $1 million to be registered when selling their stocks, but it definitely requires those firms to file a Form D.

Copies of Forms D are available for you to review from the SEC (just call 202-942-8090). This form includes the names and addresses of owners and promoters of the firms you're researching. Other information is limited. For example, a copy of the firm's audited financial statement isn't included. If a Form D isn't available, the SEC suggests you call its Investor Education and Assistance Department at 202-942-7040.

To further investigate a company, contact the securities regulator in the state where it's located and check whether any complaints about the company have been filed. An SEC listing of state regulators can be found at `www.nasaa.org/nasaa/abtnasaa/find_regulator.html`.

Several offline organizations can help you investigate before you invest, but please note that finding out what state the company is incorporated in and asking that state's secretary of state whether an annual report is on file are important steps to follow. Annual reports filed with government regulators may be different from the ones you receive in a prospectus or that you see online.

The public library in the company's locale may assist you with information about the company's payment history, lawsuits, liens, or judgments.

Who are these people? Be wary of endorsements

Some products or services may claim to be endorsed by a government agency, but such assertions should make you immediately suspicious of the organization's claims. Government agencies like the FTC, the office of the state attorney general, and comptroller of the currency don't endorse any product, organization, or offer. Some firms claim other types of government or government-related sponsorships, such as

- **State licenses:** Having a state license means that a firm has paid a fee to be allowed to conduct business in a certain state and promises to obey state laws, but it doesn't mean the state is endorsing the company.

- **State investigations:** Firms that have been investigated by a government agency aren't automatically endorsed by the examining agency. During an investigation, all information that's gathered is confidential and can't be released to the public. The government simply doesn't endorse any company or offer.

The Skeptic's Handbook: Examples of Potential Online Swindles

The National Fraud Information Center (www.fraud.org) states that many types of con games and schemes are carried out on the Internet. Some of the financial scams that have been uncovered are described in the sections that follow. *Note:* The National Fraud Information Center also provides recommendations for consumer complaints.

Going broke with unregistered brokers

Many savvy investors know how to pick high-return investments but are unsophisticated about selecting brokers or knowing where to report brokers they suspect of wrongdoing. Brokers must be registered and able to offer you references. Whenever you suspect your broker of improper dealings, don't waste time and money by hesitating to contact the SEC at www.sec.gov. The SEC also provides advice about con artists at this Web address: www.sec.gov/investor/brokers.htm.

The Web site of the National Association of Securities Dealers, Inc. (NASD) is located at www.NASD.com. If your complaint concerns an NASD broker, you can refer to this site for general help and for help with filing your complaints online. Investors also can contact the securities commissions in their respective states for assistance.

E-mail offers for get-rich-quick investments

Investors need to be skeptical about unsolicited offers. Many Internet con artists offer investments in gemstones, wireless cable, specialized mobile radio, cellular telephone or paging services, gold coins or bullion, oil and gas leases, and many other types of investments. The investments often are difficult to verify or have values that fluctuate according to world events. You need to seek the advice of someone whose financial opinions you trust before you even consider investing.

The free vacation that'll cost you a bundle

Free vacations to places like Hawaii, the Caribbean, or Disney World usually are offered by high-pressure salespeople to unsuspecting Internet users. Proving there's no such thing as a free lunch, unsuspecting vacation goers soon discover they must spend hours listening to sales presentations, and their rooms are available only on Tuesdays through Thursdays during the off season. In addition, all they have to do to receive their lovely vacation is pay a small shipping and handling charge that's almost the cost of the plane ticket.

Credit-card offers that require upfront fees

Some individuals receive e-mail offers for major credit cards or gold cards with preapproved lines of credit. The ads guarantee credit approval for thousands of dollars regardless of your previous credit history. These scams generally require large upfront fees, and the credit cards are good only for the company's catalog of goods. The Visa or MasterCard you were promised is processed separately and may require you to make a security deposit with the issuing bank. Smart consumers avoid this scam. Individuals with poor credit histories are never granted hefty credit lines by legitimate financial institutions. People seeking a secured credit card can apply directly to banks. In other words, individuals with poor credit histories don't need to pay an Internet swindler's upfront fees for services that are available for free. Complaints need to be sent to your state's Department of Consumer Affairs or the Better Business Bureau.

Paying the tab for credit repairs that never materialize

The FTC recently announced its tenth case involving fraudulent advertising for credit-repair services on the Internet. The perpetrators claim that for a fee, they can repair credit records, remove accurate but poor credit reports, and delete derogatory credit information. The FTC investigation shows that these firms didn't substantiality improve any of their clients' credit reports.

Using college financial-aid services that charge upfront fees

When many students apply for college, they look for scholarships, grants, and other types of financial aid. Many crooks are aware of this, and they charge unsuspecting individuals anywhere from $10 to $400 to assist them with finding the right scholarship or financial aid. Often the information these organizations provide is out of date, inapplicable, or not what was promised. When trying to get a refund, consumers may encounter restrictions that prevent them from getting some or all of their money back. Some refunds are returned to consumers in the form of U.S. Savings Bonds. The FTC is actively looking for these Internet frauds with its Project $cholar$cam.

Whenever you see an advertisement for "Millions of Dollars in Unclaimed Student Aid," be warned that legitimate scholarship funds and grants neither charge an upfront fee nor guarantee that you'll win a scholarship. Besides, the service being advertised may not be for a scholarship at all but rather for a search service. Scholarship search services compare your profile with their databases and provide you with a list of scholarship fund candidates. Moreover, search services never help you apply for scholarship awards, and much of their information is available for free on the Internet, at the library, or at your school's financial-aid or counseling office.

"No Credit Check" loans loaded with upfront fees

In the past, the Internet featured ads that offered consumers easy access to loans (with no credit checks) and charged an upfront fee of around $50. According to the FTC, charging any consumer an upfront fee for a loan is illegal. When the FTC finds these fraudulent ads, it forces perpetrators to remove them from the Internet.

Those age-old pyramid schemes now are online

Pyramid schemes can be promoted in newsgroups, chat rooms, and other areas of the Internet. These schemes are presented by scammers as legitimate marketing plans that require, you guessed it, an entry fee for new customers. If the company bases its profits on new recruits and not on new sales of products or services, then the investment is an illegal pyramid scheme and needs to be avoided.

E-mailed collection notices

In this scam, an individual receives an e-mail stating that he or she has an overdue account with a certain company. The consumer, of course, never has done any business with the firm, but the e-mail nevertheless threatens the recipient by stating that the matter will be referred to a collection agency if the purported debtor doesn't call the 809 number immediately. The target calls the telephone number and gets a lengthy recorded message but never has an opportunity to talk to anyone. The 809 number is likely to be for a phone located in the Caribbean and is similar to a pay-per-call line, meaning the call is charged to your account and can be very expensive. Legitimate debt collection agencies are restricted to contacting debtors either by telephone, mail, telegram, in person, or by fax. You're not required to make a pay-per-call to clear your credit record.

Save money by buying inexpensive drugs online

I receive at least ten e-mails per day offering me a wide variety of prescription drugs from online pharmacies. These fraudulent e-mail advertisements claim that I can order whatever I need, and best of all the sender's doctors will write a prescription without ever examining me, and I'll receive my order overnight for half the money I'd usually pay. Clearly, this offer is too good to be true. First, if I send these folks money, I have no guarantee that I'll ever see my order. Second, after receiving an order, I have no guarantee that what I get isn't powdered sugar pills or talcum powder. Third, buying drugs without a prescription is illegal, so I certainly can't call a law enforcement agency, such as the FTC or Federal Drug Administration (FDA) to file a complaint.

The online word-of-mouth services

Although I receive hundreds of e-mail messages every day, one of them immediately got my attention. The e-mail stated that a user was looking into my background at the sender's Web site. The e-mail went on to explain that the purpose of the Web site is to find and then communicate with people who "know and have opinions about a business or person." Why did I receive this e-mail notice? The Web site owners believe it's their responsibility to let me know what is being said about me. Curious, I visited the Web site. I soon discovered that no report or any other useful information could be found — only a notification that an anonymous contributor recently submitted an "I HAVE INFORMATION" entry on me. If I want to find out what this anonymous contributor supposedly knows, I have to part with $19.97 for a three-month subscription or $29.97 for a six-month subscription.

Right about now is when the adage "a fool and his money are soon parted" kicks in. If I subscribe and contact this anonymous person, he or she can ignore my request, claim forgetfulness, or make up any type of story. That is, if the anonymous person really exists and isn't a shill hired as an agent of the Word-of-Mouth company to stir up business. The rub is that no way exists to tap into this so-called information because the informant and inquirer are anonymous and the Web site doesn't maintain a database. Additionally, the Word-of-Mouth Web site has no control over content, so users have no recourse whenever informants spread false information. All in all, this Web site has no checks and balances to guarantee its integrity.

Who Barks and Who Bites: The Role of Online Watchdogs

The Internet is an unregulated entity that relies on the integrity of the people who use it. And yet almost daily, discussions can be heard in the halls of government about creating legislation to regulate the Internet or establish an Internet police force to ensure individual privacy, insulate children from adult entertainment or pornography, and reduce fraud.

Many Internet users believe that government intervention will reduce the effectiveness of the Internet and increase costs, and as such, individuals who use the Internet must be keenly aware of and watch out for Internet sources that represent hidden agendas. Remember, however, that you're not on your own; you can contact private organizations or state and federal agencies, and they can lend a hand.

The Better Business Bureau

The Better Business Bureau (BBB — www.bbb.org) is a private nonprofit organization that's supported by its member businesses. The organization provides reliability reports on businesses. The reports are helpful to an individual evaluating a business before making a purchase.

The BBB handles complaints about misleading advertising, improper selling practices, nondelivery of promised goods or services, misrepresentation, unhonored guarantees or warranties, unsatisfactory service, credit/billing problems, unfulfilled contracts, and other related issues.

Complaints about a specific business can be filed online. You receive an e-mail notification that the BBB received your complaint and is investigating. If the company in question doesn't respond to BBB inquiries, that fact becomes part of the record kept by the BBB and is reported to others who inquire about the company. In extreme cases, the BBB refers complaints to law enforcement agencies for further action.

State consumer fraud groups

Many states have departments of consumer affairs. These departments frequently have Web sites and accept consumer complaints over the Net. A good example of a state consumer affairs Web site is at www.dca.ca.gov, the California Department of Consumers Affairs (DCA) Web site. It includes instructions about where to file a consumer complaint, how to file a complaint, and what steps to take to resolve a complaint. California's DCA Web site also provides Internet links for specific types of complaints (automobile, insurance, investing, and so on). These links connect consumers to the appropriate organization (local consumer agencies, county district attorneys, the Better Business Bureau, and so on) and legal agencies (small claims courts, lawyer referral services, and mediation programs).

The Federal Trade Commission

The Internet revolution has created new opportunities and new dangers for consumers. If you're an online victim, the chances of getting your money back are slim. Even in cases where government agencies recover money, the consumer usually gets back less than 10¢ on the dollar. The best defense is to be an educated consumer. An educated consumer thoroughly investigates an online offer *before* putting any money down.

The Federal Trade Commission is an independent federal agency that's charged with protecting American consumers from "unfair methods of competition" and "unfair or deceptive acts or practices" in the marketplace. The FTC strives to ensure that consumers benefit from a vigorously competitive marketplace; it doesn't, however, seek to supplant competition with regulation. The commission's work is rooted in a belief that free markets work and that competition among producers and information in the hands of consumers bring about the best products at the lowest prices for consumers, spur efficiency and innovation, and strengthen the economy. The commission is, first and foremost, a law-enforcement agency.

The FTC (www.ftc.gov) inspects consumer and investment swindles. According to the FTC, the Internet has spawned an entirely new lexicon and brought the world to your living room, 24/7/365. And although opportunities online for consumers are almost endless, some challenges exist, too, as in *dot.con challenges.* Get it? Helping consumers avoid scams, the FTC provides free information about consumer issues at www.ftc.gov/ftc/consumer.htm.

Con artists have gone high-tech, using the Internet to defraud consumers in a variety of clever ways. Whether using the excitement of an Internet auction to entice consumers into parting with their money, applying new technology to peddle traditional business opportunity scams, using e-mail to reach vast numbers of people with false promises about earnings through day trading, or hijacking consumers' modems and cramming hefty long-distance charges onto their phone bills, scam artists are just a click away. If you have a consumer complaint, contact Consumer Sentinel at www.consumer.gov/sentinel.

Chapter 18

Online Insurance and Your Family's Financial Health

*E*xperts estimate that the typical American family often pays more than is necessary in insurance premiums. They estimate that the average excess is about $500 per year. In this chapter, I show you how to lower your insurance premiums by determining exactly how much insurance you need, using online calculators. I also show you how to get free, no-obligation auto, medical, residential, and life-insurance quotes online from many insurance carriers. I explain how to be a wise Internet shopper and show you how to do your homework, shop around, and compare agents, policies, and intangibles (like how you can pay your premium using a credit card or direct checking account withdrawal in monthly or quarterly payments).

The Internet provides an easy way for you to shop for the best-quality insurance company with the lowest rates. I point you to many insurance supersites that show you how insurance companies rate when compared with other companies and how to compare instant online insurance quotes. Don't worry about being pressured into buying anything. Many people shop online but purchase from a broker or agent.

This chapter provides a brief overview on the fundamentals of insurance and then divides insurance into the four most popular types of policies: auto, medical, residential, and life. Each section shows how to estimate your needs and how to use the Internet to shop for the least expensive policy.

The Essentials of Insurance: How It Works and Why You Need It

Insurance is when you strike a deal (your *policy*) with your insurance provider (the *underwriter* or *insurer*) that in return for a fee (a *premium*) you pay, the insurer agrees to take on the liabilities for your insurable (quantifiable, fortuitous) risks and guarantees you protection against loss. Your insurance policy has an *indemnification clause,* which means that you can insure yourself for more than you're worth, but you'll be paid only for the replacement costs and thus makes purchasing extra insurance useless. For example, if you insure your home for $1 million, but the replacement and refurbishment costs are only $100,000, then you can claim only $100,000.

An insurance contract has three main sections. First, the *declarations* state who or what is insured, explain the insurance premium, and list the policy dates (including times that the policy is in force and when it expires). Second, the *insuring agreement* details the obligations of the insurer, the risk covered, and the coverage amount. Third, the *conditions and exclusions* show precisely what's needed for the insurance company to pay a claim (such as filing a police report for an automobile accident and so on).

The *insurer* (sometimes called the *insurance carrier*) profits by selling as many policies as possible, which enables the insurance carrier to spread the company's risk across a large customer base. If the insurer's statistics are correct, only a few of the insured customers will suffer losses and file claims. Insurance premiums are based on the statistical likelihood of an undesirable event occurring. The pool of funds that the insurer collects in premiums from other customers is used to pay your claim. The insurer's profit comes from whatever amount is left over.

Figuring out the types of insurance

Having the right insurance is important to your personal wealth. Good financial planning can insulate you and your family against the effects of *fortuitous risk,* or the consequences of uncontrollable events or acts that can leave your family bankrupt and ruined.

Most consumers are uncertain about what types of insurance they need, how much insurance they need to carry, and what to do whenever their application for coverage is denied. Becoming educated as a consumer is important for individuals who don't understand the basics of insurance. You can learn about insurance from the Internet at Web sites that aren't tied to any specific insurance company or agent. Insurance agents frequently provide you with plenty of educational literature; however, they may not tell you about another company that has lower rates.

The Internet can help you purchase the insurance that meets your needs and suggests how you can lower the costs of your premiums. If you already have insurance, you need to check your policies at least once every two or three years. As your lifestyle changes, your insurance needs change. Insurance compilation sites like the ones I list below can assist you in making the right changes. If these insurance supersites don't provide all the answers you need, they can point you in the right direction.

- **4Insurance** (www.4insurance.com) is a free, no-obligation service. Complete the quick online questionnaire in only a few minutes, and you'll receive several quotes from different insurance carriers. This Web site includes valuable articles about auto, home, life, health, dental, disability, and annuity insurance.

- **Insurance News Net** (INN — www.insurancenewsnet.com) offers a free newsletter, news about life and health insurance and property and casualty insurance, featured articles, and news about mergers and acquisitions among insurance companies. Insurance professionals are likely to be interested in this Web site's premium-level content. The cost is $45.95 per year to become an insider and receive information from more than 12,000 sources, including full access to INN content, all sections of the Web site, hundreds of articles not published on the public site, an e-mail newswire service, and article search capabilities.

- **InsWeb** (www.insweb.com) instantly provides consumers with quotes, often more than 35 at a time. Other quotes may be sent to you via e-mail, telephone, or mail. Customer service is available online, via telephone, or by e-mail. This site also offers a glossary of insurance terms and other valuable information, such as a report on vehicle crash performance.

- **MSN House and Home** (houseandhome.msn.com) supplies articles about choosing homeowner's and renter's insurance and offers an article index. On the home page, click on "Insurance" for the overview page. You'll see insurance "Weekly Spotlights," "More Resources," and "Tips and Tools." For a good example of what you'll find at this site, click on "Homeowner's Insurance." It takes you to an article titled "What Kind of Insurance Will I Need When I Buy a Home?"

- **YouDecide.com** (www.youdecide.com) rates insurance companies and provides tools and articles about insurance. You may want to complete the lengthy questionnaire that results in better insurance quotes from approximately 15 insurance carriers. You're bound to find the high and low quotes humorous. YouDecide.com doesn't sell insurance. If you want to purchase an insurance policy, you have to go to the provider.

Assessing your risks

Through your financial planning and purchasing the right type of insurance, you can insulate yourself and your family against the effects of fortuitous risk. The following list shows how having the right insurance is important to your personal wealth. Overall, the three primary types of insurable hazards are

- **Personal risks:** These risks include loss of income caused by premature death, disability, or financial losses caused by illness or injury. Life insurance, disability insurance, and medical insurance cover these losses.

- **Property risks:** These risks include the loss of or damage to a car, a home (sometimes including its contents), or personal property. These losses are covered by automobile insurance, residential insurance, and personal property insurance.

- **Liability risks:** These risks include exposure caused by home ownership (the mailman slips on your icy walkway and sues you), car ownership and operation (you're tired, don't see the red light, and hit another car), and liability caused by negligence or malpractice related to your personal or professional life. These risks are covered by homeowner's insurance, automobile insurance, and comprehensive liability insurance programs (for physicians, consultants, and other professionals).

The Wise Online Insurance Shopper

Nearly 6,000 insurance companies do business in the United States. According to the Insurance Information Institute (III), total premiums paid annually for all types of insurance exceed $600 billion per year, with the average American family paying around $3,000 directly for annual insurance premiums and nearly $5,000 indirectly in employer-paid premiums. In terms of annual expenses, what you pay for insurance is a whole bunch of money that requires considerable time and attention.

National surveys indicate that many consumers don't care about the quality and cost of the insurance products they purchase. Savvy Internet financial researchers, like you, want companies that provide good service and charge fair prices. So, you ask, how can the Internet help? Read on.

Doing your homework on the Internet

Celent Communications (www.celent.com), a research and consulting firm, found in a recent survey that 19 percent of all personal lines of insurance are sold online. Celent predicts an increase in that number to 37 percent by 2005 or more than $200 billion in premiums. The most popular type of insurance now purchased online is automobile insurance. Personal life and health insurance attract about half as much attention as automobile insurance at this point in time.

Shopping for insurance online is similar to shopping for insurance using a toll-free (800) telephone number. Instead of providing your personal information to a customer service representative at a call center, you provide the same information in an online questionnaire. The questions you're asked are used to classify you into a risk category. The following are a couple of the types of questions you can expect:

✔ **Demographic questions:** What's your age, gender, address, and so on? These questions are asked so the insurance company can develop a framework of your risk category.

✔ **Background questions:** If you're applying for automobile insurance, you can expect questions about your driving record, the type of car you drive, and recent traffic violations or accidents.

Keep in mind that researching insurance online is free. In other words, if you complete a questionnaire, you're under no obligation to purchase. Many online insurance shoppers want to educate themselves so they won't have gaps in their coverage, while other individuals want to compare quotes and see the ratings of insurance carriers before they purchase an insurance policy. In many cases, consumers use the information they've gathered online to buy insurance from an agent. So, don't be caught off-guard. You need to take the time to find out about your insurance needs and become a knowledgeable consumer because over time doing so can save you time, money, and grief. Here are a few online sources to get you started:

✔ **Insurance Information Institute** (www.insurancescoring.info/consumers.htm) offers information about auto, home, life, health, disability, specialty, and business insurance. You discover tools, videos, online brochures, and a safety center. To find an insurance company in your state, just enter the type of insurance you're seeking in the search tool. Results are a random listing of insurance carriers in your state. Online educational information includes insurance basics, types of policies, and tips for buying and saving money.

✔ **Insure.com** (www.insure.com) is the educational part of its parent company Quotesmith.com (quotesmith.com). Insure.com serves as a marketplace, providing quotes from 200 insurance carriers. Articles on Insure.com are a combination of insurance education and news.

✔ **MoneyCentral** (moneycentral.msn.com) provides many useful articles about the value of insurance. One example is "Spot Unethical Sales Practices." Go to the home page, and in the left margin under the category titled "Planning," click on "Insurance." Toward the bottom of the page at the "Insurance Decision Center," click on "Insurance rip-offs to avoid."

✔ **Times of Money** (www.timesofmoney.com/insurance/jsp/policy_ types.jsp) supplies consumer information about the different types of life and general insurance policies. If you're unsure of the differences between term and whole-life insurance policies, this Web site is a good place for finding quick definitions.

✔ **Washington Mutual Insurance** (www.wamuins.com/en/university/ li3.html) offers information about what you need to know about buying life insurance.

Shopping for the best buy

Winning the Insurance Game by Ralph Nader and Wesley J. Smith (1993) suggests that you need not purchase the first good-looking policy that you see. The market offers a wide variety of prices and quality. As you begin shopping online for insurance, you quickly discover many Web sites that offer free, no-obligation quotes. To receive an online quote, you must complete a questionnaire.

Online questionnaires vary. Some companies claim they can provide you with a lower rate because of the detailed online information you provide. Other companies offer short questionnaires and then follow up with a telephone call the next day. Sometimes the type of insurance policy for which you're applying plays a role in how detailed the questionnaire is. The following Web sites offer suggestions for finding the best insurance buys:

✔ **Insurance Finder** (www.insurancefinder.com) offers health, life, auto, business, home, and special insurance quotes from multiple agents and brokers. The online specialty insurance quotes include insurance for computers, pets, and travel.

✔ **Insure.com** (www.insure.com) provides insurance quotes from thousands of insurance companies and up to five competitive quotes with the click of a button. On the home page, select the type of insurance you desire, type in your first name and zip code, and then click "Start Quote."

✔ **NetInsurance** (www.netinsurance.com) offers free quotes for many types of personal insurance (home, automobile, health-care, and so on). Service and support are provided from initial inquiry through the sale and postsale. A learning center and informational and analytical tools are offered throughout the site.

✔ **NetQuote** (www.netquote.com) works with hundreds of partner companies to provide quotes for the type of insurance you want based on the information you supply. NetQuote is a consumer-oriented service providing several competing quotes from different insurance companies that enable you to pursue the policy that best meets your individual needs.

Choose the type of insurance you want, answer some questions, and click to get an online quote. Quotes by different insurance carriers (and sometimes their brokers) are immediately presented. The quotes are free. The only cost to you is time.

Nader and Smith suggest that consumers be wary of an insurance company's advertising. Although insurance companies advertise deep concern, much comfort, and perpetual care, they're primarily interested in making a profit, and that means you need to make sure you follow the instructions outlined in the sections that follow.

Getting everything in writing

If the agent agrees to issue you a policy, get a binder before the formal policy is issued. A *binder* is a written commitment from an insurance company to insure a property or a certain risk. This short-term agreement provides temporary insurance coverage until the policy can be issued or delivered.

Keeping good records

If an insurance company wants more information, provide it. Keep copies of the information and the request for it in your insurance file. All other correspondence about your policy goes into the same file. Keeping your records can provide you with ammunition if a dispute later arises.

Making sure the insurance meets your needs

Use the Internet to determine the types of insurance and amount of coverage you need before you meet with the agent. Discuss your individual needs at length with the insurance company representative before you buy. Many insurance calculators can be found online to help you establish how much insurance you require. The following are a few examples of the best the Web has to offer:

- **Life-Line** (www.life-line.org/life_how_ineeds.html) is an interactive program that provides rough estimates of your life insurance requirements, for example, how much you need at death to cover immediate obligations and how much future income is needed to sustain the current standard of living for survivors.

- **MSN MoneyCentral** (moneycentral.msn.com/investor/calcs/n_life/main.asp) offers an interactive calculator that carefully helps you determine how much life insurance you need to have. By the way, the more you know about your financial position, the faster you can complete the process and the more accurate the results. Don't be discouraged, however, if you're just starting to get your financial ducks in a row. Whenever you don't know the answer to a question, you can always use the online calculator's default answer (which is based on a best-guess estimate of an average person's finances).

- **ReliaQuote** (www.reliaquote.com) covers various types of personal insurance (including health) for one-stop shopping. You can receive quotes from more than 40 different companies. All recommended insurance carriers are highly rated. The life insurance needs calculator adjusts for the correct amount of inflation so you don't have to guess.

- **QuickQuote** (www.quickquote.com) offers resource centers for life, health, and automobile insurance and features an online "Term Life-Insurance Estimator Calculator," "Health Insurance Suitability Tool," and "Automobile Coverage Analyzer."

Making sure you know what dangers exist

A peril is something that causes loss and can change from place to place. Is your home in danger of a flood for residential insurance, or is your car susceptible to theft for automobile insurance? Only buy insurance for coverage that poses a real risk for you.

Deciding how much you can spend

If you have a limited insurance budget (and who doesn't?), get the most for the least. Prioritize your insurance needs. Comprehensive policies provide a wide range of coverage. Catastrophic policies cover worst-case scenarios. You may need comprehensive health coverage but only catastrophic coverage for your old second car.

Saving money on what you buy

Several strategies that you can implement to save money include

- **Increasing your deductibles.** Higher deductibles mean lower insurance premiums, but you pay more out of pocket before your insurance kicks in.

- **Avoiding unneeded coverage.** Whenever possible, tailor your policies to cover your individual needs. If, for example, you don't have many valuables, get a slimmed-down version of your homeowner's policy, a low-premium policy that doesn't include theft.

- **Earning special savings.** Many companies lower their premiums if you meet certain criteria. Sometimes they offer two-car discounts or reduced premiums for senior citizens who take special driver-awareness classes.

- **Obtaining your insurance through a group.** You often can get lower insurance rates when you join a group than if you try to go it alone. Many professional organizations have special rates. For example, a lower insurance rate is one of the benefits of being a member of the National Association of Female Executives (NAFE), located online at www.nafe.com.

Comparing agents

The agent you want is courteous, reliable, and knowledgeable. Experts suggest that you review at least three agents to find out which one offers you an insurance package that best meets your needs. You want the best insurance policies, prices, and services. Check out the agent through the Better Business Bureau (www.bbb.org) to see whether the agent has a history of complaints. Visit the agency to see whether it's well-managed and professional. Talk with the agent face to face.

Comparing policies

The agent should provide you with a computer printout showing the advantages and limitations of different policies. If the agent doesn't provide a comparison sheet, create your own, comparing the premium price, deductible, maximum benefit, exclusions, and so on.

Every insurance company calculates its own statistics to determine levels of risk. Characteristics that are important to one company may not be of any value to another. In other words, a factor that makes you substandard at one company may not be of any importance to another insurance company.

Comparing intangibles

Other things that are important but are harder to quantify are the ease of making claims, how well you get along with the agent, and how easily you can pay the premium (automatic checking-account withdrawal, credit card, monthly, or quarterly payments).

The Web site addresses of actual insurance carriers (not brokerages or online insurance aggregation companies) are listed in several directories. Most companies will refer you to an agent in your location, or you can get the information you need straight from the source. Following are some of the directories:

✔ **Business 2.0** (www.business2.com/b2/webguide) includes an A to Z listing of life insurance companies. The directory includes 28 major insurance companies. Additionally, the directory is divided into different types of insurance carriers (auto, health, and so on). The directory lists two of the four insurance carriers I use. This handpicked directory is available only to Business 2.0 subscribers. The subscription fee is $9.99 per year. Sometimes this fee is reduced to $7.49 per year.

✔ **InsuranceLocal.com** (www.insurancelocal.com/insurancecompany.htm) offers a directory with links to more than 300 insurance carriers. This handy, no-fuss directory includes three of the four insurance carriers I use.

✔ **Yahoo Shopping Directory** (dir.yahoo.com/business_and_economy/shopping_and_services/financial_services/insurance) provides a listing of insurance carriers divided into several interesting categories. You can search for an insurance company alphabetically or by region, category, or popularity. The alphabetical listing, which includes about 200 insurance carriers, also includes two of the four insurance carriers I use. Additionally, some of the firms listed are brokerages or lead-generating Web sites.

Comparing finalists

After you finish your comparisons, three or four insurance policies will stand out. Follow these three steps for making your final comparison:

1. **Check the insurance company's rating.**

   For instance, you can check out the firm's "Best Insurance Report" at A.M. Best (www.ambest.com). Reports also are available at your local library, and your insurance agent should have a copy at his or her office.

2. **Check the consumer complaints about the insurance company.**

   Usually your state's department of insurance keeps a list of insurance consumer complaints (a good example is the Illinois Department of Insurance located at www.ins.state.il.us/Complaints/Complaints.htm. At the "Complaints Statistics Compiled by the Department of Insurance" section, click on the most recent year. Next see the "Complaint Statistics of Insurance Companies by Coverage Types," and select the type of coverage you're investigating. Note the number of policies issued, the total number of complaints, and the ratio of complaints to policies (for example, 125 complaints per 1,000 policies).

3. **Rank the finalist companies.**

   How you rank the finalists depends on your personal requirements, needs, and desires.

Private rating agencies grade insurance companies. The ratings are only opinions and aren't 100 percent foolproof. Ratings can provide important information about how others view the financial health of your insurance carrier. Look at how several companies rate your insurance carrier. Additionally, you may want to check how the ratings for insurance companies have changed during the last several years. The sites that follow are some of the better ones:

✔ **A.M. Best Company** (www.ambest.com/ratings/index.html) provides insurance information and company ratings. Among other things, Best has a "Resource Center" with reviews of insurance issues and analysis. The ratings from this well-known company provide an in-depth look at the financial strengths and weaknesses of insurance companies.

✔ **Moodys.com** (www.moodys.com) includes ratings for insurance companies. Registration is free. You receive your user ID almost instantly by e-mail. Log on and go to the dialog box on the left. In the dialog box, select "Insurance." At the Insurance home page, select "Insurance Financial Strength Ratings" on the right. You'll discover a long list of rated insurance companies. For a more in-depth look, click on the name of your insurance carrier.

✔ **Standard & Poor's Ratings Lists and Claims-Paying Ability Reports** (www.standardandpoors.com/RatingsActions/RatingsLists/ Insurance/InsuranceStrengthRatings.html) is a search engine that finds ratings on insurance companies. Look up the name of a company from which you're thinking about purchasing insurance. The report indicates whether the insurance firm has a new rating, whether that rating was raised (or lowered) from the previous month, or whether its Credit Watch is positive, developing, or negative. The S&P Web site also provides explanations of its rankings.

Keep in mind that paying a low insurance premium won't get you very far if your insurance company isn't financially strong. These rating agencies investigate and analyze the risks that can affect an insurer's long-term survival. Competitive forces, changing marketplace fundamentals, and operational failures can directly affect you and your family, so selecting a company that you know will be able to pay future claims or benefits is important. Most insurance companies have an *A* rating. Companies with *B* ratings or lower shouldn't be considered. You'll probably discover that the best-rated companies usually have the best insurance products.

Automobile Insurance: Find the Right Ticket Online

How much you pay for automobile insurance depends on several factors:

✔ **Where you live:** In most situations, the territory in which you reside establishes the base rate of your automobile insurance.

✔ **Your age, gender, and marital status:** These affect how the automobile insurance underwriters categorize you.

- ✔ **The number of miles per day that you drive:** The more miles you drive per day, the greater the risk of an automobile accident.

- ✔ **Your driving record:** The habits of drivers with poor driving records often don't improve.

- ✔ **The kind of car you drive:** This is based on the car's age, original cost, and ease of repair. For example, a Mercedes is more expensive to repair than a Chevrolet.

- ✔ **The extent of your insurance coverage:** This is based on the amount of your deductible (whether high or low), limits of liability, whether you carry comprehensive coverage, and so on.

Edmunds (www.edmunds.com/advice/insurance/articles) offers tips and advice for individuals who are new to the automobile insurance game. For example, the article that asks, "How Much Auto Insurance Do You Really Need?" looks at minimum insurance requirements on a state-by-state basis. You also can find suggestions about how to be adequately insured but pay the lowest amount for automobile insurance.

For more ways to save money on your automobile insurance, check out "Nine Ways to Lower Your Auto Insurance Costs" at the Federal Citizens Information Center located at www.pueblo.gsa.gov/cic_text/cars/autoinsu/autoinsu.htm. This article provides help advice and links online sources that can assist you in getting a lower rate.

If you don't have medical insurance, make sure that your automobile insurance has a large amount of medical coverage. If you're injured in an accident, this coverage may make all the difference in the quality of care you receive (for example, being admitted to a county or private hospital).

Many individual insurance companies provide quotes online, but the following online resources can give you quotes from multiple insurance companies:

- ✔ **Insweb.com** (www.insweb.com/auto/) is a good Internet source for information and online automobile insurance quotes. This site provides frequently asked questions (FAQs) on automobile insurance, liability insurance, and insurance in general. Its research center provides company ratings, glossaries of automobile insurance terms, and an article archive of papers provided by consumer affairs and educational organizations. After you complete the insurance quote form, the online service matches your information with criteria set by participating insurance companies. The service delivers quotes online, by e-mail, and by U.S. mail.

- ✔ **4Insurance.com** (www.4insurance.com/auto/resources.asp) offers information about the ins and outs of purchasing automobile insurance and tips on how to lower your insurance premiums. Complete the questionnaire, and you'll receive multiple quotes from several insurance companies competing for your business.

✔ **Insurance.com** (`www.insure.com/auto`) provides consumer information about personal insurance needs. Topics range from automobile safety-testing results to the minimum requirements of each state for automobile liability insurance. This site includes information about auto, home, and life insurance. It provides Standard & Poor's ratings of insurance companies and has model-by-model statistics on automobile theft.

If you're thinking about buying a new or used car, check with your insurance company first. Some brands and types of cars have lower insurance rates.

Medi-Clicking for Insurance

Many experts believe that medical insurance is the most important insurance you can buy. If you die without life insurance, your family, with the help of relatives and employment, can go on. If your uninsured property is destroyed and you're healthy and continue to work, you may be able to replace it. A long-term illness, however, can be devastating. For example, if you have a long, uninsured illness followed by a long uninsured convalescence period, you may end up homeless and bankrupt.

Exploring the types of health insurance

You have three primary medical insurance options: traditional health, health maintenance organizations (HMOs), and prospective payment organizations (PPOs). The following sections briefly explain each type of medical insurance and discuss the differences among them.

Traditional health plans

Traditional health plans enable patients to select any doctor or hospital they desire and use a fee-for-service system that has these three parts:

✔ **Hospitalization.** *Hospitalization* covers defined expenses incurred while the covered individual is in the hospital. Some traditional health plans have an indemnity payment plan, which restricts payment to a fixed sum. This sum usually is below the amount charged by the hospital.

✔ **Medical/surgical services.** These covered services include doctor visits or treatment charges that usually require copayments. *Copayments* are payments paid by the insured that usually are 20 percent of the doctor's fee.

✔ **Catastrophic or major medical.** These coverages usually feature a lifetime maximum of payments that the insurance company will pay after hospitalization and medical/surgical plans are used up.

Health maintenance organizations

Health Maintenance Organizations (HMOs) mean the insured person pays one premium and receives all health-care services at no additional cost or at a nominal additional cost. HMOs cost more to purchase and require more out-of-pocket payments from the insured. Some HMOs own their own clinics and hospitals. The biggest difference between an HMO and a traditional health insurance plan is that the doctor works for the cost-conscious HMO and not for you.

Preferred provider organizations

The aim of *preferred provider organizations (PPOs)* is to provide the services of traditional health plans and the money savings of HMOs. They pay high benefits as a reward for using their preselected doctors or hospitals.

Health insurance info online

The list that follows includes a few of the Internet sites that are sources for health insurance information:

- ✔ **Alliance for Affordable Services** (www.affordableservices.org/benefits.asp) provides information on health-care benefits, savings, fitness, legislative issues, news, and links to related sites. The site also features articles on ways to control health-care costs.

- ✔ **Health Insurance Savings** (www.healthinsurancesavings.com/default.asp?app=GGLA) offers immediate access to affordable health insurance, life and dental insurance for the self-employed, and money-saving benefits to you, your family, and your small business. Members of the National Association of the Self Employed (NASE) qualify for these benefits. Access-level membership is $96 per year, and Premier Resource Level is $420 per year. Visit the NASE Web site at www.nase.org for more details.

- ✔ **eHealthInsurance.com** (www.ehealthinsurance.com) lists frequently asked questions about health insurance. If you have a question, you'll probably find an answer here. Check the bottom of the home page for information about health-insurance basics, frequently asked questions (FAQs), and "Ask the Experts."

- ✔ **Health Insurance Consumer Guides** (www.healthinsuranceinfo.net) includes consumer alerts, information about how to handle disputes with your health insurance providers, and news about the protection consumers have (or the lack of it) as they seek to purchase and hold on to private health insurance.

For millions of Americans who are out of work or without health insurance, the Internet is an important resource for health information. In a recent survey by Kaiser Permanente, the nation's largest nonprofit health plan, 62 percent of respondents stated they'd turn to the Internet for medical information. Of this population, 18 percent prefer Web referrals to relevant community health services, and 16 percent of those surveyed said they'd use the Internet to both research and treat nonurgent conditions. The top worries of respondents were obesity (which affects 190 million Americans), cancer, heart disease, being overweight (which can be a forerunner to obesity), and diabetes.

What health insurance ought to cover

When reviewing health-insurance plans, what features are best and which ones should you look for? The following is a list of items that may need your attention when you evaluate a medical-insurance plan:

- **Attempted suicide:** If you attempt suicide and are unsuccessful, you may have to pay for your medical care.

- **Cosmetic surgery:** Your medical insurance may cover a mastectomy but not reconstructive surgery. However, when the cosmetic surgery results from a birth defect, it may be covered.

- **Hospital services:** Full coverage of hospital services needs to include a semiprivate room, board, emergency-room costs, nurses, medicines, X-rays, rehabilitation therapy, and lab tests.

- **Mental illness:** Some policies cover a limited amount of psychotherapy. Others pay only for mental illness that has an organic (bodily) source.

- **Nursing homes:** At least part of a nursing home's expenses for convalescing patients needs to be covered.

- **Older children:** If your children go on to college, you may need to cover them up to age 23 or 25.

- **Pregnancy:** If you're planning a family, make sure your policy covers pregnancy and complete coverage starting from birth for infants.

- **Prescription drugs:** Many policies don't cover medications. Some may require a nominal copayment that can end up being expensive.

- **Preventive care:** Routine annual physicals and tests may not be covered.

- **Substance abuse:** Many policies exclude injuries or disabilities that are related to abuse of narcotics or illegal drugs.

- **Surgery:** Full cost of surgery needs to be covered. Some surgical coverage doesn't include outpatient care or anesthesia.

Reading the fine print

When checking health insurance policies, several clauses require your special attention. The items you need to focus on are listed below in no particular order:

- ✓ **Coinsurance.** Reject any open-ended coinsurance policy; you don't want to be responsible for 20 percent of an $80,000 hospital bill.

- ✓ **Deductibles.** A deductible is the amount paid out of pocket for a doctor's visit or lab tests before your insurance plan pays. Does each family member have to pay $1,000, or does the insurance kick in when your family has cumulatively paid $1,000?

- ✓ **Exclusions.** In an insurance policy, *exclusions* refer to certain areas under the insurance umbrella that aren't covered, such as medical care if you travel abroad.

- ✓ **Preexisting conditions.** If you apply for a new insurance policy, it may not cover an illness that began at an earlier time.

- ✓ **Renewals.** You may not have the right to renew your insurance policy, which means that you may not be able to get another policy that covers your existing illness.

- ✓ **Time requirements.** Your policy may require a waiting period for benefits to begin.

Instant online medical insurance quotes

The Internet provides a variety of sources for instant medical insurance quotes. The following are just a few:

- ✓ **Insweb** (www.insweb.com/health/) is a good Internet source for more information and online medical insurance quotes. Answer eight questions to view instant health insurance quotes from more than 111 companies. The site provides answers to FAQs on health insurance, liability insurance, and insurance in general. Its research center provides company ratings, glossaries of medical-insurance terms, and an article archive of papers provided by consumer affairs and education organizations.

- ✓ **4Insurance.Com** (www.4insurance.com) provides free insurance quotes for health, auto, life, renter's, motorcycle, home, health, watercraft, and retirement insurance. The health questionnaire is relatively short and takes about five minutes to complete. It provides an insurance guide and helps you find an agent in your area.

✔ **Answer Financial** (www.answerfinancial.com) believes that everyone needs health insurance. Complete the online form at Answer Financial to get an apples-to-apples comparison of multiple health plans from leading health-insurance companies. The questionnaire includes about six questions and takes less than five minutes to complete. At the home page, under "Personal" in the "Products & Services" section, click on "Healthcare."

Shopping for Property Insurance on the Internet

Experts believe that renters and property owners alike need to have residential policies. If you own a home, it may be the largest asset that you have. If you rent your home, you want to protect your property. The Internet can assist you in your search for a quality policy and broaden your understanding of residential insurance. The following are a few examples of sites that can help:

✔ **Insurance Information Institute** (www.iii.org) provides a wealth of residential insurance articles that show different ways to lower your homeowner insurance costs. At the home page click on "Home."

✔ **Insurance.com** (home.insurance.com/insurance_options/home/ home_ins_index.asp?sid=2651) provides free home-insurance quotes from several leading insurance carriers in addition to the ABCs of home insurance, tips for new homeowners, and more answers to home-insurance questions.

✔ **MS MoneyCentral** (moneycentral.msn.com/content/insurance/ insureyourhome/p35340.asp), provides information about the basics of home insurance. Be sure to read the article about why one of every three homes is underinsured.

Residential insurance policies are relatively stable but exist in a competitive market, which means that prices vary. The annual premium for $300,000 worth of residential insurance policy ($200,000 for the house and $100,000 for the contents) ranges from $500 to $700 per year. Experts suggest that you get upward of ten quotes before you buy.

The average deductible is $250, but you save money if you can live with a higher deductible. Basic liability protection generally is sufficient, and the amount of money needed to replace your home need not include the value of the land. In most situations the land won't be destroyed; therefore, it won't need to be replaced. For more information about the basics of homeowner's insurance, see Homesite at `www.homesite.com/insbasics.htm`. Homesite Insurance is geared for homeowners, renters, and condominium owners. The Web site offers information about homeowner's insurance, moving, tips on buying a home, and the benefits of homeowner's insurance. Take the homeowner's insurance IQ quiz to see whether you're an educated homeowner's insurance shopper.

Because of the Terrorism Risk Insurance Act of 2002, homeowners now have the right to purchase insurance coverage for losses from acts of terrorism (as defined in the Act). Any in-force exclusions for acts of terrorism, as defined in the Act, that are already contained in your policy were nullified as of November 26, 2002. For more information about this change, see the Web site for the National Association of Insurance Commissioners (NAIC) at `www.naic.org/pressroom/releases/EmergencyResponse.htm`.

Among the many discounts that you may want to use to your advantage are

- **Multiple policy discount:** You use the same company for your automobile insurance and liability policies.

- **Safety device discount:** If you have smoke detectors and a burglar alarm system, you may save money.

- **Nonsmoker's discount:** Some insurance companies offer discounts to nonsmokers. (They're not likely to go to sleep with a lit cigarette.)

- **Fire-resistant material discount:** Houses that are constructed using fire resistant materials (cement block, brick, and related materials) can often get a discount.

- **Mature homeowner discount:** Some companies award longevity and maturity with a discount.

- **Loyal customer discount:** Certain companies reward long-term customers.

Shopping for Life Insurance on the Internet

Life insurance is designed to replace loss of income that results from a premature death. As a general rule, American families don't have enough life insurance. Usually only one family member (the one who works full time) is insured. Other family members may be providing part-time income, care giving, cooking, or cleaning services, and hiring someone to provide those services can become expensive. That means family members who aren't the principal wage earners also need to be insured.

Using the Internet to get in the know about life insurance

Among the several models of life insurance that are available, the list that follows provides a brief overview of the primary types:

- **Term insurance:** Sometimes called temporary insurance, it insures a person for only a specific time, or a term. It is a stripped-down model of insurance that doesn't include any extras and generally is simpler and less expensive than whole-life policies. Benefits are paid if the insured dies within the time period. When the term ends, the policy expires just like automobile or homeowner's insurance. Term life insurance doesn't have any cash value or any right to a refund.

- **Whole life (or cash-value insurance):** Over time, some insurance policies accrue a cash value. Whole-life policies are expensive types of forced savings accounts. You get a better return with another long-term investment. Yet some individuals use them for tax and estate-planning purposes. Many whole-life insurance policies are issued by mutual companies and accrue dividends. Some policies accrue interest or earnings on investments. If a death occurs, the insurance company pays the death benefit and doesn't have to pay any cash value. If the policy is canceled, the accrued cash value is paid to you. You also can borrow against the cash value while the life insurance is in full force.

Playing the longevity game

Check out Northwestern Mutual's Longevity Game at www.nmfn.com. The Longevity Game gives you a sneaky peek into your future. The game identifies factors that lead to a longer life and compares those factors to the most current information gathered by the life insurance industry, public health organizations, and scientific studies. No one can actually see into the future, but the factors you encounter in the game significantly affect how long you will live. At the home page, click on "Learning Center." Next click on "Calculators" and scroll down the page to Longevity Game. *Note:* If you're running a pop-up blocker you won't be able to play the game.

Life insurance is designed to provide security for your family, protect your mortgage, and take care of your estate-planning needs. According to *Consumer Reports,* term life insurance premiums are the lowest in years. To my way of thinking, the Internet provides access to information and compares online quotes from a variety of insurance companies, making term life insurance a great value. Consider this: If all your plans fail, you still can protect your family after your death. The Internet provides plenty of advice about life insurance. The following sites are good resources:

- **Acordia Life Insurance Services** (www.acordia.com) provides information about hard-to-place individual life insurance cases. If you have ever been turned down for insurance, this site can be helpful.

- **Insurance Information Institute** (www.iii.org) shows individuals what insurance is and how it works. The Web site is well organized and easy to navigate. If you're interested in insurance, you can spend hours at this authoritative Web site.

- **Insure.com** (www.insure.com) can provide you with a life insurance quote in a matter of minutes. To get started, at the home page click on "Life."

- **NAIC** (www.naic.org/insprod/catalog_pub_consumer.htm) supplies consumer guides to auto, home, and life insurance. You also find information about medigap, cancer, and long-term care insurance. The cost for each shopper's guide is between 50¢ and 90¢. The cancer insurance shopping guide is free.

If you own a small business or are self-employed, you may want to consider purchasing a disability insurance policy. Disability insurance benefits are payments to you, at a rate of no more than 70 percent of your current income, if you're unable to work or run your business. For details about disability insurance, see the ABC's of Small Business at www.abcsmallbiz.com.

Estimating your life insurance needs

The basic amount of life insurance every person needs is based on how much money you've already accumulated and the amount your heirs will need to recover from the loss of your income.

You may want to calculate your life insurance needs in several ways. The first approach is determining what your heirs will need in the first year after your death. The second needs estimate looks at what your heirs will require five years later, and a third estimate looks at your family's needs ten years later. Keep in mind that as time passes, your family's needs and expenses change, and the amount they require to maintain their current standard of living changes. For example, you may want to consider the cost of private schooling or college tuition. Completing three estimates enables you to fine-tune your assessment of the amount of life insurance you need for the long term. These three Web sites provide ways to estimate your life insurance needs:

- ✔ **Life-Line** (www.life-line.org/life_how_ineeds.html) offers an interactive program that provides you with a rough estimate of your life insurance needs. The easy-to-use online calculator can save you time and money.

- ✔ **FinanCenter** (partners.financenter.com/consumer/calculate/us-eng/lifeins01.fcs) offers a "How much life insurance do I need?" online calculator that shows how much life insurance coverage your family may need to cover future expenses in the event of your untimely death.

- ✔ **Intelliquote** (www.intelliquote.com/how-much-life-insurance-do-i-need.asp) offers an online life insurance needs calculator. Keep in mind that the old rules for purchasing life insurance often don't take into consideration current assets, your working spouse, and any special needs you and your family may have.

Part VI
The Part of Tens

The 5th Wave

By Rich Tennant

"I read about investing in a company called UniHandle Ohio, but I'm uneasy about a stock that's listed on the NASDAQ as UhOh."

In this part . . .

In this section of the book, I provide you with tips that explain how you can use the Internet to help you stop living from paycheck to paycheck and cite ways to get your debt under control.

Chapter 19

More Than Ten Resources and Tips for Online Financial Success

*F*inancial success isn't the result of only one action, such as spending less money. The road to personal wealth has many twists and turns no matter who you are. Your personal path to financial freedom may be different from that of your neighbor, but you can tilt the odds of being able to create wealth in your favor by using the resources on the Internet and by following a few simple guidelines.

Creating Something to Invest

You need to know what you already have before you can start creating wealth. Organizing an inventory of your assets and your liabilities is the first step. The second is finding the difference between your assets and your liabilities, or your net worth. Your net worth is your personal wealth.

I know, I know, it's work, and you have a thousand reasons to procrastinate. However, if you truly want to be financially successful, you must take the time and get started right away. For more help on determining what you can invest, check out

- **The Federal Reserve Bank of Dallas** (www.dallasfed.org), which offers a tool called "Building Wealth" to assist you with building your plan for financial success.
- **CalculatorWeb** (www.calculatorweb.com/calculators/netwcalc.shtml), which provides a variety of online calculators. The Net Worth Calculator is great for developing a quick snapshot of your current financial position.

Budgeting with Care

The only way you can grow wealthy is to have something to save and invest, and the only way to have something to save and invest is to build those characteristics into a budget so that you're not living from paycheck to paycheck. By tracking your current income and day-to-day expenses, you can find out how much extra you're spending on unnecessary items that are putting a drain on your pocketbook. After finding the leaks, you can look to the Internet for plenty of ways to make savings and investments a part of your budget. Then you can sit back and watch the money flow in. Here's what the Internet has to offer:

- **FinanCenter.com** (www.financenter.com/consumertools/calculators/#budget) offers a variety of online budgets. Let the Internet do the math for you.
- **About.com** (financialplan.about.com/od/budgeting/index.htm?terms=budget) provides budgeting information, advice, tips, worksheets, and resources to help you set up a successful budget, understand the psychological aspects of money and spending, and stay motivated.

Setting Your Financial Goals

Write down your financial goals. What exactly do you want? Be careful about what you wish for and how you plan to attain your goals. Use realistic goals so that you don't set yourself up for failure. Wealth creation is a long path, so you need to create deadlines and milestones that let you know whether you're heading in the right direction and when you need to make changes. Check out these Web sites for help in setting your financial goals:

- ✔ **FinanCenter** (www.financenter.com/financenter/plan/planner 01.fcs) offers an extensive financial planner that tells you whether you're saving enough for your retirement years.

- ✔ **SmartMoney** (www.smartmoney.com/retirement/planning/index. cfm?story=intro) offers an extensive retirement planner, an online worksheet on which you try out different scenarios that can include beginning or delaying your retirement or saving more money today to have a greater impact on your lifestyle when you retire.

Saving and Investing

After you develop a budget, you know how much you can save each month. Each dollar you save is a brick, a paver in your pathway to financial freedom. These Web sites can help you get started:

- ✔ **Allstate** (termlife.allstate.com/afs/aaAssetCalc01.asp) offers a survey of 12 questions. Enter your answers, and the online calculator suggests an investment allocation strategy that suits your current needs and situation.

- ✔ **Dinkytown Investment Profile** (www.dinkytown.net/java/Investor Profile.html) is an investment profile questionnaire that's designed to help you create a balanced portfolio of investments. Your age, investment characteristics, and several other factors are used to calculate your investment profile. Your profile, and its associated asset allocation, is an excellent place to begin creating a well-balanced investment portfolio.

Haste Makes Waste! Starting Slowly!

Invest your savings so that your money makes more money. You've probably heard stories about janitors and dishwashers who saved everything they could for years and retired with million-dollar portfolios. These stories are not myths. Instead, they can be attributed to the power of compound interest, tax-advantaged accounts, and long-term investing.

Keep in mind that no matter what type of savings and investing plan you use, the sooner you put your plan into effect, the better your chances of financial success. The following Web sites are examples of the sources where you can get more information about maximizing investments.

✔ **Smart Pros** (http://finance.pro2net.com/x32994.xml) can help you build an emergency fund so you can get to your savings quickly and without any fees or penalties.

✔ **Morningstar.com** (www.morningstar.com) provides information about stocks, mutual funds, and personal finance.

✔ **SmartMoney.com** (www.smartmoney.com/compoundcalc/?nav= LeftNav) offers an online compound-interest calculator, personal finance advice, and more.

Controlling Your Debt

Debt is a useful tool for large purchases like a house or a vehicle. Borrowing money to pay for nonessential everyday items can lead to debt overload. Many people are in bondage, tied down because of their debts. Debt reduces your net worth, your personal wealth, by the amount you've borrowed, and to top it off, you'll have to pay interest on your debt. When you're debt-free, you can save and invest the interest you'd otherwise pay on your debt. The Internet provides valuable information about staying out of debt. Here are a few examples:

✔ **Nolo** (www.nolo.com) offers a timely article titled "Avoiding Financial Trouble: Ten Tips." On the home page under the "Free Information & Tools" tab, click on "Legal Encyclopedia," and then click on "Debt & Bankruptcy." You'll find the article beneath the heading "Avoid Overspending."

✔ **Insider Reports** (www.insiderreports.com) provides a helpful article titled "10 Reasons Why Most People Don't Achieve Financial Success." Find out if you're unconsciously setting yourself up for failure.

Protecting Your Assets

Your financial plan needs to be monitored and may need to be updated when your financial situation changes. The Internet can help you protect your assets. Here are a few Web sites that can help:

✔ **Yahoo!** (planning.yahoo.com/unfor2.html) includes information about insurance coverage and describes which bases you need to cover.

✔ **Kiplinger.com** (www.kiplinger.com/planning/estate) offers a number of useful online calculators that help you determine your net worth, how much insurance you need, and how much raising a child will cost.

Chapter 20

Almost Ten Ways to Reduce Your Out-of-Control Debt

According to Experian (www.experian.com), the average credit-card debt held by households is $4,663. In 2003, U.S. households charged $412 billion, a 185 percent increase compared with five years ago, according to Standard & Poor's. When your credit cards have an APR of 18 percent and you have $4,000 in credit-card debt, you're paying $720 per year in interest fees. Many credit-card companies also are adding annual or membership fees and other charges that make using credit cards and maintaining outstanding credit-card balances even more expensive and put much more pressure on individuals who already owe large amounts of debt.

The following ten strategies and online sources can help you combat a tidal wave of debt. Remember getting out of debt is the first step toward becoming fiscally fit. With a little determination, self-discipline, and the right online tools, you too can get there.

Determine How Much You Owe

Collect all your credit-card statements and go to the CNNMoney Debt Reduction Planner at cgi.money.cnn.com/tools. At the CNNMoney home page, click on "Calculators" in the left margin. At the Calculators page, click on "Debt Reduction Planner." The Debt Reduction Planner is a simple information tool that's geared toward helping you understand and analyze your debts. Overall, the planner can help you develop an action plan to reduce your debt. *Note:* Results are based on averages and may not be entirely accurate for your unique situation.

Pay More than the Minimum

Using your credit card wisely helps you protect the quality of your credit and saves you money. Here's an example of how someone could end up paying $5,397 for a computer that's worth only $1,750. That person charges the computer to a credit card at 18 percent APR interest and then pays only the minimum $35 per month. At that rate, it's going to take that person 264 months (that's 22 years) to pay off the computer. This example shows how not using credit correctly can cost you. MyVesta (www.myvesta.org) offers a useful online calculator that indicates how long it will take you to get out of debt if you pay only the minimum amount per month. If you make minimum payments, how long will it take you to pay off your debt?

Get a System for Debt Reduction

Visit Auriton Solutions (www.auriton.org) to check out its five signs that you're on your way to a financial crisis. One sure sign is taking cash advances to pay your bills. You can also create a monthly spending plan for reducing your debt at this Web site. After you've paid off the first priority debt, make the needed adjustments to allocate more money to focus on paying off your next priority debt, and so on. Eventually you'll be debt-free.

Negotiate with Credit-Card Companies

A recent study by U.S. Public Interest Research Group (PIRG, www.USpirg.org) indicates that a 1998 Federal Reserve survey of 2,000 credit card holders found that 81 percent thought the interest rates (APRs) on their cards were too high. In January 2002, state PIRGs conducted a survey showing how consumers can save thousands of dollars by merely asking for reduced rates.

About 50 PIRG volunteers called their credit-card issuers and requested a lower APR. The results from this national study indicate that by merely making this one five-minute telephone call, about half the volunteers received lower APRs. The average APR of the study group was 16 percent. After the telephone calls, the average APR of the study group was 10.47 percent. Three of the consumers within the study group were paying APRs that were over 23 percent. These individuals were able to reduce their APRs by 15 percent.

A number of factors contributed to the success of the requests for lower rates. For example, the length of time the cardholder had been with the credit-card issuer improved the chance of getting a better rate (the longer the better). Likewise, the cardholder's credit limit on the card (the higher the better), the unpaid-balance-to-limit ratio on the card (the lower the balance ratio the better), lower outstanding balances (the lower, the better), and whether the cardholder was ever late or missed a credit-card payment all factored into whether the rate was reduced and by how much.

Contact Your Creditor about Your Situation

Fair-Debt-Collection located at `www.fair-debt-collection.com/Dealing_with_Creditors/phone-script.html` offers a telephone script you can use for contacting your creditors about your financial situation. This script let's you know in advance what you need to ask and what information you need on hand when you contact the credit-card issuer. This helpful Web site also offers templates for writing contact letters to creditors and sending e-mail messages.

Determine How Much You Can Pay Each Creditor Each Month

You need to create a budget for now and for later to pay your creditors and curb your nonessential expenses. Estimate what your cash flow would be if you were laid off (including severance and unemployment payments). How many months can you survive? Use Credit.about.com (`Credit.about.com`) to help you come to grips with your budget and make your own credit repairs. At the site, you'll discover how to deal with creditors and find links to financial management articles. Additional information includes warnings about debt consolidators and moving debt from one credit card to another.

Pay Off Credit Cards with the Highest Interest First

Pay the minimum payment plus any additional amount you can afford on your highest-interest-rate credit card. When that debt is paid off, cancel the credit card. If you want to understand the ramifications of paying off credit cards on your overall credit score, see Nolo.com (`www.nolo.com`). Click on "Debt & Bankruptcy" to find several ways to get out of debt. You'll find free, reliable, everyday legal advice for everyday people.

Consider Using Some of Your Savings to Pay Off Your Credit Cards

If you're thinking about using some of your savings to pay off your credit-card debt, be sure to refer to CNN Money's Money 101, Lesson 9 Controlling Debt (`money.cnn.com/pf/101/lessons/9/page4.html`). You certainly don't want to borrow from your 401(k) and end up losing the tax-deferred compounding of your money and tax-deductible contributions and the ability to pay yourself back with after-tax dollars. Borrowing from your retirement account probably will make contributing new 401(k) contributions much harder while you're repaying the loan you made to yourself.

Stop Using Your Credit Cards

Using credit to finance normal purchases or to splurge on those little extras is a sign that you're mismanaging your personal finances. You need to make a pledge to yourself that you'll use your credit cards only for essentials. According to Bankrate (`www.bankrate.com/brm/news/credit-management/debt-toomuch.asp`), a useful rule to follow is that your debt, excluding your home, should not exceed 20 percent of your take-home pay. Bankrate points out that debt is like hot sauce: It's great in small doses, but too much is like playing with fire.

Index

X

Y

Z

Notes

BUSINESS, CAREERS & PERSONAL FINANCE

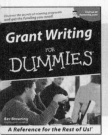

Grant Writing For Dummies
0-7645-5307-0

Home Buying For Dummies
0-7645-5331-3 *†

Also available:

- Accounting For Dummies †
  0-7645-5314-3
- Business Plans Kit For Dummies †
  0-7645-5365-8
- Cover Letters For Dummies
  0-7645-5224-4
- Frugal Living For Dummies
  0-7645-5403-4
- Leadership For Dummies
  0-7645-5176-0
- Managing For Dummies
  0-7645-1771-6

- Marketing For Dummies
  0-7645-5600-2
- Personal Finance For Dummies *
  0-7645-2590-5
- Project Management For Dummies
  0-7645-5283-X
- Resumes For Dummies †
  0-7645-5471-9
- Selling For Dummies
  0-7645-5363-1
- Small Business Kit For Dummies *†
  0-7645-5093-4

HOME & BUSINESS COMPUTER BASICS

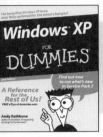

Windows XP For Dummies
0-7645-4074-2

Excel 2003 For Dummies
0-7645-3758-X

Also available:

- ACT! 6 For Dummies
  0-7645-2645-6
- iLife '04 All-in-One Desk Reference
  For Dummies
  0-7645-7347-0
- iPAQ For Dummies
  0-7645-6769-1
- Mac OS X Panther Timesaving
  Techniques For Dummies
  0-7645-5812-9
- Macs For Dummies
  0-7645-5656-8

- Microsoft Money 2004 For Dummies
  0-7645-4195-1
- Office 2003 All-in-One Desk Reference
  For Dummies
  0-7645-3883-7
- Outlook 2003 For Dummies
  0-7645-3759-8
- PCs For Dummies
  0-7645-4074-2
- TiVo For Dummies
  0-7645-6923-6
- Upgrading and Fixing PCs For Dummies
  0-7645-1665-5
- Windows XP Timesaving Techniques
  For Dummies
  0-7645-3748-2

FOOD, HOME, GARDEN, HOBBIES, MUSIC & PETS

Feng Shui For Dummies
0-7645-5295-3

Poker For Dummies
0-7645-5232-5

Also available:

- Bass Guitar For Dummies
  0-7645-2487-9
- Diabetes Cookbook For Dummies
  0-7645-5230-9
- Gardening For Dummies *
  0-7645-5130-2
- Guitar For Dummies
  0-7645-5106-X
- Holiday Decorating For Dummies
  0-7645-2570-0
- Home Improvement All-in-One
  For Dummies
  0-7645-5680-0

- Knitting For Dummies
  0-7645-5395-X
- Piano For Dummies
  0-7645-5105-1
- Puppies For Dummies
  0-7645-5255-4
- Scrapbooking For Dummies
  0-7645-7208-3
- Senior Dogs For Dummies
  0-7645-5818-8
- Singing For Dummies
  0-7645-2475-5
- 30-Minute Meals For Dummies
  0-7645-2589-1

INTERNET & DIGITAL MEDIA

Digital Photography For Dummies
0-7645-1664-7

Starting an eBay Business For Dummies
0-7645-6924-4

Also available:

- 2005 Online Shopping Directory
  For Dummies
  0-7645-7495-7
- CD & DVD Recording For Dummies
  0-7645-5956-7
- eBay For Dummies
  0-7645-5654-1
- Fighting Spam For Dummies
  0-7645-5965-6
- Genealogy Online For Dummies
  0-7645-5964-8
- Google For Dummies
  0-7645-4420-9

- Home Recording For Musicians
  For Dummies
  0-7645-1634-5
- The Internet For Dummies
  0-7645-4173-0
- iPod & iTunes For Dummies
  0-7645-7772-7
- Preventing Identity Theft For Dummies
  0-7645-7336-5
- Pro Tools All-in-One Desk Reference
  For Dummies
  0-7645-5714-9
- Roxio Easy Media Creator For Dummies
  0-7645-7131-1

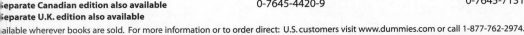

* Separate Canadian edition also available
† Separate U.K. edition also available

Available wherever books are sold. For more information or to order direct: U.S. customers visit www.dummies.com or call 1-877-762-2974.
U.K. customers visit www.wileyeurope.com or call 0800 243407. Canadian customers visit www.wiley.ca or call 1-800-567-4797.

 WILEY

SPORTS, FITNESS, PARENTING, RELIGION & SPIRITUALITY

0-7645-5146-9

0-7645-5418-2

Also available:
- Adoption For Dummies
  0-7645-5488-3
- Basketball For Dummies
  0-7645-5248-1
- The Bible For Dummies
  0-7645-5296-1
- Buddhism For Dummies
  0-7645-5359-3
- Catholicism For Dummies
  0-7645-5391-7
- Hockey For Dummies
  0-7645-5228-7

- Judaism For Dummies
  0-7645-5299-6
- Martial Arts For Dummies
  0-7645-5358-5
- Pilates For Dummies
  0-7645-5397-6
- Religion For Dummies
  0-7645-5264-3
- Teaching Kids to Read For Dummies
  0-7645-4043-2
- Weight Training For Dummies
  0-7645-5168-X
- Yoga For Dummies
  0-7645-5117-5

TRAVEL

0-7645-5438-7

0-7645-5453-0

Also available:
- Alaska For Dummies
  0-7645-1761-9
- Arizona For Dummies
  0-7645-6938-4
- Cancún and the Yucatán For Dummies
  0-7645-2437-2
- Cruise Vacations For Dummies
  0-7645-6941-4
- Europe For Dummies
  0-7645-5456-5
- Ireland For Dummies
  0-7645-5455-7

- Las Vegas For Dummies
  0-7645-5448-4
- London For Dummies
  0-7645-4277-X
- New York City For Dummies
  0-7645-6945-7
- Paris For Dummies
  0-7645-5494-8
- RV Vacations For Dummies
  0-7645-5443-3
- Walt Disney World & Orlando For Dummies
  0-7645-6943-0

GRAPHICS, DESIGN & WEB DEVELOPMENT

0-7645-4345-8

0-7645-5589-8

Also available:
- Adobe Acrobat 6 PDF For Dummies
  0-7645-3760-1
- Building a Web Site For Dummies
  0-7645-7144-3
- Dreamweaver MX 2004 For Dummies
  0-7645-4342-3
- FrontPage 2003 For Dummies
  0-7645-3882-9
- HTML 4 For Dummies
  0-7645-1995-6
- Illustrator CS For Dummies
  0-7645-4084-X

- Macromedia Flash MX 2004 For Dummies
  0-7645-4358-X
- Photoshop 7 All-in-One Desk Reference For Dummies
  0-7645-1667-1
- Photoshop CS Timesaving Techniques For Dummies
  0-7645-6782-9
- PHP 5 For Dummies
  0-7645-4166-8
- PowerPoint 2003 For Dummies
  0-7645-3908-6
- QuarkXPress 6 For Dummies
  0-7645-2593-X

NETWORKING, SECURITY, PROGRAMMING & DATABASES

0-7645-6852-3

0-7645-5784-X

Also available:
- A+ Certification For Dummies
  0-7645-4187-0
- Access 2003 All-in-One Desk Reference For Dummies
  0-7645-3988-4
- Beginning Programming For Dummies
  0-7645-4997-9
- C For Dummies
  0-7645-7068-4
- Firewalls For Dummies
  0-7645-4048-3
- Home Networking For Dummies
  0-7645-42796

- Network Security For Dummies
  0-7645-1679-5
- Networking For Dummies
  0-7645-1677-9
- TCP/IP For Dummies
  0-7645-1760-0
- VBA For Dummies
  0-7645-3989-2
- Wireless All In-One Desk Reference For Dummies
  0-7645-7496-5
- Wireless Home Networking For Dummies
  0-7645-3910-8

HEALTH & SELF-HELP

0-7645-6820-5 *†

0-7645-2566-2

Also available:
- Alzheimer's For Dummies
  0-7645-3899-3
- Asthma For Dummies
  0-7645-4233-8
- Controlling Cholesterol For Dummies
  0-7645-5440-9
- Depression For Dummies
  0-7645-3900-0
- Dieting For Dummies
  0-7645-4149-8
- Fertility For Dummies
  0-7645-2549-2

- Fibromyalgia For Dummies
  0-7645-5441-7
- Improving Your Memory For Dummies
  0-7645-5435-2
- Pregnancy For Dummies †
  0-7645-4483-7
- Quitting Smoking For Dummies
  0-7645-2629-4
- Relationships For Dummies
  0-7645-5384-4
- Thyroid For Dummies
  0-7645-5385-2

EDUCATION, HISTORY, REFERENCE & TEST PREPARATION

0-7645-5194-9

0-7645-4186-2

Also available:
- Algebra For Dummies
  0-7645-5325-9
- British History For Dummies
  0-7645-7021-8
- Calculus For Dummies
  0-7645-2498-4
- English Grammar For Dummies
  0-7645-5322-4
- Forensics For Dummies
  0-7645-5580-4
- The GMAT For Dummies
  0-7645-5251-1
- Inglés Para Dummies
  0-7645-5427-1

- Italian For Dummies
  0-7645-5196-5
- Latin For Dummies
  0-7645-5431-X
- Lewis & Clark For Dummies
  0-7645-2545-X
- Research Papers For Dummies
  0-7645-5426-3
- The SAT I For Dummies
  0-7645-7193-1
- Science Fair Projects For Dummies
  0-7645-5460-3
- U.S. History For Dummies
  0-7645-5249-X

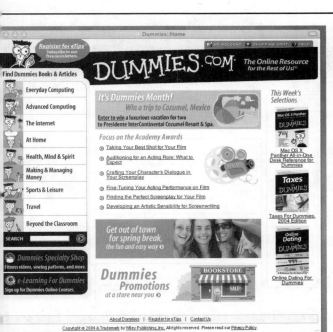

Get smart @ dummies.com®

- **Find a full list of Dummies titles**
- **Look into loads of FREE on-site articles**
- **Sign up for FREE eTips e-mailed to you weekly**
- **See what other products carry the Dummies name**
- **Shop directly from the Dummies bookstore**
- **Enter to win new prizes every month!**

Separate Canadian edition also available
Separate U.K. edition also available

Available wherever books are sold. For more information or to order direct: U.S. customers visit www.dummies.com or call 1-877-762-2974.
U.K. customers visit www.wileyeurope.com or call 0800 243407. Canadian customers visit www.wiley.ca or call 1-800-567-4797.